HOMELESS

POLITICS AND CULTURE IN MODERN AMERICA

Series Editors:
Margot Canaday, Glenda Gilmore, Michael Kazin, and Thomas J Sugrue

Volumes in the series narrate and analyze political and social change in the broadest dimensions from 1865 to the present, including ideas about the ways people have sought and wielded power in the public sphere and the language and institutions of politics at all levels—local, national, and transnational. The series is motivated by a desire to reverse the fragmentation of modern U.S. history and to encourage synthetic perspectives on social movements and the state, on gender, race, and labor, an on intellectual history and popular culture.

HOMELESS

POVERTY AND PLACE IN URBAN AMERICA

ELLA HOWARD

PENN

UNIVERSITY OF PENNSYLVANIA PRESS

PHILADELPHIA

Published by
University of Pennsylvania Press
Philadelphia, Pennsylvania 19104-4112
www.upenn.edu/pennpress

Printed in the United States of America on acid-free paper
2 4 6 8 10 9 7 5 3 1

Library of Congress Cataloging-in-Publication Data

Howard, Ella.
    Homeless : poverty and place in Urban America / Ella Howard. — 1st. ed.
        p.   cm. — (Politics and Culture in Modern America)
    ISBN 978-0-8122-4472-4 (hardcover : alk. paper)
    Includes bibliographical references and index.
    1. Homelessness—New York (State)—New York—History—20th century. 2. Skid
Row. 3. Bowery (New York, N.Y. : Street). I. Title. II Series.
    HV4506.N6 H73   2013
    362.5/92097471—pcc   2012014390

CONTENTS

INTRODUCTION

I N 1961, New York City Mayor Robert Wagner announced a major renewal initiative for the city's infamous skid row. Based on research conducted by social scientists, Operation Bowery would develop and implement policies designed to end urban homelessness. Explaining the plan, Wagner asserted, "We will be rebuilding men and making possible the rebuilding of a blight area at the same time." Wagner's comment revealed the rhetorical fusion of the city's "broken" men and the street where they lived. In a period of optimism and faith in governmental research and programs, officials were confident in their abilities to survey, analyze, and repair the poor as well as their decrepit neighborhood. The ambitious project followed on the heels of the federal urban renewal program, which had similarly attempted to revitalize the nation's skid rows, but focused on their buildings rather than their occupants. Homeless individuals dutifully cooperated with researchers and officials in both initiatives, but expressed little hope for change, or even much desire to leave skid row. As one homeless man remarked, "I won't leave the Bowery 'till I die."[1]

By the 1960s, homelessness seemed a permanent feature of the Bowery, having defined the street since the turn of the twentieth century. As the city's skid row, it housed religious missions, public shelters, cheap hotels, greasy restaurants, dive bars, pawn shops, used clothing stores, and, of course, the homeless men and women who frequented them. These businesses and their patrons lined the Bowery's sixteen blocks, from Chatham Square in Lower Manhattan north to Cooper Square, giving shape to a distinctive, if poorly understood, culture of homelessness.

Reformers and politicians had long criticized the Bowery. As far back as the nineteenth century, when it had housed theaters and amusements for the

Figure 1. By the turn of the twentieth century, the Bowery was home to many organizations serving the homeless, including the Hadley Rescue Hall, which offered a free supper and invited guests to "come as you are." George Grantham Bain Collection, Prints & Photographs Division, Library of Congress.

working classes, some of the city's respectable citizens had decried it as a den of sin. Police raids during the 1880s and 1890s temporarily closed the poolrooms and gambling halls, leading to the regular arrests of dozens of area prostitutes. Investigators were horrified by the lodging houses for homeless men. In the words of one observer, "The filthy bed-clothing, scarcely more filthy floors, the offensive odor resultant from a lack of ventilation, and the foul air laden with the odor of poor gin and poorer tobacco, makes the places vile and unhealthy resorts as it is possible to conceive of." Investigative journalist and social reformer Jacob Riis offered similar commentary, describing the area's cheap lodging houses as sites of corruption for naïve young men:

> As a matter of fact, some of the most atrocious of recent murders
> have been the result of schemes of robbery hatched in these
> houses, and so frequent and bold have become the depredations

of the lodging-house thieves, that the authorities have been
compelled to make a public demand for more effective laws that
shall make them subject at all times to police regulation.[2]

Such graphic narratives told of cheap, dirty accommodations used by desperate men of limited means and questionable motives.[3]

Despite this critical attention, the neighborhood remained remarkably unchanged for decades. What explains the tenacious longevity of such a filthy and dangerous district? This book answers that question by analyzing the experience and politics of homelessness. Skid rows were established in response to changing economic conditions, as increasing numbers of migrant workers and unemployed men took up residence in urban centers. Their continued existence over the ensuing decades resulted from the overlapping and conflicting solutions that were offered to "the problem of homelessness," each reflecting a distinct understanding of the situation and construction of the problem.

For the homeless, the problem often centered on insufficient food and shelter, as well as the callous indifference of politicians and the general public alike toward their plight. As a result, the homeless crowded onto the nation's skid rows in search of meals, beds, showers, bars, and companionship. Many politicians identified the problem as that of potential crime and disorder perpetrated by the homeless. In response, they supported crackdowns on panhandling, vagrancy, and public drunkenness, and invited policing practices that discouraged the homeless from living outside skid row by punishing their behavior more severely when they ventured away from the district. The homeless had migrated to skid rows and many city officials were intent on keeping them confined there.

Some groups saw skid rows themselves as part of the problem of homelessness. Owners of homes and businesses located nearby often agreed with Chamber of Commerce members that the presence of the homeless on the streets lowered property values and harmed the neighborhood. They described the homeless as volatile, threatening, and unpredictable—unfit to occupy valuable urban space. As a result, they tried to eradicate skid rows, supporting urban renewal initiatives designed to raze skid-row districts and displace the homeless from city centers. Similarly, many social scientists saw the skid-row homeless as an especially maladjusted population, unable to survive in mainstream society. They conducted massive research projects in search of the elusive sociological explanation for homelessness. Their work focused on a better understanding of human development, but they also hoped to contribute to the effort to end homelessness and, thus, skid rows.

Most Americans misunderstood the journey that led individuals to inhabit skid rows. Over the course of the twentieth century, homelessness was a more fluid category than is commonly recognized. Many impoverished individuals and families moved into and out of homelessness. In some cases, specific life events sent them to the streets, but general economic trends also played a major role in the trajectory of many. With few exceptions, however, the dominant explanations of homelessness placed blame solely on individuals. As a result, assistance programs did not attempt merely to help one survive, nor did they offer broader social and economic critiques. Instead, they focused on reforming the behavior, morality, or character of the homeless. The proposed causes of homelessness changed over time, ranging from laziness, a lack of religiosity, and poor socialization, to alcoholism and drug use. Usually, though, a single theory was privileged, regardless of the diverse individual circumstances.

Skid rows fueled these narrow understandings of homelessness and its causes. Living apart, the homeless had only infrequent contact with the middling and upper classes. The splintering of skid rows from the core of city life reflected one aspect of the late nineteenth-century segregation of the city by class, race, and ethnicity. The resulting geographic and cultural boundaries between the homeless and the rest of the nation's urban populations influenced policy decisions. For one, the separation enabled officials to develop policies largely outside of the public eye. The homeless could find basic services on skid row, even if they were denied resources through other channels. As a result, skid rows allowed city officials to avoid developing alternative assistance programs. More significantly, the lack of contact between middle-class city residents and the homeless strengthened the fusion of people and place in the phrase "skid-row bum," which inscribed culturally and historically specific meanings onto impoverished individuals and the place where they lived. At times thought of as the carefree tramp, at other times the culpable alcoholic, the menacing potential mugger, or the romantic, sensitive street poet, the image of the "skid-row bum" held sway over the popular imagination.[4]

This book focuses on the Bowery, the nation's best-known skid row, and seeks to add to the political and urban history of New York. The Bowery also offers a useful lens through which to understand national trends, as most of the nation's skid rows rose and fell in remarkably similar patterns. They faced similar debates over public versus private funding, the role of labor in relief programs, urban renewal projects, and shifting diagnostic approaches to poverty.[5] Local, state, and national perspectives are necessarily inextricable, as debates over poverty's underlying causes in City Hall, the State Assembly, or the halls of Congress influenced local homeless policies and, indeed, the experience of homelessness itself. In order to trace the historical relationship between national debate, local policy, and personal experience, this book thus leaves the Bowery at times. Decisions made in Albany or Washington, D.C., had dramatic effects on skid row. Facilities constructed outside the city, including labor camps and residential shelters, also comprise part of the story of Bowery homelessness and are necessary in understanding not only who was not there but also some reasons for and consequences of their absence. More than a neighborhood history, the development of the Bowery lends insight into the meaning of homelessness and poverty in twentieth-century America.[6]

Focusing on the homeless offers a new perspective on the development of the nation's modern welfare system. As male, unemployed, and often heavy drinkers, the skid-row homeless tested the limits of postwar liberalism. Even in New York, one of the nation's most politically liberal cities, most lasting programs to combat urban poverty offered little aid to the poorest of the poor. This pattern of neglect reflected the political realities that defined liberal programs, whose proponents routinely abandoned the urban homeless when supporting them might be unpopular with a voting public committed to specific visions of a work ethic and economic self-sufficiency.

Using skid row as its focal point, this book explores the complex relationship between poverty and place in nearly a century of the modern city by tracing the controversies surrounding the space allocated to New York's poorest residents. The city's system of care for the homeless has been perennially incomplete; services have remained partial due to fundamental tensions between administrators' desires to assist and their unwillingness to appear overly generous. For decades, the Bowery served these conflicting impulses, affording both a refuge for the homeless and a tool for city officials intent on disciplining them. Offering meager and decrepit facilities, the area provided a standard of living so low that it sparked relatively little outrage from working- and middle-class New Yorkers.[7]

Geographers and historians alike have analyzed the groups claiming "public space" in the American city over the course of the twentieth century. During the skid-row era, the creation of a separate homeless district translated into specific policing practices, as the homeless were held to different standards of conduct than were other urban residents. But who decides the most appropriate use of an urban area? To what extent should private profit be the determining factor, versus the pursuit of the common good? These debates would play out on skid row, as individual entrepreneurs, urban planners, welfare administrators, and politicians jockeyed for power.[8]

Other scholars have also explored the exclusion of the homeless from urban spaces and political processes in recent years. Since the end of the skid-row era, the significance of many of these themes has become evident. On the contemporary streets of America's cities, police and neighborhood associations feud with the homeless over appropriate uses of space, through anti-sleeping and anti-panhandling ordinances. The history of skid rows reveals the ways prior generations mediated such conflicts over policy, poverty, and place. It highlights the fact that our current web of urban programs and legislation is not only historically specific, but also subject to change.[9]

Throughout the period under study, administrators emphasized moral rehabilitation as the means of returning the homeless to mainstream society. Public agencies instituted work programs requiring the poor to perform either useful or symbolic labor in exchange for assistance, arguing that such activity would restore both their physical and moral health, while also instilling the work ethic in a population long considered lazy and irresponsible. Some religious programs also required physical labor, while others offered housing and meals to those homeless men willing simply to attend lengthy sermons. The fusion of aid and moral reform on the part of both religious and public institutions reinforced the stigmatization of poverty.

Shifting social attitudes toward the use of alcohol and controlled substances also shaped the services offered to the skid-row population. Moralistic discussions of substance abuse permeated debates on work, relief, and shelters for the homeless, fostering an atmosphere of suspicion and a push for regulation. Both public and private organizations strove to convince the homeless to modify such behaviors as a condition of assistance. Alcohol-oriented programs sponsored by religious missions and public agencies on skid row, as well as research conducted into the consumption habits of the homeless, reveal fundamental connections between perceptions of poverty, public welfare, and the social construction of alcoholism.

This single-issue understanding of homelessness continues to limit the effectiveness of many social service programs. During the 1980s, one homeless woman criticized the approach by many social workers toward their homeless clients:

They're intelligent, but you just know that they don't give a goddamn because they don't know how to listen. They sign you in then they forget about you. As soon as the poor person starts rattling off their problems, and that's the main thing they need when they are like that, someone to listen to them instead of talking to a wall like always, the workers change the subject back to liquor. They ask you in a soft voice, "You're not going to take any more drinks?" And the people reply, "But a guy came up and hit me over the head and my wife died. . . ." That's when the worker goes through the ceiling.[10]

The history of twentieth-century homelessness is, in large part, one of institutions, governments, and regulatory forces. My research took me through the archives and publications of religious missions, city, state, and federal governmental records, and the elaborate data files built by social scientists who analyzed skid-row life. But the tools of policy history alone cannot uncover the shifting meanings of skid-row homelessness. Portrayals of the Bowery, other skid rows, and the homeless in the popular media offer an additional lens through which to view the era's developments. Drawing on political as well as cultural history, we gain a better understanding of not only the policies that were enacted, but also the ways those policies were informed by subjective perceptions of the causes and realities of homelessness.

The history of the Bowery is also that of thousands of individuals, ranging from activists, impoverished people, missionaries, merchants, and politicians who used skid row to various ends. Although skid rows did not fulfill all of the criteria generally associated with "communities," they did foster beneficial relationships between individuals. One contemporary homeless man who lives in a transit station describes the importance of such ties: "These people, when I got down here, these people reached out to me because they knew, they already knew what it was like. They're not afraid to help their fellow man. As soon as I got down here I met Ron and the fellows and they didn't push me away. I mean I didn't know where to go, I didn't know where to eat, I didn't know where to sleep. They just invited me right in."[11]

Tracing the histories of so many actors, many of whom were never well-known historical figures, proves complex. In 1936, the former administrator of a federal transient camp predicted that future historians of homelessness would struggle with false sources: "Later this mass of questions and answers will be broken down and books will be written on what makes a transient.

The fault with the conclusions drawn will lie, not in the ability of the person writing the book, but in the fact that not ten percent of the information on which he based it is correct." In fact, administrative and institutional data concerning homeless programs are vast, if widely scattered. Some homeless individuals surveyed by social scientists suffered from the usual lapses in memory, perhaps exaggerated by substance abuse, while others may have had reason to intentionally obscure the details of their experience. Most researchers, however, recorded only subjects' initials or used pseudonyms, offering participants a measure of anonymity. Studies have shown that homeless respondents lie no more or less often than their non-homeless counterparts.[12]

More difficult for this research has been the relative paucity of recordings of the words of the homeless themselves. Social scientists visited the Bowery and other skid rows to talk, often in great depth, with their residents. The methodologies of most research teams, however, required investigators to record the answers that respondents gave to a specific set of questions. Often, the resulting reports are filled with rich detail, but are narrated in the third-person style of an investigative document. Reading through such findings, one catches only glimpses of the personality or sense of humor of an individual respondent. The sensationalized, mass-market paperbacks on the subject published in the 1960s included more direct quotations allegedly from the homeless, and I have incorporated a few here where relevant to the narrative. More reliable are books released since the 1980s that contain profiles of homeless individuals, often with significant portions left in their own words.[13]

The term "homelessness" reflects a historically specific understanding of poverty and carries a different connotation than other related terms, such as "vagrant" and "transient." This terminology has been used in various ways over the course of the twentieth century, complicating efforts at quantitative analysis. Historically, the term "homeless" often described not only people sleeping directly on the streets, but also those on cots in dormitory-style halls and in private lodging-house cubicles topped with chicken wire. I present such data here, explaining the methods used by researchers as much as possible.

Contemporary census projects seeking to count the homeless struggle not only to locate the now disparate urban poor, but also to define the parameters of homelessness for each study. In the modern context, an individual sleeping on a friend's sofa is considered homeless under some definitions.

The toll such a lifestyle takes on individuals is often underestimated. A homeless HIV-positive man in his thirties who suffered from manic-depression described his situation:

> I mean I would give anything just to be someplace where I feel
> I'm in control of my own environment, and where I don't have to
> worry that it's going to be gone. See I just stay with people now,
> anyone who will take me in until I find work and a place. And I'm
> so tired of living in temporary situations. You know, one bedroom
> to the next, one living room couch to the next. You don't have
> a choice. It's that or suicide—suicide is always just a convenient
> device away. [14]

The chronic instability of this lifestyle justifies the categorization of even such temporarily domiciled individuals as homeless.

Some terms reflect political distinctions. For the purpose of funding, "local homeless" were long distinct from "transient homeless," who might include, especially during the Depression, both "transient families" and "unattached transients." As hinted at by these terms, the structure of most social assistance programs kept women and children separate from men. Drawing services from separate divisions of even the city Department of Welfare, historically, women with children were rarely considered to be "homeless," even if they were housed using public funds. This distinction has certainly limited our understanding of the true landscape of poverty and public assistance. [15]

Most cities' skid rows were nearly exclusively male enclaves. The location of New York City's women's shelter on the Bowery meant there was a female presence on the street. But the more private habits of homeless women, as well as neglect by social scientists, journalists, and period observers, rendered the female homeless population nearly invisible. Broader perceptions of gender roles also shaped the programs that officials and service providers designed for the down and out. Such developments reflected the continued power of theories relegating men to the public sphere and women to the private. As one homeless woman described the gendered division of homeless services, "There's so much more available for the men who are down and out than for the women. That's because they figure a woman can always get a man." [16]

In this project, I include discussion of homeless women when they appear among the data gathered by social scientists or journalists studying the Bowery. I also analyze the ways in which women's presence on the streets shocked and alarmed even many hardened observers during the Depression and during the 1980s, prompting new understandings of urban poverty. Still, the Bowery was primarily a male enclave, and full study of the experience of homeless women awaits further research.[17]

The Bowery was also primarily home to white homeless men. Skid rows across the country tended to reflect the "racial" and ethnic composition of the broader population, and also displayed effects of local attitudes toward race. Although they shared many traits with their African American counterparts, many homeless whites remained violently racist in their outlook. Barred from entry to many of the neighborhood's facilities by racist policies, some African American homeless individuals sought shelter from organizations in Harlem, or gathered on the outskirts of the neighborhood. I follow their journey uptown, but thorough analysis of African American homelessness remains a worthy subject of its own study.

My work is indebted to the emerging body of scholarship analyzing the role of homelessness in the development of poverty policy. Historians have traced the influence of homeless vagrants on evolving systems of social welfare. As industrial capitalism expanded its influence over American society, various elites feared possible violent actions by the poor. They also worried that others might be lured away from respectable employment and working-class life by the model of a vagrant enjoying life without labor. Such suspicions of a migrant body of nonconformists propelled politicians to establish social and economic safeguards, especially during the late nineteenth- to early twentieth-century era of the "tramp" and "hobo." Focusing on the Bowery, I add a level of detail to our understanding of urban homelessness, while situating the narrative in the context of New York's specific history.[18]

Influenced by the ongoing renewal of urban history initiated by scholars interested in social history and the production of space, I pay attention to the local landscape. Skid row proved not only the backdrop for the history of twentieth-century urban homelessness, but also a central factor in its development. The Bowery and other skid rows offered the resident homeless places to eat, drink, socialize, find work, and sleep; they also carried the stigma of shame, degradation, despair, and immorality. Throughout the period under study, those acting on a charitable impulse to aid the poor nearly always coupled their effort with one to reform behavior. The policies of public and private organizations toward the residents of skid row lend insight into the broader relationships between social control, charitable assistance, and public welfare in American culture. Urban renewal czars like Robert Moses conflated people and place, hoping to erase poverty from the landscape through good urban design. More than a neighborhood, skid row became a socioeconomic class and a marker of identity, bearing connotations concerning morality, character, and social worth.

In the end, the forces of gentrification rather than federal policy, crusading City Hall, or technocratic experts terminated the Bowery's life as skid row. Area boosters had tried for decades to market the Bowery as the next frontier of downtown living. Until the late 1970s, such efforts had failed, hampered first by the grim elevated trains that left the area dark and foreboding, and later by the persistent presence of homeless men. Ultimately, however, the real estate market shifted, and even skid row became a desirable destination. Trendy rock clubs, artists' studios, and increasingly expensive apartments announced the East Village's consumption of the Lower East Side, and the Bowery proved no exception. The homeless did not, of course, disappear with their former habitat. Instead, they scattered across the landscape of the city's five boroughs, becoming at once more visible to most New Yorkers and less centralized for the purposes of study, attempted diagnosis, and assistance.[19]

These changes on the Bowery, coupled with large historical developments in the culture of homelessness, prompt me to end this narrative in the early 1980s. One development, the controversial verdict in the *Callahan v. Carey* case, committed the city to meeting homeless men's "right to shelter" on request. Following the decision, city officials scrambled to meet its terms, changing the nature of the debate over local homelessness. More significantly, by the early 1980s the demographics of the city's homeless population had shifted dramatically. As increasing numbers of young men, ethnic minorities, women, and entire families became homeless, the single, male "skid-row bum" was no longer the face of homelessness. As a result, the solutions offered by skid rows, as unsatisfying as they had always been, were no longer viable.

Homelessness and the Bowery in the Nineteenth Century

The institutions that address poverty embody the values of their creators. Officials developed almshouses early in the nineteenth century to help the homeless while also regulating their behavior. Administrators hoped the regimented schedules of institutional life would prepare residents to rejoin the labor force. The plan may have benefited young, healthy individuals, but it proved torturous for many children as well as elderly, ill, mentally ill, and disabled adult residents. Almshouses developed in the context of the era's broader institution-building movement. Historian David Rothman has described the motivations behind such institutions as a "fantasy of re-habilitation." Treating the homeless as flawed individuals in need of repair, the almshouse system conflated the poor population into an undifferenti-ated mass. Almshouses also restricted the movement of the poor, a factor that became increasingly important as the century progressed.[20]

The dramatic expansion of the nation's rail systems during the late nine-teenth and early twentieth centuries offered the homeless employment as well as unprecedented mobility. The laborers who had constructed the railroads and other symbols of modern life comprised what historian David Court-wright has called "the floating army" of dispossessed workers.[21] Officials and charity reformers worried about such transience, fearing that it threatened the nation's social order. Many migrant homeless performed day labor, a fact overlooked by those characterizing them as dangerous nonworkers. Such perceptions shaped the policies of public and private agencies for decades.[22]

The era's leading charity reform group, the Charity Organization Society (COS), established in 1877, strove to prevent the homeless from inspiring oth-ers to pursue lives outside the rapidly industrializing work force. The organi-zation opposed the "unearned" relief system that had routinely been available to the city's homeless during nineteenth-century economic crises. Instead of breadlines and soup kitchens, the COS proposed a new system grounded in labor rather than direct relief.[23]

Setting out to modernize New York's homeless policy, the COS opened a Manhattan woodyard in 1884. Homeless men chopped firewood in exchange for tickets redeemable for meals and lodging. Through woodcutting, admin-istrators contended, men proved their willingness to work. During its first winter, the yard employed over six hundred men, and during the next, near-ly one thousand. Homeless women worked in the facility's laundry, which served as a "work test" while also offering employment and industrial edu-cation.[24]

By 1886, state legislators had paved the way for the establishment of a Mu-nicipal Lodging House. One did not open for another decade, however. In the interim, the COS established a "wayfarer's lodge" that slept one hundred woodyard laborers on West 28th Street.[25] When the muni finally opened in 1896, the city police closed the lodging rooms they had previously made avail-able to the homeless. COS administrators asked police sergeants to differenti-ate carefully between "professional beggars" and "what might be termed the 'worthy' poor." Men of the higher classes were to be referred to the woodyard, while those representing the "ordinary vagrant class" would be sent to the muni for brief lodgings and then were encouraged to leave town.[26]

Charity workers and the homeless criticized the woodyard's operations. Although the facility's director estimated that most men could chop the requisite amount of wood in less than four and one-half hours, some clients required nearly eight hours to complete the job. Some charity workers accused the COS of using the woodyard to test a man's ability to work, rather than his willingness. In 1909, one man described his negative experience in the woodyard: "I work from 10 in the morning to 5:30 and they gives me a slip of paper which means 35 cents after I walks way over to the East Side and cashes it in at a restaurant. Me half starved and not been to a decent bed for five nights before. I'll drop dead and go to the Morgue before I goes to the Woodyard for any more charity 35 cents again."[27]

Yet COS officials continued to urge city residents to distribute woodyard tickets to the homeless in lieu of cash. Issued in booklets to donors, the tickets entitled recipients to a woodyard shift, a night's lodging, and two meals. Administrators promoted the tickets as a guilt-alleviating salve for urban dwellers uncomfortable at the sight of their suffering fellow city residents: "In our experience a comparatively small number of men who received these tickets ever present them, but the gift of a ticket to an able-bodied man who applied to you for relief discharges your conscience from leaving such a man without shelter or food."[28]

Another, more dramatic response to homelessness arose in 1895, when a bill in the New York State legislature called for the "detention of paupers" in a farm colony outside the city. Men between sixteen and forty years old would be sent to the facility if convicted of habitual drunkenness, disorderly conduct, or vagrancy. Josephine Shaw Lowell, Chair of the Committee on Vagrancy of the National Conference of Charities and Corrections, one of the forces behind the bill, blamed the city's lodging houses for corrupting the poor by allowing them to survive without employment. She urged investigators to probe the backgrounds of the homeless carefully and to monitor their behavior. Her plan would imprison anyone remaining in the city longer than one month without a home. Officials hoped farm colony sentences would reform homeless men's behavior by reacquainting them with discipline and hard work. Plans for the colony fizzled.[29]

After the economic crisis of 1907, some (probably inflated) estimates described thirty thousand homeless men in New York. City officials proudly announced the construction of a modern municipal shelter accommodating up to one thousand men. Residents worked eight hours every other day, as stewards, laundry staff, housekeepers, and janitors within the facility, or at the woodyard. While administrators praised the muni's expansion, a State Legislature bill revived the farm colony plan. The Department of Public Charities Commissioner acknowledged that "vagrancy is not exactly a crime," but argued that "men owe a duty to society not to allow themselves to fall into vagrancy, and that when they do reach that point society must protect itself against them, and against the results apt to follow the application of the doctrine that 'necessity knows no law.'" Temporarily homeless men would stay at the muni, required to perform only moderate work tests. Those deemed incorrigible vagrants would receive longer terms of farm labor.[30]

Although officials never established the farm colony, the prospect generated enthusiasm for over fifteen years.[31] Its continued popularity reflected interest in requiring labor from the homeless while removing them from the city. The plan, as well as the era's launch of the municipal lodging house, also testified to the expanding efforts of public agencies to care for the poor. Munis were opening in cities across the country, signaling the commitment of public funds to the problem of homelessness. Chicago opened a muni in 1901; by 1910, cities ranging from Washington to Kansas City, Louisville, and Pueblo had followed suit. At the dawn of the twentieth century, city, state, and charity officials struggled to reconcile their visions of the duties of an individual toward society and the social responsibility of a community toward its members.[32]

By the early twentieth century, some welfare administrators and other observers believed that an expanded government role in American life would effectively prevent homelessness. Frank Laubach's 1916 Columbia University study, "Why There are Vagrants," supported the prohibition of alcohol, increased use of eugenics, and improved industrial education and social insurance to end homelessness. He also urged establishment of a federal employment agency.[33]

The development of homeless services in New York had been halting and contested. Yet by 1915, a Washington social worker referred to humane assistance programs, breadlines, generous food at the muni, and clothing distribution programs as a "New York view" of the issue. Earlier theories had warned that such relief practices would lead to dependency. Increasingly, service providers sought to keep homeless men healthy and strong until they again found work. John Kingsbury, Commissioner of Charities, praised the muni's expanded employment program as "a repair shop for rebuilding broken lives." He also urged a broader appreciation of the diversity of experience on skid row: "There is as much difference in temperament, disposition, and so on among a hundred occupants of the Municipal Lodging House as among a hundred patrons of a Fifth Avenue hotel."[34]

New York's homeless population gravitated toward the Bowery by the late nineteenth century, drawn to necessary services and lodgings. The Bowery's relationship with alcohol began early; by the eighteenth century, it housed numerous taverns. During the nineteenth century, the Bowery served as a saloon and entertainment district, providing nightlife diversions for the city's working classes. In the antebellum era, "Bowery Girls" joined their male counterparts, modeling finery and enjoying the area's commercial entertainments.[35]

In the postbellum era, the Bowery's transformation accelerated. Saloons remained a mainstay of the neighborhood culture. Some bars drew prostitutes and thieves who infamously used "knockout drops" to rob unconscious patrons. By the 1870s, much of the area's "legitimate" entertainment had migrated to the Tenderloin district, as the Bowery came to be associated with opium dens and dive bars. "Rat baiting" enjoyed popularity in saloon backrooms, as area gamblers wagered on dogs' ability to kill rats crowded into a pen. By 1891, the Bowery and Park Row housed one-sixth of the city's saloons, most of which drew few women who were not prostitutes.[36]

Legends and local characters added notoriety to the area's establishments. Throughout the 1890s, McGurk's Suicide Hall, above Houston Street on the Bowery, was the site of frequent suicide attempts by impoverished prostitutes. Steve Brodie, who claimed to have survived an 1886 leap from the Brooklyn Bridge, opened a nearby Bowery saloon. His story was immortalized in the 1894 musical, "On the Bowery," in which he starred. As an encore, he performed the song, "The Bowery," from Charles M. Hoyt's 1892 "Trip to Chinatown." The song included the popular refrain, "The Bow'ry, the Bow'ry! They say such things, and they do strange things on the Bow'ry! The Bow'ry! I'll never go there anymore!"[37]

By the 1880s, the homeless had begun to gather in specific neighborhoods in major cities including Philadelphia, Chicago, San Francisco, Minneapolis, and New York. In *How the Other Half Lives*, Jacob Riis estimated that the Bowery housed over 9,000 homeless men. He described robbery, crime, and vice in the area's lodging houses, including a gruesome tale of a beggar mutilating a young boy with a heated iron and acid to make him a more sympathetic

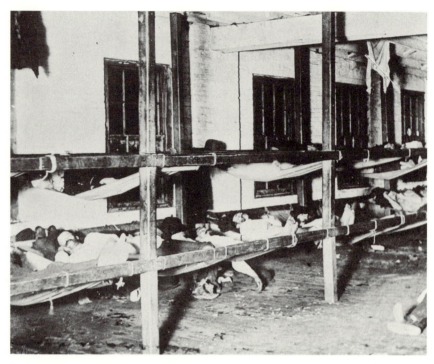

Figure 2. Homeless men with few resources slept in crowded hammocks as skid rows formed in the nation's cities. Richard Hoe Lawrence, "A Seven-Cent Lodging House in the Bowery," c. 1895. Copyright Museum of the City of New York.

panhandler. Riis offered a gritty description of the shabby beds offered in the seven- to ten-cent-a-night lodging houses: "A strip of canvas, strung between rough timbers, without covering of any kind, does for the couch of the seven-cent lodger who prefers the questionable comfort of a red-hot stove close to his elbow to the revelry of the stale-beer dive." The 1896 Raines Law allowed bars with at least ten rooms for rent to serve alcohol with meals on Sundays. As a result, dive bars opened prostitution-oriented hotels to increase profits.[38]

Twenty years after the publication of Riis's work, I. L. Nascher labeled the Bowery "the backbone of Povertyville." He saw improvements in the area, but also persistent despair. Nascher catalogued the declining theater district, long past its heyday. The former Bowery Theater had been converted to a German theater in 1897, and catered to a Russian Jewish audience by the early twentieth century. Pastor's famous Opera House of the 1860s had housed the German Volks Garten in the 1870s, and had been the site of the Jewish People's

Figure 3. A thriving commercial district at the turn of the century, the Bowery was connected to the wider city by loud, dirty elevated trains. Stereograph Card Collection, Prints & Photographs Division, Library of Congress.

Theater since the early 1880s. The area's English-language theaters, the London Theater and the Miner's Theater, offered low vaudeville and burlesque performances. The area also featured penny arcades of mechanized amusements ranging from slot machines, photographs, and X-ray machines to automatic banjos and pianos. Wax museums and anatomical museums stood beside those focused on a single gimmick, such as one charging ten cents for a glimpse of the "8th wonder of the world," a four-legged chicken.[39]

As other popular entertainment destinations, including Brooklyn's Coney Island, drew the working classes further from the Lower East Side, the Bowery became the city's skid row. By 1920, few women frequented the Bowery;

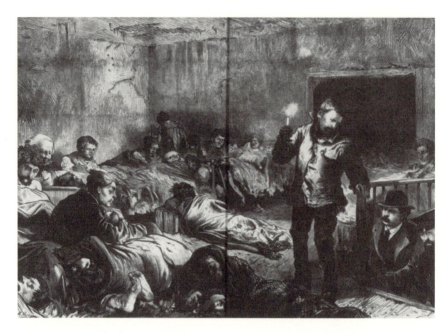

Figure 4. During the late nineteenth century, many homeless individuals found shabby accommodations in crowded lodging houses. Matthew Somerville Morgan, "Life Sketches in the Metropolis—Our Homeless Poor—A Midnight Visit to One of the Cheap Lodging Houses in Water St," 1872. Prints & Photographs Division, Library of Congress.

even prostitutes rarely appeared. Nascher observed, "With the exception of the Jewish theaters, the Atlantic Garden and dives, its places of amusement are intended for men alone." Prohibition closed the area's legitimate saloons, but dive bars and backroom speakeasies flourished.[40]

In the early twentieth century, Bowery accommodations ranged from better hotels, such as the Occidental, which charged a dollar per night, to a nickel spot on the floor at a Park Row lodging house. Between these extremes, one with more than a quarter might rent a room with curtains and carpets, a room the size of a closet with less than a quarter. Ten-cent rooms, either stalls or dormitory cots, meant a communal bathroom and a shared towel, comb, and brush. A similar range of restaurants advertised meals costing from one to five cents.[41]

Religious missions remained area fixtures, providing crucial services to

Figure 5. At the start of the twentieth century, the Bowery Mission provided coffee to homeless men willing to participate in religious instruction. George Grantham Bain Collection, Prints & Photographs Division, Library of Congress.

Bowery homeless. Established in 1850 by the New York Ladies' Home Missionary Society of the Methodist Episcopal Church, the Five Points Mission offered religious and charitable services to the area's poor into the Depression years. During its long tenure it had provided a wide range of services, including a controversial adoption service, but by the 1930s the mission distributed food and clothing to needy area families and offered classes and religious services to the local immigrant community.[42]

Other religious institutions like the Doyers Street Mission, Madonna House, All Night Mission, Hadley Mission, Holy Name Mission, and Volunteers of America facility offered meals and lodgings to the area's poor. The pioneering Jerry McAuley Water Street Mission, established in 1872 as the first in the city to assist needy men rather than children and families, had been joined a decade later by McAuley's Midtown Cremorne Mission.[43]

Established in 1879, the Bowery Mission moved to a former coffin factory at 227 Bowery in 1908. The mission operated a 1:00 a.m. breadline from Thanks-

Figure 6. Some Bowery lodging houses, such as this one photographed between 1908 and 1909, provided reading rooms that were popular with homeless men who had nowhere else to spend much of the day. George Grantham Bain Collection, Prints & Photographs Division, Library of **Congress.**

giving to Easter each year. In order to avoid violating lodging house regulations, mission staff moved men through the late night breadline, then into an overnight religious service, followed by coffee and bread served at 5 a.m. During the early 1920s, the mission also expanded its efforts to "Americanize the immense foreign population" of the neighborhood through children's programs.[44]

The YMCA opened its first Bowery facility in the 1870s, offering lodgings, reading rooms, and an employment bureau. Many welcomed its arrival to the neighborhood; at the opening, a donor announced, "Let us rejoice that the Gospel has come into the Bowery and that it has come in the genial and sensible form that it has." By 1915, the organization had moved to East Third Street, where it remained for over thirty years. The seven-story building housed one large dormitory room of nearly two hundred beds, over one hundred and fifty private rooms, a cafeteria, a five-cent restaurant, a laundry, tailor shop, barber shop, fumigation room, employment department, large auditorium, reading room, and game room. The organization also briefly dabbled in industrial work, sponsoring a workshop for disabled men.[45]

Originally established in England, the Salvation Army arrived in New York City in 1880, focusing its evangelical Christian outreach program on the city's poor. The Bowery Corps, originally called "New York Number Nine," opened on Fourth Street in 1893. The Army's approach to rehabilitating the poor combined material relief with a labor program. As early as 1897, the Army's "Salvage Corps" operated "industrial plants." Client workers collected discarded furniture, clothing, and appliances from city residents, then repaired and refurbished them at Army plants for resale through secondhand stores. In exchange for their work, men received room, board, and sometimes cash. The Army's administration considered the innovative industrial program "a two-way salvage service," working to rehabilitate both used goods and "maladjusted" men.[46]

This developing cluster of missions highlighted the Bowery's late nineteenth-century transformation from a relatively respectable entertainment district to a skid row. As the theater district moved uptown and much of the vice trade moved west, the Bowery's function narrowed, as its lodging houses, missions, and restaurants became home primarily to impoverished, single white men. By the turn of the century, the municipal shelter was in operation uptown, as the city committed public funds to combat homelessness. Critics attacked such services as overly generous and called instead for work colonies and other distant facilities, but life on the Bowery continued largely unchanged for decades. The arrival of the Depression would, however, crush the existing system, forcing officials to question everything they thought they understood about homelessness.

CHAPTER 1

THE CHALLENGE OF THE DEPRESSION

DURING the 1920s, Urbain Ledoux opened "the Tub" on St. Mark's Place on the Lower East Side. Known as "Mr. Zero," the businessman turned philanthropist offered meals and lodging to New York's homeless men. A Buddhist, Ledoux felt called to work among the poor. He had begun his efforts in New England, selling the unemployed at "slave auctions" on Boston Common. By March 1928, Ledoux reported lodging over 1,140 men nightly in steamer chairs while feeding 2,000 from a five-cent basement soup kitchen and a ground floor cafeteria. Espousing his own brand of radical politics, Ledoux proposed outlandish schemes such as auctioning the labor of the unemployed to Midwestern farmers, who might repay him in grain to use to feed the poor.[1]

As the Depression deepened, Ledoux used publicity creatively to highlight the plight of the Bowery's homeless. Large Thanksgiving meals earned the Tub mention in the annual newspaper coverage of charitable holiday programs. In the spring, Ledoux led a contingent of homeless men marching in the famous Fifth Avenue Easter parade. The bedraggled marchers inspired journalists to contrast New York's wealthy and its poor: "Mr. Zero and the 'boys' from the Tavern arrived in front of St. Patrick's Cathedral at noon and displayed what the unemployed man will wear this season. Their garb was traditional, in keeping with last year and the years before it—battered plug hats, lumberjackets, frayed trousers and shoes that had more than their share of walking the streets."[2]

Ledoux's colorful efforts reflected the collapse of the city's relief system. By 1929, the existing network of charitable assistance and commercial lodgings, sufficient for decades, had strained and broken under the crushing tide of pov-

Figure 7. In this iconic work for the Federal Arts Project, Berenice Abbott photographed the extensively detailed menu of inexpensive food served on the Bowery. "Blossom Restaurant, 103 Bowery, Manhattan," 1935. Copyright The New York Public Library/Art Resource, NY.

erty and homelessness. City officials and charity administrators looked on in horror as poor people spread across the urban landscape, squatting in shacks, lining up for bread, begging for cash, and marching in protest. Who should provide assistance to these crowds of people? Some were the established poor, who had been homeless even before the Depression had begun. Previously, they had been helped, as the poor of other cities had also been, by a network of ethnic and religious associations bolstered by a few public organizations. Now, as throngs of the newly poor—pushed out of the security of the middle- and working classes by the economic devastation brought on by the Depression— crowded into such institutions, the existing networks could not keep up with the demand. The dramatic increase in poverty during the late 1920s and early 1930s shocked city and state officials into action, prompting them to begin developing a new, increasingly publicly funded, philosophy of relief.

Life on the Bowery

In the 1920s, a young white man without shelter might spend the night at the Bowery Branch YMCA on East Third Street. The organization promoted Protestant Christianity, but nearly half the residents were Roman Catholic. If admitted, he could attend lectures, discussion groups, and weekend trips to the country and the beach with other members, half of them under thirty. Most likely, though, he would find the casework approach of the YMCA invasive, and would continue looking for a facility offering him a bit more freedom.[3]

Leaving the YMCA and walking south down through the Bowery, he would encounter an array of establishments vying for his business. He might pause to read the menu painted in the windows of a corner restaurant. He might stop in at the Holy Name Mission for counsel or a place to rest. If he hoped for simple lodging and to be left alone, he might rent a room next door at the Arcade Hotel. Walking farther, he could see used suit jackets hanging in secondhand clothing shops, and might buy one for an upcoming job application. He could visit one of the many barber shops and barber schools that lined the street, their characteristic striped signs promising a discounted shave or haircut. Below Bleecker Street, flophouses and missions lined the streets. Between Houston and Delancey Streets, the eye was overwhelmed by the sea of signs announcing hotel names, including the Montauk, Savoy, and Puritan. Along the sidewalk, an informal "thieves' market" of used and stolen goods was thriving. Next door to the Salvation Army's Memorial Hotel, the Bowery Mission had occupied 222 Bowery since 1908. The building's second-floor stained-glass windows reminded those inside and out of God's constant presence there.

Looking uptown from Houston Street, peering between the elevated railroad tracks and the four-story Bowery facades, he would see the stately Metropolitan Life building silhouetted against the sky. Although only a few miles apart, mostly prosperous Midtown and the gritty Bowery hardly seemed part of the same city. Near Grand Street, he would see remnants of the area's own deep and eclectic architectural past. Several businesses occupied the ground floors of Federal-era townhouses. Everyone noticed Stanford White's bold Roman classical style 1895 Bowery Savings Bank. The building's massive fluted Corinthian columns were topped by a pediment featuring figures sculpted by Frederic MacMonnies. Such grandeur seemed out of place on skid row.[4]

One had to walk gingerly to avoid tripping on the products displayed in front of hardware and fixtures stores, the sandwich boards promoting inex-

Figure 8. Photographer Berenice Abbott captured the shadowy realm of the Bowery, where the sun rarely penetrated beneath the tracks of the elevated trains. "El, Second and Third Avenue Lines," 1936. Copyright Museum of the City of New York.

pensive meals, or the groups of men sitting or sometimes collapsed on the sidewalk. Near Canal Street, one also had to avoid the huge bales of paper outside the Jewish Press Publishing Company. Both sides of the street were crowded with jewelry stores and more cheap hotels, barber colleges, bars, and movie theaters. The journey down the Bowery concluded past the Owl Hotel, where tattoo studios also offered to conceal black eyes. Near Chatham Square, the Bowery's official terminus, the All-Night Mission offered salvation and soup to those who sought help.

The Bowery was not the only place in the city where homeless white men found accommodations and assistance. In one notable example, the Mills Hotel Trust operated three large facilities downtown, containing a total of more than 4,000 rooms and costing from thirty to fifty cents per night. On Blackwell's Island, the New York City Home for the Aged and Infirm housed invalid men and women, and others unable to work. When full, the massive facility lodged over 900 men and nearly 1,200 women. The muni on 25th Street also continued to welcome both men and women. But the Bowery had developed into a skid-row district, attracting the homeless not just to a single facility, but to sixteen blocks of flophouses, missions, cheap restaurants, and bars.[5]

White women found far fewer options on the Bowery. If she had money, a homeless white woman might dine in area restaurants, or drink in bars alongside her male companions. Many flophouses did not permit women residents. If she was over fifty and had twenty-five cents, however, she might spend the night at the Glendon Hotel at 243 Bowery, six doors north of the Bowery Mission. Beginning in 1898, the facility had been maintained by the Salvation Army, but by the mid-1920s it was privately owned. Flanked by a dingy restaurant and a shop selling store fixtures, the five-story building housed approximately sixty women, most of whom worked as peddlers or maintenance workers. Entering the hotel door, she would immediately mount a steep staircase to the second-floor cashier's window. The sitting room drew lodgers, who clustered around a black stove or sat near the windows. The hotel operator sympathized with her charges, yet described them as feisty: "I feel sorry for them myself. If one of them does get a little drunk I don't chase her out if I can handle her. I try to get her quiet and put her to bed. It's not so easy, running the house, believe me! My husband's got a man's lodging house next door. He'd rather run that than this any day. One drunken old woman can rave and cuss so she wakes up the whole dormitory, and first thing you know they're all shouting and cussing at one another."[6]

Young white women found aid across Manhattan. The Children's Aid Society sponsored an array of facilities, including the small Shelter for Women with Children on East 12th Street. Some organizations offered lodgings for a fee. Up to one hundred and ten "respectable, self-supporting young women under 40" could be lodged in double rooms at the Eastside Anthony Home. Spanish-speaking young women were welcome at the Fourteenth Street Casa Maria, sponsored by the Augustinian Fathers of the Assumption. A few facilities were remarkably open in their admissions policy, such as the City Federation Hotel on 22nd Street, which offered board and lodging for up to fifty-six women of any race. Other facilities focused on working-class women, such as Maedchenheim on East 62nd Street, home to "domestic service girls."[7]

Some institutions had restrictive and starkly class-based policies. The 104th Street Association for the Relief of Respectable Aged and Indigent Females home refused applicants who had "lived as servants." Entry also required a $300 fee and the promise of all one's property at death. In the Bronx, the West Farms Peabody Home for Aged and Indigent Women welcomed up to thirty-two Protestant women over age sixty-five, but cautioned, "domestic servants and colored women excepted."[8]

African Americans found few welcoming facilities on the Bowery. Many hotels and restaurants discriminated against non-whites. Charitable organizations also maintained segregated referral systems, sending African American applicants most often to Harlem, the Bronx, and Brooklyn for aid. Facilities like the Brooklyn Home for Aged Colored People, for instance, welcomed those over sixty-five.[9]

African American women's charity resources clustered in Harlem. St. John's House for Working Girls (sponsored by the Cathedral of St. John the Divine) offered lodgings to "worthy but poor colored girls," as did the Sojourner Truth House and the White Rose Mission and Industrial Association. The YWCA had operated in Harlem since 1905. It ran smaller residences until it opened Emma Ransom House in 1926, with over two hundred beds and impressive amenities including an elevator and laundry service.[10]

These mostly smaller, private charities reflected the commitment to individualism and voluntarism that typified American philanthropy before the Depression. Many organizations were designed to aid individuals of a specific ethnicity, which usually emerged from a mixture of ethnic pride and reaction to prejudice. The Norwegian Evangelical Lutheran Emigrant Mission and Emigrant Home on Whitehall Street, for instance, offered temporary lodgings to arriving Norwegians.[11]

Jewish New Yorkers developed especially elaborate charity networks that reflected two distinct religious and cultural philosophies of assistance. German Jews established the Homeless Men's Department of the Jewish Social Service Association in 1922. The organization used intensive screening interviews and background checks before providing assistance and referrals. By contrast, the Hebrew Immigrant Aid Society (HIAS), established by Eastern European community leaders, did not ask applicants about their backgrounds. The organization's predecessor, Hachnosas Orchim on Essex Street, was so-named for providing hospitality to wayfarers in need of kindness. That facility's philosophy was described in 1894:

> It is up to us, the Russian Jews, to help our poor countrymen and keep them from being insulted by our proud brethren to whom a Russian Jew is a schnorrer, a tramp, a good-for-nothing. . . . In the philanthropic institutions of our aristocratic German Jews you see magnificent offices, with lavish desks, but along with this, morose and angry faces. A poor man is questioned like a criminal. He trembles like a leaf, as if he were standing before a Russian official.

By 1919, HIAS clients were fed and lodged in a three-story Lafayette Street building equipped with a dormitory, kitchen, dining room, laundry, showers, synagogue, and employment service.[12]

Catholic charities also helped the era's homeless, having expanded to aid the influx of destitute Catholic immigrants in the nineteenth century. Although most focused on children's services—in opposition to the efforts of Protestant "child-savers" to remove children from poor Catholic parents— some organizations assisted homeless adults. The Bowery's Holy Name Mission conducted basic casework services, while Madonna House offered simple accommodations and meals with no background investigation to up to 250 men. By the early twentieth century, public funds supported Catholic charities through carefully developed agreements ceding organizational control to Catholic administrators.[13]

The Bowery establishments thus coded the area early in the twentieth century as catering to the needs of poor white men. The homeless survived largely through the use of a patchwork system of assistance that had evolved out of the distinct priorities of various charitable organizations. Racial prejudice divided some of the area's skid-row institutions, as did an array of religious ideals and a variety of theoretical understandings toward the needs of the poor. Although this complex and often overlapping system had been sufficient for decades, it would be shattered by the unprecedented scale of the Depression. As New York City and the nation faced economic disaster, all accepted wisdom about the nature of poverty would be challenged.

The Dawn of the Depression

During the early years of the Depression, Americans struggled to understand their situation. Rural families often reported a lack of awareness of the crisis. Ed Paulsen recalled, "Everybody talks of the Crash of '29. In small towns out West, we didn't know there was a Crash. What did the stock market mean to us? Not a dang thing. If you were in Cut Bank, Montana, who owned stock?" Similarly, many previously homeless urban residents found life largely unchanged as the 1930s began. For many members of the nation's vulnerable working classes, however, the economic downturn proved devastating, driving them to already crowded urban shelters and food distribution programs.[14]

Industrial employment had been declining even prior to Black Tuesday in October of 1929, when the stock market tumbled dramatically, sending investors into a panic and the economy into a tailspin. As the initial downturn evolved into a recession and then a depression, unemployment would rise to dramatic heights, leaving one in four Americans unemployed by winter 1932. Unable to pay mortgages on homes and farms, thousands of families and individuals found themselves rootless, as they abandoned properties and set out on the roads in search of opportunities. Many of these newly dispossessed individuals and families poured into the nation's cities.

As New York's homeless population increased, the Bowery continued to offer many vital services, housing over fifty of Manhattan's eighty-two lodging houses. By early 1928, service providers estimated the Bowery's homeless population close to 5,000. The city had not endured such dramatic homelessness since the depression of 1914, when annual muni lodgings had topped 300,000. By 1930, the muni housed 750 men each night in bunk beds on three floors, as well as 150 women and children on a separate floor. That winter, city officials opened an East River annex to accommodate additional clients. By February 1931, both facilities were filled to capacity, lodging 3,150 individuals and feeding 12,000 on a single evening. A second annex at the South Ferry terminal lodged and fed an additional 750. By the end of the year, the muni and its annexes provided more than half the 9,000 local beds available.[15]

Although many people migrated to the area in search of better opportunities during the Depression, most of the city's homeless men were New York residents. Most of those who hailed from other states had not traveled far, venturing from Massachusetts, Pennsylvania, New Jersey, or Connecticut. Their national origins were unremarkable, reflecting those of the city's male population. The vast majority described themselves as unmarried, although some were undoubtedly lying to avoid charges of desertion. New York's homeless were older than those of many other cities; the median age of homeless Bowery men was forty-one, while that of their counterparts in Houston, Los Angeles, Washington, D.C., and Pittsburgh ranged from thirty to thirty-four. Homeless African American men were significantly younger than their white counterparts, with an average age of thirty-one.[16]

Homeless youth captured much of the national spotlight during the Depression, but relatively few appeared in New York City. Most remained in the South; youths comprised 28 percent of the homeless in the Southeast, but less than 4 percent in New England. Young, homeless New Yorkers also largely avoided the Bowery. The small population had historically received assistance from facilities like the Children's Aid Society Brace Memorial Newsboys' House, which had lodged homeless boys since 1854; by 1933 it accommodated up to 150 boys per night.[17]

Unskilled workers, frequent victims of layoffs, comprised the majority of the era's Bowery men. A study of nearly 20,000 homeless men found that a large proportion were laborers and sailors, although a range of skilled trades was also represented[18] (Table 1).

As the Depression began, private religious charities like the Salvation Army continued to provide vital services. The Army established a Midtown Transient Service Bureau, whose staff routed both poor and indigent clients to the Army's area hotels. The Booth Memorial Hotel, on the Bowery since 1913, housed over 600 cubicle rooms that accommodated both relief cases and those able to pay thirty-five to fifty cents. By March 1930, in order to maximize the building's capacity, the staff allowed an additional 400 men to "flop" on the building's floors. Outside, they distributed up to 2,000 meal tickets in a daily breadline. The Army also operated an innovative Sixth Street "Cheer Lodge." Equipped with facilities for cleaning clothes, including washtubs, heaters for drying, and irons, the lodge also offered space for socializing, playing games, and reading.[19]

Table 1. Central Registration Bureau Applicants by Occupation,
Sample Taken in 1931–32

Laborer	6, 832
Seaman	339 (+ 2,005 registered with seamen's agencies)
Porter and houseman	779
Kitchen worker	730
Cook	626
Painter	585
Clerk	484
Fireman (furnace)	447
Machinist	380
Longshoreman	338
Waiter	306
Chauffeur	274
Hospital worker	272
Carpenter	255
Salesman	248
Plumber	156
Hotel helper	135
Electrician	126
Printer	126
Iron worker	124
Handyman	106
Baker	100
Agricultural worker	94
Tailor	89
Janitor	82
Rigger	71
Shoemaker	69
Trainman	59
Truck driver	58
Factory worker	57
Watchman	57
Butcher	54
Metal worker	50
All other and not reported	3,348

Anderson, *Homeless in New York City*, 268–69.

Figure 9. The Salvation Army's Booth Memorial Hotel accommodated hundreds of homeless clients during the Depression. Courtesy of Salvation Army National Archives and Research Center.

Figure 10. The Salvation Army's Gold Dust Lodge, a temporary facility used during the Depression, housed and fed thousands. Courtesy of Salvation Army National Archives and Research Center.

The Army also opened the Gold Dust Lodge in 1931, turning a building on loan from Gold Dust Flour into an emergency homeless shelter. The large facility lodged up to 2,250 men, while staff served up to 4,800 daily meals. It housed a barbershop, tailor shop, shower and locker rooms, laundries, libraries, and facilities for film screenings and lectures. By the end of 1932, Lodge residents hailed from forty-three states and forty countries and ranged in age from twenty to over seventy. Each resident worked onsite one day each week in exchange for an extra meal. In 1933, the facility's course offerings included English, arithmetic, bookkeeping, salesmanship, navigation, Bible study, and English as a second language, as well as recreational activities from baseball, chess, and checkers to band concerts and a glee club.[20]

"That's Where I'd Go," proclaimed the cover of a Depression era brochure for the Bowery YMCA. Photographs depicted members' journey through the stages of their stay. Entering shabby and destitute, they emerged clean, poised, employed, and enjoying life in private rooms. Rather than offering clients charitable assistance, the Bowery YMCA issued loans based on an elaborate system of credit. The organization provided a client's room, board, and job search expenses, but officially expected him to repay their value once established in a job. Administrators hoped the system would prevent clients from feeling dependent on charity, empowering them to envision their return to economic self-sufficiency.[21]

This financial system led the organization to struggle during the Depression, as employment opportunities for members declined. In 1927, the Bowery YMCA provided aid to over 3,000 men, at a cost of nearly $24,000 in extended credit. Members repaid an impressive 70 percent of those expenses. In 1932, the organization aided over 6,000 men through $48,000 in credit, less than half of which was repaid. The organization sponsored thirty-two New York City locations, including a Harlem branch, which moved to a new facility in late 1932, where it housed 243 sleeping rooms.[22]

Compared to the city's other ethnic populations, the Jewish community fared relatively well during the Depression, largely due to high rates of white-collar employment. Discriminatory hiring practices barred many Jews from finding work, however. Also, as the Depression began, President Hoover discouraged immigration of those likely to become public charges, reinforcing the commitment of the Hebrew Immigrant Aid Society to its mission. Enlarging its programs, the organization served nearly 66,000 meals in 1929, 156,000 in 1931, and over 438,000 in 1932. Transients comprised 40 percent of the men lodged during 1931, reflecting the organization's continued efforts to aid both recent immigrants and other poor.[23]

As the economic crisis continued, Jewish charities struggled to meet the needs of applicants. Some leaders lobbied for the integration of private and public relief efforts, while others hoped to continue the community's tradition of self-reliance. Maurice Karpf, president of New York's Graduate School for Jewish Social Work, noted, "It has been a source of pride of

Jewish communities and of Jewish social workers that we do not have a pauper population." Others voiced pragmatic concerns over the effect of public administration on programs designed to meet the community's specific needs; by 1931, the Lower East Side hosted a Kosher kitchen and two Kosher breadlines.[24]

Although established religious organizations continued to provide the bulk of assistance to the city's poor during the early years of the Depression, other modern religious charities arose in response to the crisis. The Greater New York Gospel Mission opened in 1929 on Greenwich Village's Eighth Street. Mission administrators hoped the location would encourage clients to leave the Bowery. Housed in a four-story brick building, the Mission offered lodging, dining, and prayer. Up to sixty men slept in the second-floor dormitory, another twenty-nine in convalescent beds on the third, and twenty-five employed men on the fourth. The mission offered restrooms but lacked bathing facilities; every ten days, residents bathed at the muni.[25]

The institution's sermons, like those of other missions, often employed nostalgic rhetoric designed to inspire guilt and subsequent conversion. In one example, a preacher harshly questioned the men's original ambitions: "Don't tell me that you ever sat down in that little home of yours, with that pure, sweet mother, and sister perhaps, around the fire-side, and deliberately planned in your mind and determined that the one ambition in your life would be to become low and homeless and penniless—a derelict undesired by society on the Bowery of New York City."[26]

Although some men found such an approach helpful, not all clients praised the mission's work. Most clients did not stay long; in May 1931, almost 60 percent left after a week or less. Several lamented the lack of bathing facilities, an obvious failing. Others seemed most troubled by their proximity to fellow homeless men. In the words of one client, "A place like this will run any respectable man nuts, all this worrying, associating with bums, and knowing you are an object of charity." Or, in the straightforward terms of another, "The place gets on my nerves."[27]

Charity administrators struggled even more dramatically to meet the needs of homeless white women. Prior to the Depression, the women had been something of a rarity and few resources had been developed to meet their needs. Program administrators and city officials were unprepared to understand the nature and causes of female homelessness, or the reasons for differences in the behavior of homeless women and men. One stark difference was a woman's vulnerability to both sexual assault and social con-

demnation. Fearful of being attacked or judged, many single women carefully avoided drawing attention to themselves. As a result, they were often
overlooked by officials.[28]

Because relatively few white women had been homeless in New York pri-
or to the Depression, few established facilities were prepared to lodge them.
The Traveler's Aid Society opened a Central Registration Bureau for women,
but placements proved difficult. Private shelters initially reserved nearly four
hundred beds for women, but filled many with homeless children. Administrators referred women suffering from mental and emotional problems to the
muni, a prospect some protested. Elderly homeless women ineligible for state
old-age pensions found themselves relegated to the muni or the City Home.
Dreading such facilities, some supported themselves by panhandling. Racially biased institutional policies also limited the clientele at many shelters; very
few women's institutions accepted African American clients.[29]

Overall, the city's homeless women shared the national origins of their
male counterparts; most were American born, and the vast majority of those
born abroad were Irish. Yet the city's homeless women were older than its
men; 40 percent were over fifty, versus 25 percent of men. Such figures conflated two distinct groups of homeless women: middle-aged whites and younger African Americans. In a trend that would continue throughout the century, widows comprised over a third of the city's homeless women. By contrast,
widowers made up only 9 percent of the homeless male population. The
economic vulnerability of older women, especially those unable to support
themselves through work, rendered many destitute during the Depression.[30]

Many service providers described the era's homeless women as more
"difficult" to work with than men. Sociologist Nels Anderson observed,
"Unlike the homeless men, the homeless women are aware of their 'rights.'
Often they come and go at will, disrespecting the time limits set by the institution." But most of the era's observers described homeless women as
deeply ashamed of their poverty and especially fearful of public scrutiny.
Reflecting on the New York City breadlines in a 1933 *New Republic* essay,
Emily Hahn asked, "Where were the women?" She noted that most social
workers found that impoverished women, more often than their male peers,
avoided requesting assistance. Waiting until they teetered on the brink of
total financial and physical ruin before seeking assistance, she argued, rendered women more vulnerable to mental breakdown. While in the past,
an unmarried woman over thirty-five might have been taken in by family
members as a "poor relation," she argued, financially independent mod-

ern women faced unprecedented challenges. She described even the prostitution labor market as "overcrowded." In part, the appearance of single
women and single mothers among the homeless reflected their increasing
financial independence, as more middle-class white women, especially, had
joined the American work force in recent decades. Now they, like their male
colleagues, were unemployed.[31]

Service providers, too, worried that gender roles prevented needy women
from applying for aid. In response, some established facilities began specifically targeting homeless women. The Salvation Army's Women's Emergency
Lodge offered three daily meals, overnight accommodations, and employment referrals, while its women's food depot, sponsored by Mrs. E. F. Hutton, distributed meals and food baskets. In December 1930, the Army opened
a Midtown canteen and "rest room" serving women and girls. The institution offered leisure space to women seeking employment; administrators described it as an alternative to browsing aimlessly in department stores. The
Army magazine highlighted the specific challenges faced by homeless wom-
en: "A man can sleep in the parks, the steps of buildings, and the like, but will
a woman do these things?" Such deeply practical, dramatic concerns shaped
many efforts to address women's basic needs.[32]

Other initiatives reflected more complex psychological interpretations of
women's motivations. In 1930, a philanthropist opened a free East Side lunchroom for needy women. "The Good Samaritan" served coffee and sandwiches
to approximately one hundred women referred daily by churches and charitable
organizations. The New York Times characterized the clientele as more "proud"
than their male counterparts, speculating that they patronized the lunchroom
only because its curtains concealed them from public view. Before seeking assistance, the Times assured readers, these women endured great suffering to
preserve their reputation and self-esteem: "It was the first time they had ever
accepted charity. To be identified with a 'Bowery' atmosphere was too much
for them. . . . Once inside they felt better. The tables, though white-topped, were
small, woman-size tables. There were even a few flowers."[33]

Muni staff were able to place a higher proportion of women residents
than men in jobs by 1930; while women made up only 3 percent of the institution's lodgings, they received 37 percent of the work assignments. The
jobs they filled were primarily the service positions still available during the
early years of the Depression (Table 2). As women's employment possibilities
dwindled, opportunistic households hired domestic workers at discounted
wages, sometimes paying as little as $5 per week.[34]

Table 2. Principal Occupations of White and
Black Women at Central Registration Bureau, Sample Taken in 1931–32

Occupation	White	Black
Domestic	311	68
Cook	35	12
Assistant nurse	33	2
Factory worker	32	6
Hospital worker	31	0
Dressmaker	29	5
Laundry worker	26	1
Housekeeper	25	1
Hotel worker	20	0
Clerk	14	1
Saleslady	14	0
Typist	14	1

Anderson, *Homeless in New York City*, Table 12, 33.

As employment became increasingly scarce, the long-running debates over women's right to perform wage labor intensified. Some homeless men blamed their situation on women's presence in the workforce, seeing the competition for jobs as detrimental. One former envelope addresser who had stayed at the muni intermittently for the past decade concluded bitterly, "There is no more addressing to be done. They used to advertise for all manner of it. . . . Most addressing work is done now by machines and women. Petticoats are putting us fellers on the bum." Such debates also played out in the popular media. Rebutting a 1933 letter to the editor of the *New York Times* that protested the continued employment of "white-collar women," one author argued eloquently: "The majority of women who work for a living are pressed thereto by hard economic necessity. They do not work for the love of it nor to keep a man out of a job. They work because they have to in order to eat and live."[35]

Homeless women were challenging residual nineteenth-century social norms that relegated them to the domestic sphere. Unprepared for the arrival of large numbers of female applicants, private and public agencies catered to an idealized vision of middle-class white femininity. Shy and ashamed, the model client accepted food only when it was offered in a genteel environment. The poor and working-class women who comprised most of the era's homeless, however, bore little resemblance to charity officials' visions. Often widows, workers, and other financially independent women, they were openly requesting assistance and protesting its shortcomings.

The effects of the Depression thus reflected the existing economic and social structure of American society. A person's experience was determined not only by socioeconomic class, but also by gender and racial identity. The African American community of Harlem struggled especially intensely with homelessness. As extended unemployment exacerbated existing social inequality and poverty, homelessness became an increasingly fluid category in the neighborhood. According to the 1930 census, African Americans made up only 5 percent of the city's male population, yet comprised over 15 percent of muni applicants.[36]

As the Depression intensified and tenant evictions became commonplace, many Harlem families and individuals found themselves on the verge of homelessness. In one case, a musician left home in 1931, offering no forwarding address. His widowed mother, whom he had previously supported, had never worked outside the home. By the time she owed six weeks of past rent, a caseworker described her as "terrified lest she be dispossessed." The *New York Age* also publicized stories such as that of Venus Eleazor, a pregnant mother of two deserted by her husband. She lived with her brother and sister-in-law until all three lost their jobs and were evicted. As the family split, Eleazor was fortunate to find friends with whom she and her children could live, narrowly avoiding homelessness.[37]

Educationally, the era's homeless African Americans remained less prepared than their white counterparts; most of the men were unskilled laborers. They worked often in the city's jobs deemed less desirable by whites—as porters, cooks, chauffeurs, kitchen workers, and waiters.[38]

The leading private charities initially attempted to address the mounting crisis in the African American community. The Charity Organization Society launched a Central Bureau to administer emergency relief in the Mt. Morris and Harlem districts. The Salvation Army opened a Harlem lodging house in 1931. Their five-story Hotel for Colored Men on 124th Street held 150 relief lodgers. After applying for assistance at the Welfare

Council Central Registration Bureau (CRB) in lower Manhattan, clients granted a two-week stay walked nearly eight miles to the housing facility. By 1936, the hotel would lodge well over four hundred men, and the organization would serve a staggering 234,333 free meals and provide almost 86,000 nights of lodging.[39]

By December 1932, African Americans comprised nearly one-quarter of all new CRB cases. Administrators attempting to make appropriate referrals faced racist institutional policies. While some African American women stayed at Club Caroline or the YWCA, those not matching the client profiles of those organizations were relegated to the muni, a prospect objectionable to many. Men and women who were refused lodgings were often forced to sleep in public. Many remained in Harlem, sleeping along the banks of the East River, in subway stations, or among the rubble on Park Avenue north of 134th Street. Several city parks also proved popular campsites for homeless African Americans, including Mount Morris Park, Colonial Park, St. Nicholas Park, and lower Manhattan's Battery Park.[40]

Innovative programs tried to harness the rising frustration of the African American community. The Harlem Cooperating Committee on Relief and Unemployment launched a remarkable 1930 campaign to mobilize community resources toward the assistance of the poor. Citing the approximately 1,000 eviction notices issued locally over a three-month period, the organization's fund-raising appeals asked employed Harlem residents to contribute at least 1 percent of their earnings to assist "destitute families of their own race." More than a simple appeal to racial unity, the campaign reflected growing community concern over the unjust treatment of African Americans. In a 1931 letter to the Mayor's Official Committee, one Harlem resident voiced her frustration with such official neglect. "My husband has been jobless for eighteen months," she explained, "but since we have no children, no one can offer him aid. In Harlem our rents are exorbitant, because we want to live decently, and when we pay a low rental we are forced to live like rats in holes. Is no one interested in the Harlem Negroes?"[41]

African Americans and Puerto Ricans who received assistance during the Depression often battled prejudice from white administrators who frequently believed that race, ethnicity, or nationality was somehow causing their poverty. One charity worker speculated that Puerto Ricans lacked both skills and motivation: "To me it seems as though they regarded the C.O.S. as a kind and sympathetic parent—their only resource in their time of need. I grant there are pitifully few resources available to the Porto Rican group. Nevertheless, I wonder if they have the initiative and the 'guts' to go after them, if there were." Officials' biases exacerbated the tensions surrounding relief distribution.[42]

Those African Americans who had migrated recently from the South and Mid-Atlantic states without financial resources faced especially limited prospects during the Depression. Not only could they access few resources and support networks, they did not fit the established relief categories of either "transients" or "local homeless." As the crisis worsened, some families and individuals abandoned plans to remain in the city and returned to the South.[43]

The plight of "J. S." and his family reflected that of many of the era's African American migrants. Born in Louisville, Kentucky, in 1886, he left school at fourteen, on his father's death, to support his younger siblings. He married, fathered two children, and came to New York in 1927, working for eighteen months to earn enough money to bring his family to the city. They lived together in Harlem for nearly a year, until he lost his job as a kitchen helper and could not find another. In 1931, the family's destitution inspired neighbors to donate the train fare for his wife and children to return to Louisville. Now alone in the city, J. S. frequented various homeless facilities. The Harlem YMCA and CRB repeatedly sent him to the muni, but he preferred the Bowery Mission, where he enjoyed the religious services and mission atmosphere. Remarkably, even after facing difficult circumstances, discrimination, and simple bad luck, J. S. blamed himself for his predicament, estimating that two-thirds of the era's homeless had caused their own ruin. "We have been careless," he insisted, "we could have saved a dollar or two instead of spending all we made." Steeped in the era's culture of individualism, he also expressed little interest in Communism, and even felt that some "foreigners" attempting to incite revolution in the United States should be killed.[44]

Twenty-one-year-old "M. L." planned a similar reverse migration to the South. After hitchhiking to New York from South Carolina, he found employment only through making deliveries for $6 per week. Unable to live on the wage, he quit, shined shoes, and performed odd jobs, sleeping in a downtown cellar or in St. Nicholas Park. Having exhausted his resources, he planned to return to South Carolina before winter.[45]

African Americans who returned to the South were abandoning their plans to build better lives in New York and other northern cities. Lured by the promises of the Great Migration, they had encountered cities plagued by racial prejudice and discrimination, problems only exacerbated by the emerging crisis. The scarcity of resources during the Depression highlighted existing inequalities, whether based on class, gender, or race.

As the economic crisis began, Americans had no way of knowing how long it would last. Many initial forecasts were far too conservative, predicting a swift resolution to the nation's financial troubles. As one year stretched into two and three, however, the existing relief structure began to crumble. The ethnic and religious organizations that had fed and sheltered the poor for decades simply could not muster the resources necessary to meet the rising demand.

Private charities would continue to provide vital services to the nation's poor, driven by a desire to spread their religious messages while alleviating human suffering. Increasingly, however, they would partner with local governmental organizations in order to achieve their goals. These emerging relationships did not dramatically alter the types of services that were provided to the poor, yet they would ultimately contribute to the development of a new popular understanding of the role of government in American life.

A System Out of Control

The uneven system of relief pieced together by private charities and municipal agencies increasingly drew criticism as the Depression worsened. Overlapping mission statements meant duplication of services, which seemed wasteful to many observers. Others called for disciplining panhandlers and other poor individuals who refused to follow official relief protocols. Some questioned the loose organization of aid programs, calling first for government regulation and, ultimately, government funding of aid to the nation's poor. Many of the initial critiques, however, originated out of sheer disgust at the existing conditions.

As early as 1928, mounting poverty and homelessness already meant severely overcrowded facilities. New York City officials tried to regulate private relief efforts, including the one sponsored by Mr. Zero (Urbain Ledoux). The Tub was temporarily closed in April by City Health Commissioner Louis Harris; the Rescue Mission, the Hadley House Mission, and the All-Night Mission were also briefly shut down for violating health and safety codes. In particular, they lacked adequate fire exits, toilets, bathing facilities, and beds.[46]

Some observers insisted that closing such facilities merely exacerbated the suffering of the homeless. The week after the closures, the facilities were reopened. *Daily News* reporter Martin Sommers embarked on an undercover, three-night Bowery research trip to evaluate them. Posing as a homeless man from Ohio, Sommers adopted the "nom de bum" Joseph Stephens. Reporting on his stay, he described the missions in question as "not 100 percent sanitary or healthy." Although critical of the conditions of such lodgings, he questioned the logic of their closure: "But where, if these missions are closed, are the bums and job hunters to sleep?"[47]

Far worse than the closed flops, in his opinion, were the "spilkies" or speakeasies that allowed men to stay overnight after purchasing alcohol. He described conditions in graphic terms:

> The Black Hole of Calcutta would have been a garden spot
> compared with that Spilkie, it seemed to me when we entered. A
> single room about as long and narrow as a subway train. Ten or
> twelve rickety chairs crowded as close together as chairs can be.
> Sleeping derelicts tumbling against one another, groaning and
> snoring and coughing. Fifteen others asleep on a floor that literally
> was slimy. . . . In a rear room behind the bar ten other bums
> coiled in sleep. . . . Wedged between two bums with a proclivity
> for falling together, I slept only about an hour that night. Their
> scratching, writhing, and cursing made sleep impossible.[48]

Spilkies were not a new invention; men had "flopped" for decades in back rooms of Bowery saloons. In 1914, investigators described saloons in which "the men were allowed to expectorate promiscuously on the floors," and poor hygiene and improper ventilation left the atmosphere "foul-smelling" and "nauseating." Despite the unappealing atmosphere, spilkies attracted homeless men. A 1930 census found over seven hundred men lodged in speakeasies. Especially for men who resented the regulations of the muni and the moralizing of the missions, spilkies offered a brand of freedom, access to alcohol, and camaraderie.[49]

Even harder for officials and charity administrators to regulate were the city's panhandlers. In 1930, the Welfare Council Committee on Unemployment warned that panhandling posed not only "a serious nuisance," but also "a real menace." A year later, the Council "Committee on Street Begging" cautioned that, without appropriate and swift action, the city would "revert to creating and maintaining a pauper class." The Council urged city residents not to give cash to the homeless but to refer them to the Central Registration Bureau.[50]

The director of the Emergency Shelter distributed 15,000 books of tickets redeemable for lodging and meals, encouraging city residents to give them to panhandlers in lieu of cash. Even this action proved controversial, as the Welfare Council worried the tickets might somehow lure additional panhandlers to New York from other cities. The homeless, the Council warned, treated such tickets as commodities, wagering them in card and dice games. Despite such criticism, the Emergency Unemployment Relief Committee issued booklets of tickets that winter, entitling recipients to food and shelter from their choice of nineteen locations throughout the five boroughs. Charity officials used such tickets as a litmus test of panhandlers' motivations. Anyone who refused them risked being branded a "professional beggar."[51]

Similar anti-begging campaigns had been waged periodically since the turn of the century. In 1916, psychologists with the police department Mendicancy Squad had argued that most individuals in breadlines appeared fit enough to work. The Squad insisted that most homeless refused employment, even as many homeless insisted that job offers often proved to be scams. Such crackdowns on begging had increased during the 1920s, when the Mendicancy Squad targeted beggars in the Times Square theater district, many of whom were disabled. Convicted beggars received workhouse sentences ranging from one to three months. Subsequent waves of such arrests garnered headlines describing "wealthy," "moneyed," and "well-to-do beggars." Allegedly, some wore "fur coats and diamonds in their hours of ease," while others panhandled while possessing over $12,000. One young panhandler from a wealthy Revere, Massachusetts, family, who sold penknives on the subways, reportedly boasted of a plan to return to Boston to "take it easy as soon as I get enough out of the suckers here." The media also relished tales of ingenious panhandlers posing as "legless" or "fit-throwers" to garner higher profits.[52]

The campaign against panhandling in New York City during the Depression, while less severe than those of prior eras, effectively frightened many of the city's homeless away from the practice. Asked if he would consider begging on the streets, one homeless man replied, "If I thought the cops wouldn't bother me I would go for it. I wouldn't do it unless I was out of work and needed something to eat." A frequent muni client remarked, "I don't ask nobody for money. I'm afraid. Fellows tell me that if you ask people the cops will club you to death." A young African American man answered, "Panhandle? No. You're not allowed. If you were allowed, I would. But if the law catches you they half kill you." The fear of police violence, coupled with a sense of futility, caused a middle-aged homeless immigrant to avoid the practice: "I nev-

FLEISCHMAN'S BREAD LINE

Figure 11. Breadlines, such as this December 1913 example, were common sights in American cities during times of economic hardship. George Grantham Bain Collection, Prints & Photographs Division, Library of Congress.

er mooched on the street. I am afraid of the cops. Men told me they get beat up in the street. Everybody is broke. Who are they going to mooch. People, if they are all dressed up, got no money. . . . I am a working man; I made my living. I don't believe in mooching. You have got to get soup on the Bowery when you can't get it anywhere else."[53]

Personal shame kept other homeless people from panhandling. A young African American man expressed his reservations: "I just ain't got the nerve to go up to a man—me a great big man—and ask him for a nickel. They wouldn't give me nothing no how. I look too big and able, like I can take care of myself." An elderly man explained, "No, I do not ask men for money; I don't have the guts. I have tried it several times, but when a guy looks at me I walk away. I can't even bum an eye-opener (morning drink). If the first place I ask refuses me I do without it." Raised to fulfill the socially accepted role of the breadwinner, many homeless men struggled to beg on the city streets. Those who did faced prosecution.[54]

The parallel explosion of breadlines in the early years of the Depression dramatized the scale of the era's suffering, and frustrated officials' efforts to control

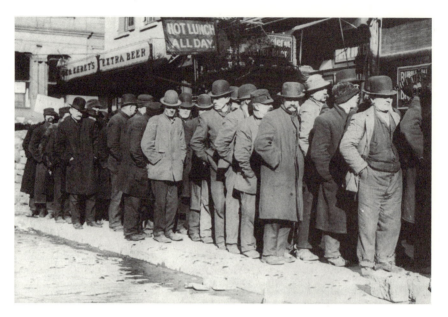

Figure 12. On February 7, 1910, Bowery men awaiting bread packed themselves tightly into orderly lines. George Grantham Bain Collection, Prints & Photographs Division, Library of Congress.

the relief system. Quickly becoming the most recognizable symbol of urban poverty, breadlines sparked fear, empathy, and shame in observers. American realist painter Reginald Marsh depicted men hunched in crowded lines. Marsh titled one etching with Hoover's infamous phrase, "No one has starved," to highlight the ironic contrast between the suffering of the poor and the seemingly glib optimism of federal officials. Marsh's subjects, their repeated forms clad in battered raincoats and shabby hats, some embittered, others forlorn, emphasized the dehumanizing nature of public relief distribution.[55]

Long-time city residents would have recalled the breadlines from the depression of 1914. In the spring of that year the *New York Sun* had operated a daily storefront breadline. The New York Association for Improving the Condition of the Poor (AICP) had opposed the practice, calling breadlines "always unwise," due to their risk of causing "demoralized character." Worse still, the *Sun* had allowed women and children to participate in the breadline. The paper featured stories of young girls in the breadlines aiding bedridden mothers, and of others suffering from tuberculosis and malnutrition. The

AICP argued that women applicants should be referred to other social welfare agencies rather than "subjected to the demoralizing effect on themselves and on their homes of appearing in public in a breadline."[56]

AICP officials worried that children in the breadlines were not only exposed to a "demoralizing atmosphere," but also risked being lured into a life of panhandling. Administrators warned that such children "take the first step in mendicancy which is too often never retraced." Instead, they argued, schools should expand reduced-price school lunch programs, in order to provide children with access to healthy food without risking their self-respect.[57]

During the Depression, breadlines welcoming women and children continued to disturb many observers. Salomon Lowenstein, chairman of the Welfare Coordinating Committee on Unemployment, urged relief administrators to keep children out of breadlines, calling instead for home relief for such families, "so that their poverty will not be advertised." When the Mayor's Official Committee required families to line up for food distribution at area police stations, many criticized the system as "inconsiderate and demoralizing." One observer cited both the corporeal and psychological exposure of recipients: "The long lines at the police stations, often standing for hours in cold and rain with scanty clothing, meant physical hardship as well as humiliation. All the neighbors knew who were there."[58]

As the crisis of the Depression mounted, the breadlines snaking the city's streets struck many observers as emblems of a relief system out of control. As early as 1930, President Hoover's Emergency Committee for Employment, established to communicate information about the economic crisis, advocated a relief registration system to reduce fraud. Without such procedures, officials argued, some recipients might spend their days traveling from one breadline to another, consuming up to six meals. Some worried that such access to food would keep the poor from seeking employment, and might even attract homeless people from other cities. Yet not everyone shared these concerns over duplicative relief. When the Welfare Council instituted a registration process for relief applicants, a Salvationist remarked wryly, "It is hoped that some such scheme may operate this winter, but the basic principle remains—that the hungry must be fed, and it is not regarded as a major catastrophe if a man should happen to get two bowls of soup instead of one."[59]

By early 1931, approximately 70,000 daily meals were provided at 79 New York breadlines, including 3,500 meals served in the parks by the Emergency Work Bureau and 19,000 packaged meals distributed through the Salvation Army food depots. Officials coordinated the mealtimes of the various food stations, hoping to limit repeat diners. Such systems could not exert control over breadlines sponsored by individual philanthropists. Inspired by newspaper articles chronicling the suffering of the homeless, wealthy area resident Mrs. Irving T. Bush solicited donations from friends to purchase clothing, YMCA meal tickets, and vouchers for medical care. She distributed these items at a twice weekly winter breadline that sometimes swelled to fifteen hundred. Branding her "Lady Bountiful," media reports emphasized the caring, personal, feminine attention Bush paid male recipients. In her own accounts, Bush downplayed the scale of her operation, remarking, "I can only go on trying to give a little relief in my simple, homespun way."[60]

Even with the expanding regulations, though, the existing systems of homeless assistance were soon not enough to meet the mounting need. Convinced that private philanthropy would provide the solution, New York City's political and social elites embarked on an ambitious, unprecedented campaign of quasi-public fundraising. First, in 1930, the mayor's official committee, aided by the police department, gathered information about the city's needy and distributed food and small cash supplements. City workers donated a portion of their salaries to fund the program. A similar fund sponsored by employees of the city schools facilitated free school lunch programs to children and occasional small cash supplements to needy families.[61]

That year, two moralistic organizations established to address nineteenth-century poverty, the Charity Organization Society and the Association for Improving the Condition of the Poor, formed the Emergency Unemployment Committee, headed by Seward Prosser. The Prosser Committee raised $8.6 million toward relief efforts, distributing some funds to selected social welfare organizations, including the Salvation Army, Jewish Social Service Association, and Catholic Charities. The Prosser Committee Emergency Work Bureau also created jobs for residents. Satisfied with this progress, the Welfare Council coordinating committee, led by former New York state governor Alfred E. Smith, urged both public and private organizations not to open additional lodging houses or breadlines. Describing the existing system as adequate, Smith cautioned, "New York City cannot, however, be expected to provide shelter for homeless men or families coming here from other communities." Other cities, too, were ending breadlines; by early 1931, less than one-fifth of the nation's cities continued to maintain them.[62]

By 1931, the economic crisis was worsening, and the city's poor were beginning to protest their spartan living conditions. A dramatic Communist-sponsored "hunger march" spanning several boroughs brought protesters to the City Free Employment Bureau on Lafayette Street. From there, they proceeded to the Bowery. Marchers called for free utilities for the unemployed, unemployment insurance, and an end to evictions. They also suggested using the city armories and vacant buildings as temporary lodgings. When the three or four thousand marchers passed the Salvation Armybreadline, an altercation left a police officer's jaw broken. On another occasion, two trucks filled with bread, cookies, and jelly rolls donated by a bakery parked beside a breadline outside the Salvation Army's Bowery Hotel. Hungry and tired, the waiting men mobbed the trucks, forcing the police to quell the "pastry riot."[63]

The muni, in particular, drew protests over the city's treatment of the poor. A Trade Union Unity League demonstration of 1,000 homeless and unemployed men protested the five nights per month limit on stays. Facility superintendent J. Mannix refused to confirm the policy, insisting: "We are never full, and I believe the reason more do not come here is that they object to taking a bath." A series of meetings ensued; the crowd at one voted to request from welfare commissioner Frank Taylor unlimited lodging, indoor areas for those awaiting meals, three meals each day, use of public buildings and armories for additional lodging space, and free clothing and use of laundries for the unemployed. The *Daily Worker* reported that Mannix responded by posting a woman at the entrance distributing candy and encouraging the homeless to "cheer up," noting, "Angered at this cheap insult, many of the jobless threw back the cheap candy."[64]

By late 1931, the city's Gibson Committee, chaired by Harvey P. Gibson, set out to raise $12 million over five months to further the work of a variety of relief organizations. The Committee's program employed workers three days per week in the city's parks and similar locations. Divisions focused on women's needs, the outer boroughs, and white-collar employment. The Committee avoided helping transient homeless men, concentrating instead on men with dependents and single women. Some homeless men resented such favoritism toward married men by the city's employment and relief programs. A middle-aged Irish alcoholic who had lived in the city since he was seventeen years old commented wryly: "I'm not married. But I'm going to get married. I'm going to pick up some woman in the park and marry her so that I can get one of those jobs that they are handing out."[65]

President Hoover praised the Gibson Committee's work as a shining example of the "traditional American spirit of community solidarity in times of stress." It exemplified the power of private philanthropy: "A cold and distant charity which puts out its sympathy only through the tax collector yields a

very meager dole of unloving and perfunctory relief." Hoover's reaction to the
Gibson Committee reflected his continued conviction that charitable assistance should be carried out by private entities on a voluntary basis. Hoover's
President's Emergency Committee for Employment was transformed that
year to the President's Organization for Unemployment Relief (POUR). In its
new form, the Committee used advertisements to solicit charitable donations
for aiding the nation's poor. Members of the administration fervently hoped
such measures would prevent the need for direct federal aid. As it became
apparent that voluntarism would not meet rising needs, the administration
gradually extended its role in public relief. Under the 1932 Emergency Relief
and Construction Act, for instance, the administration provided federal aid
to state relief programs, although it limited support to those who successfully
navigated an intensive application and screening process.[66]

The eventual shift of the Hoover administration toward expanding the
role of the federal government in the nation's relief system reflected both the
gradual deepening of the crisis and an attempt to address the president's in-
credibly poor public image. As the crisis mounted, Hoover acquired a reputation as being cold and heartless. These perceptions only intensified with his
disastrous handling of the "Bonus Army" of military veterans seeking early
payment of their bonuses scheduled for dispersal in 1945. When General
Douglas MacArthur's troops drove the veterans and their families from their
campsite, Hoover's image sank to new lows. Ironically, the violent altercation
followed by only a day Hoover's signature on the Emergency Relief and Construction Act, eradicating the goodwill he might have attained.[67]

During the early 1930s, cities across the country followed the same pattern
as New York, as private charities floundered in the face of crushing demand.
Ann Arbor officials, like their Detroit counterparts, tried to alleviate the suffering of the poor, gradually expanding the city government's role in relief
efforts. Prior to the Depression, Ann Arbor was home to little public relief,
as private charities shouldered the burden of caring for the poor. Concerned
mayor Edward Staebler had commissioned an unemployment committee
(the Community Fund) as early as 1928, asking them for policy recommendations to counteract the city's dwindling employment opportunities in construction, retail, and industry. As the crisis worsened, the Community Fund
focused increasingly on distributing food and clothing to the poor, but by
1931 the organization could not meet local needs. By 1932, Ann Arbor began
to take on a larger role not only in fundraising efforts and regulating employment services, but also in hiring the unemployed on public work projects.[68]

Figure 13. In this February 1937 FSA photograph of Howard Street, a skid row in San Francisco, Dorothea Lange captured the despair felt across the nation. Farm Security Administration—Office of War Information Photograph Collection, Prints & Photographs Division, Library of Congress.

Philadelphia witnessed a similar evolution of its relief system, as the elaborate network of private charities established during the nineteenth century gave way by 1932 to calls for federal aid to the poor. As manufacturing and construction jobs disappeared by 1930, Philadelphia was hard hit by the Depression. Home to eighty breadlines and soup kitchens, Philadelphia's initial attempts at extending services focused on coordinating the efforts of private and religious charities. Banker Horatio Gates Lloyd led the Committee for Unemployment Relief, which hoped to coordinate and raise private donations to avoid instituting a system of public relief. Despite the Lloyd Committee's impressive campaign, the funds proved insufficient to meet Philadelphia's dire need. Lloyd oversaw five subcommittees, targeting direct relief, work relief, a loan fund, breakfasts for schoolchildren, and a shelter for homeless men. The men's shelter, housed in an eight-story factory building, was furnished with 3,000 cots from the War Department and kitchen equipment from the Red Cross. Men were asked to work a half-day in exchange for meals and lodging. Such elaborate relief cost more than private coffers could bear; by 1932, Philadelphia officials had abandoned their conservative stand, and called for direct federal assistance for the needy.[69]

As New York State's quasi-public efforts funded vital programs, some officials correctly predicted that they would never keep pace with the rising need. Governor Franklin Delano Roosevelt and his allies proposed state funding of local relief. The 1931 Wicks Act made New York the first state to channel public funds to needy localities. The Temporary Emergency Relief Administration (TERA), headed by social worker Harry Hopkins, allocated $20 million toward work relief and home relief programs for state residents who passed a means test. The commitment of state funds marked a significant turning point in the approach to poverty, establishing a precedent of funding and control. Under TERA, the state reimbursed up to 40 percent of the funds that localities spent on unemployment relief. State-level administrators also acquired the power to "make and enforce rules" regarding such aid.[70]

Emboldened by these developments, New York City social workers and relief officials began to lobby for federal aid in the fall of that year. Not all states and cities supported such initiatives, however. In the words of Atlanta mayor James Key, "We do not want a government dole or a Federal breadline. . . . Atlanta can take care of her own if outsiders do not rush in, and every effort will be made to confine relief strictly to our own people." Such fear of the transient homeless limited efforts to meet their needs, as local officials insisted that only local autonomy would preserve their interests.[71]

The fear of outright rebellion of the poor proved a final factor in the shift toward acceptance of broader public relief systems. Some commentators worried that the degradation of sustained poverty, exacerbated by the public and humiliating nature of contemporary relief practices, would radicalize the poor. Communists and other radicals rallied around the cause of homelessness, staging mass demonstrations and marches on both private and public agencies. On the radical stage, Claire and Paul Stilton's play "1931—" revolved around an unemployed factory worker who slid down the social ladder, eventually landing in a breadline. The play depicted jobless men on the Bowery, shoveling snow on Fifth Avenue and repeatedly applying for the dwindling number of factory positions. One critic called it "harrowing," noting that its subject matter inarguably reflected "the now and here of the life we are leading."[72]

In San Francisco, Communist political rallies drew homeless men. Participant Ed Paulsen recalled, "I remember the demands: We demand work, we demand shelter for our families, we demand groceries, this kind of thing." Although the crowds of homeless men stated such demands, Paulsen remembered them as largely apolitical: "We weren't greatly agitated in terms of society. Ours was a bewilderment, not an anger. Not a sense of being particularly put upon. We weren't talking revolution; we were talking jobs."[73]

Caught in an unprecedented economic crisis, homeless people struggled to comprehend their lives. Raised in a culture celebrating the moral value of hard work and thrift, many could not reconcile their unemployment and lowered standard of living with their established belief systems. More broadly, even as the crisis of the Depression worsened, most Americans did not embrace Communism or other radical causes, maintaining, for the most part, a commitment to individual responsibility. The homeless, like other Americans, held a variety of opinions regarding their individual culpability for their current situation.[74]

Some homeless people were angered by the treatment they received from the religious missions. One former client remarked bitterly, "You don't get nothing at the Salvation Army. . . . They give them boiled cabbage one day, and the next day they want them to saw wood for four hours. By God, it's an outrage. You can't get a pair of socks with holes in them unless you pay for them." A Russian immigrant dissatisfied with his stay at an area mission commented, "Bed bugs. They preach too much. No good. Every night Jesus Christ, Jesus Christ! No good. Never helps me. You get poorer. The soup is all mixed up with water. You get plenty of bread; that's one thing that you can say. I was there two or three weeks. I never slept on a bed—I slept on the floor all of the time." The homeless shared such useful evaluations through friendship networks. A former migrant laborer reported learning from "the boys" that "the Gold Dust Lodge was all right when it first opened but is getting punk now," since the institution of work requirements.[75]

Many homeless individuals harbored equally deep distrust toward employment agencies. Agencies often charged workers a five-dollar fee, shared by the agency and the employer, in exchange for jobs lasting only a few days.

Men assigned to work outside the city through such agencies also paid exorbitant room and board rates. Reverend Walter Britt of the Greater New York Gospel Mission referred to such employment agents as "arrogant grafters," who, "like spiders," "fatten on the prey" of the destitute. The homeless called them simply "sharks."[76]

Worried that the homeless would prove dangerous, officials commissioned neuro-psychiatric examinations of nine hundred homeless men in 1931. Researchers described not simmering radicals but surprisingly "apathetic," "cooperative," and "indifferent" subjects. Some doctors characterized the homeless under study as "a rather dull lot" and "shiftless," but one observed that "the great majority would be able to carry on successfully in ordinary times." Another noted that "in a period of depression the less fit show up as less fit than they would under normal economic conditions."[77]

Indeed, the disabled homeless fared especially poorly during the Depression, having few advocates. One man described as emotionally retarded, physically limited, and of low intelligence registered with the Bowery YMCA, but misunderstood the instructions for finding a job, resulting in dismissal from the program. Despite these challenges, he blamed himself, describing his predicament as "due to my own dumbness. If you got sense you can always get a job. A man should be able to meet any situation." "J. K.," a middle-aged Irish American laborer born in Jersey City, experienced a similar situation. Nearly unemployable due to cataracts in both eyes, protruding hemorrhoids, and a partly amputated thumb, he could not read an employment slip given him at the muni. Confused by the instructions, he left for the day instead of reporting for work. Banned from the muni for a year, he stayed at the Bowery Mission, in area speakeasies, along the riverfront, and in the Delancey Street subway station.[78]

Mental illness and depression also plagued many homeless. Some accepted a degree of depression as a reasonable response to their desperate plight. One summarized the effects of prolonged poverty on his outlook: "Sometimes hunger makes me a little depressed. In fact, I think a fellow would be an imbecile going around smiling in this crisis. A fellow expects every day to find a job somewhere, even if it's only cleaning out a cellar."[79]

Social investigators asked New York's homeless to analyze the reasons for their present circumstance. Many described basic difficulties maintaining their personal hygiene and professional appearance. One middle-aged man replied, "I got down like this by continually looking for work and having no new clothes to replace the old ones. I could get something, I am sure, if I looked better. I have no appearance to go anywhere for work. As soon as you lose your appearance you lose everything." Another observed, "I think that appearance is the main thing that is keeping me back. I have always been credited with being a fairly good worker." An elderly man who had recently spent his first night at the muni complained bitterly of its fumigation process, "I'd rather be dead. At the Municipal Lodging House they put your clothes in the stove a couple of times; after that they rot. I'd work for anything if I could keep clean. This suit is fearful. I'm ashamed to walk around in it."[80]

Other homeless individuals criticized the relief system more broadly. After an intake interview at the Central Registration Bureau, one man complained about the insensitivity of the staff: "When a man is down he feels about as low as he can, I don't see why these organizations that are supposed to help him try to step on his knees. Why don't they give him a word of encouragement—slap him on the back and say, 'Well, old man, things will break your way in a few days? Instead of that, they use sarcasm or yell at him and make him feel lousier than he already feels." Another eloquently expressed frustration over a social service provider's decision to contact his family and inform them of his plight: "Had I desired to solicit my relatives and friends in any way it would not have been necessary for me to invoke the aid of an outside agency. I have been trying to make 'the grade' in the vernacular, without calling on those near and dear to me. It was the very thing I wished to spare them."[81]

Frustrated by the increasingly regulated relief system, many of the city's homeless avoided established programs. Eschewing formal lodgings, they slept instead in unsanctioned encampments and abandoned buildings. Police raids of such areas often resulted in vagrancy arrests and month-long work-house sentences.[82]

Such squatter colonies were not a new development. During the nineteenth century they had been a common sight in the city, as substantial numbers of squatters occupied areas ranging from Manhattan's Upper East Side and Upper West Side to Red Hook, Brooklyn. By 1880, Manhattan officials had been aggressively evicting squatters, through use of the courts, police, and bureaucratic measures requiring them to pay costly water and sewage fees. Although many squatters paid rent to property owners according to informal leases, the Manhattan courts sided with the landlords. By the turn of the century, Brooklyn officials, too, began evicting large numbers of squatters, making way for urban development projects, including the construction of Ebbets Field. By the 1920s, nearly all vestiges of squatter communities had been cleared from the city's landscape.[83]

But with the crisis of the Depression, such encampments appeared again across the country. Sarcastically termed "Hoovervilles," in mockery of the president's callousness toward the suffering of the poor, such temporary structures housed nearly 16,000 men and almost 2,000 women nationwide by March 1933. In Cleveland, as the Depression struck the African American and Eastern European immigrant communities, shantytowns were built on Whiskey Island and elsewhere throughout the city. By 1933, Cleveland was home to nine shantytowns. The largest, lodging mostly African Americans at the foot of East 13th Street, contained 42 shanties and over two hundred residents. Shantytown dwellers fished, gardened, and scavenged for food in the city dumps. The city razed some encampments repeatedly throughout the Depression.[84]

In New York, officials similarly cracked down on large or semipermanent shantytowns. In 1932, homeless people erected over one hundred huts in a Spring Street vacant lot, only to lose them in a police raid. Later that year, homeless military veterans built a shantytown near Riverside Drive and 79th Street. The community's leaders prided themselves on the militaristic code of order and discipline they instituted.[85]

Central Park's lower reservoir housed the city's most visible and solid shantytown. Unemployed skilled laborers constructed sturdy shacks of lumber, tarpaper, linoleum, and even brick foraged from area construction sites. A September 1932 police raid sparked protest from residents, who pointed to the care with which they had built and maintained the dwellings. Asked his plans after the demolition of the encampment, one resident replied, "I don't know where we'd go. Doorways, I guess. I'd sooner die than go to the municipal." For highly independent homeless individuals, shantytowns offered freedom from invasive regulation and some opportunity for leadership.[86]

As the Depression plunged more middle-class Americans into poverty, the mingling of the "old" and "new" homeless challenged prevailing understandings of the nature of poverty and subsequent relief strategies. As early as 1928, *New York Times* articles noted that mission breadlines drew no longer the routine "Bowery derelicts," accommodating instead many men who were "better dressed and of a higher caliber." A 1930 essay cautioned that the economic crisis posed psychological dangers unique to the middle classes:

> "White-collar" workers . . . have an anguished, haunting look of
> fear which is not seen in the day worker, the laborer, the man

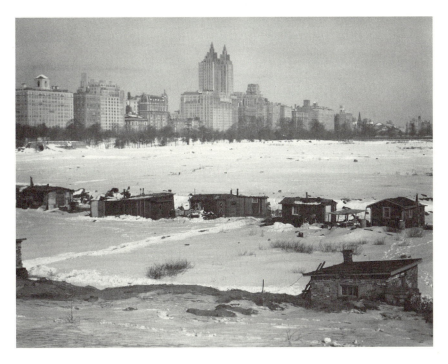

Figure 14. During the Great Depression, homeless New Yorkers built a substantial encampment in Central Park, photographed here against the skyline of wealth. Nat Norman, "Hooverville, Central Park, ca. 1930s." Copyright Museum of the City of New York.

> more or less used to vicissitudes in employment and who has
> learned to accept them, if not philosophically, at least with a
> certain defensive adroitness. But to the white-collar man the
> situation which he has seen coming slowly and inevitably nearer
> as his savings disappeared, means shame and chagrin.[87]

Chicago faced a similar situation, as private charities tried to meet stagger-ing demands. By winter 1932, over 175,000 Chicago families were receiving relief.[88] Researchers at the University of Chicago set out to understand how families found themselves on assistance. Their study found that poor and working-class families were falling on hard times, no longer able to afford the rent on even their small, overcrowded apartments. Before applying for assistance, families were exhausting available credit, borrowing money, asking friends and family for help, and selling their possessions. One Chicago shelter resident described his fall down the socioeconomic ladder:

> I went from door to door trying to sell hosiery. But I finally couldn't make it. In the winter of 1933 I couldn't even make my room rent and money for food. Then I worked in restaurants. I pawned my trunk to pay for my rent. I sold my pawn ticket. The last straw was when I was bawled out by a girl on Clark street. She called me a dirty bum. That settled it. If I was to be a bum, I'd be one. So I gave up the struggle and applied for relief.[89]

Other men applying for aid had long been in a precarious situation, often due to mental illness and problem drinking. One shelter resident recalled, "I went to hell when my wife died. I lived with my wife for ten years. We had no children, but we got along very well together. We were exceptionally happy. After she died I kind of went to hell. I didn't give a damn whether I worked or not. Then after I lost my job I started hanging around North Clark Street, mostly around the cheap dance halls and taverns."[90]

These converging needy populations overwhelmed the relief bureaus of the nation's charities, causing officials to gradually abandon long held beliefs about the causes of poverty and the appropriate role of local and national government. Observers accustomed to the suffering of historically impoverished groups bridled at the sight of their middle-class peers enduring embarrassingly public, demeaning aid distribution. Yet even as some objected to the seemingly undifferentiated treatment of the era's poor, the experience of poverty and homelessness in the nation's cities remained profoundly shaped by an individual's race, ethnicity, gender, profession, age, and religious background. The Depression was exacerbating existing inequalities, forcing the working classes into poverty and the poor into destitution.

The early years of the Depression brought rising unemployment and increasing numbers of homeless individuals and families. By January 1933, over 1.5 million Americans were homeless. As they flooded into the nation's cities, private charities struggled and ultimately faltered in the face of the massive unemployment and mounting poverty of the Depression. Charity administrators were forced to renegotiate their relationship with the emerging welfare state. New York City's Jewish charities, for instance, had long been proud of their ability to provide for the needy in their community. But by 1931 the

Jewish Social Service Association was receiving public funds. By 1933, public organizations provided assistance to many Jewish Americans. Relinquishing control of many relief programs, Jewish community leaders joined Catholics in supporting public welfare initiatives.[91]

Public officials and private relief administrators struggled to understand the motivations of the era's shifting poor and homeless population. Nineteenth-century charity reformers had distinguished between the unworthy and worthy poor, and such logic remained deeply influential during the Depression. Many officials feared that assistance of the poor would foster "pauperization" and a lingering habit of seeking aid. Some also worried about increasing political radicalism. Ledoux's antics might have been harmless, but the rising trend of radicalism in cities across the country caused politicians and charity administrators to fear that poor and homeless individuals might not merely expect assistance, but also demand it. In reality, relatively few homeless New Yorkers could be identified as radicals. Some participated in marches and demonstrations, but most relied on the American logic of individualism, blaming themselves for their poverty.[92]

Until governor Franklin D. Roosevelt's 1931 launch of the TERA, New York City's relief system, like those of other cities, had remained a local affair. Public and private programs assisting the homeless and poor had multiplied and evolved, but administrators had clung to long-established philosophies, as religious missions and charity reform organizations had remained at the center of relief efforts. As traditional systems of poor relief proved incapable of meeting the era's dramatic need, however, social workers, politicians, and relief administrators at the municipal, state, and federal levels proposed bold, increasingly public strategies.[93]

CHAPTER 2

A NEW DEAL FOR THE HOMELESS

I N an April 1932 campaign speech, Democratic presidential candidate Franklin D. Roosevelt announced his commitment to projects "that build from the bottom up and not from the top down, that put their faith once more in the forgotten man at the bottom of the economic pyramid." Roosevelt called for reform of agricultural and tariff policy and of mortgage lending practices in an effort to stabilize the American economy. Once in office, the Roosevelt administration delivered on these promises, enacting a wave of policies and programs designed to ease the suffering of the poor while regulating the economic and political realms. Identifying the migrant homeless as another area of risk, the administration set out to assist them.[1]

In the tumultuous environment of the Depression, the Roosevelt administration enjoyed unprecedented latitude in forging programs with ambitious agendas. Even in this climate, though, efforts to aid the homeless were constrained by political realities. As the expansion of the scope of the federal government brought national administrators into operations carried out at the state and local levels, power struggles erupted. More significantly, Americans questioned the nature of the assistance that should be offered to the homeless. Their definition of appropriate aid was grounded in their understanding of the causes and demographics of homelessness. During the depths of the Depression, which propelled middle- and working-class Americans into poverty, the nation was willing to extend unprecedented generosity. Such programs did not last, however, unable to withstand the rhetorical and political evolution of the New Deal.

The New Deal on Skid Row

As the Depression deepened, America's cities were unable to provide assistance to the swelling ranks of the homeless population. During the winter of 1931–32, New York's Central Registration Bureau referred 45,000 men to the muni. By the time of Roosevelt's 1932 election, the muni was providing nearly 80 percent more nights of lodging than it had the previous year. Homeless women, especially, applied for relief in record numbers, at a rate more than double that of 1931. White-collar workers also appeared more often in assistance lines, changing the face of homelessness from a migrant worker to one's former middle-class neighbor. Entire families continued to hit the road in desperation. This grim situation was replicated nationwide; over thirteen million Americans were unemployed, and some estimated the total number of transients at two million.[2]

During the initial stages of the Depression, President Hoover had maintained faith in voluntarism and the self-regulatory ability of the private sector. As the crisis worsened, though, even the Hoover administration began to embrace expanded government intervention into the economy. The Reconstruction Finance Corporation initially lent funds to banks and railroads, then expanded its mission to include lending money to state relief programs for public works projects. When state governors, including Pennsylvania's Gifford Pinchot, complained of the difficulty in receiving funding, social work expert and economist Edith Abbott asked, "Why are state and national government fighting over the responsibility levels while poor people are in need of relief? How much is tradition, how much 'principle'?" Impatient in the face of stark destitution and rising homelessness, many called for decisive action.[3]

Offering direct relief to the poor struck many as a disastrous plan. During the late 1931 and early 1932 U.S. Senate hearings leading to the passage of the Emergency Relief Administration statute, representatives of Hoover's President's Organization on Unemployment Relief and the U.S. Chamber of Commerce opposed the relief bills, calling them a "dole." Linton Swift, executive director of the Family Welfare Association of America, refuted their claim: "I wish to make clear my conviction as a social worker that proposals for Federal aid have no relation to the establishment de novo of a dole. A dole is a dole, whether it is given by an individual, a private charitable agency, a city, a state, or the Federal government. It is a dole whether it is given in cash or in kind." But direct federal relief to the poor in particular continued to be singled out and branded a dole long after the hearings.[4]

Looking at the era's homeless and other unemployed, officials and middle-class observers felt a mixture of empathy and fear. Many were disturbed by the fact that the newly poor seemed to be, on the whole, average Americans. In a 1933 speech to the National Conference of Social Work, social worker and head of the Federal Emergency Relief Administration Harry Hopkins observed, "We are now dealing with people of all classes. It is no longer a matter of unemployables and chronic dependents, but of your friends and mine who are involved in this. Every one of us knows some family of our friends which is or should be getting relief." These shifts would affect programming, unless middle-class Americans falling on hard times were to receive the same treatment as "Bowery bums."[5]

On a broader scale, many also feared that long-term unemployment would destroy the nation's character. In 1932, YMCA administrator Ernest Poole worried that direct relief programs were encouraging moral decay. Poole described three stages of unemployment. On losing a job, a man typically maintained hope, earnestly looking for another position. But over time he became embittered and increasingly frustrated. The era's widespread unemployment, Poole reasoned, led men quickly to defeatism, leaving many unwilling even to accept employment, much less seek it out. A young man who would have felt uncomfortable among the homeless in better times might, in the context of the Depression, succumb readily to lowered ambition and self-esteem.[6]

By the cold months between Roosevelt's election and inauguration, the depths of the Depression had been reached, as more individuals and families lost jobs and drained their remaining resources. Over a third of New York's workers found themselves unemployed as the winter began. By early 1933, the TERA funds, initially predicted to last two years, were nearly exhausted, as public and private relief agencies struggled to continue operations. Roosevelt retreated from his early rhetoric describing a government concerned with the foot soldiers of the nation's "economic army," ending his campaign with cautious, vague statements. Yet as he took office, social workers and service providers optimistically awaited the actions of their newly elected ally.[7]

The Roosevelt administration inherited a complex system of laws governing aid to the homeless. Local settlement ordinances rendered many transients ineligible for public assistance. Most states shared New York's one-year residence policy, but requirements varied. New Hampshire required seven years of residence for public assistance eligibility, for example, and Rhode Island ten years. Even travel between counties, in some states, could disqualify one from public relief. In addition to such legal barriers, local resentment of "outsiders" left transients especially vulnerable. Elliot Chapman, a young transient, described the situation, "But as for getting any steady job, it is pretty near impossible because in the different communities they say, 'We have so many of our own here in the city we are looking after, we cannot very well care for anyone else.'" In response, the National Association of Travelers Aid Societies encouraged communities to return transients to their place of residence. This approach reflected the continued definition of homelessness as a local problem.[8]

States and municipalities that provided assistance only to those who had established residency left tens of thousands of homeless transients without aid in cities across the country. In order to remedy the situation, the 1933 FERA classified the homeless into three groups: local homeless, state homeless who had established one year of residence in a given state, and transient homeless who lacked state residency. Migrant laborers were not to be considered transients, so that states would not simply deflect the cost of their support to federal funds. Under the Federal Transient Program (FTP), launched in August 1933, the government allocated $15 million toward reimbursement of approved state plans to care for individuals without state residency. The administrators hoped to establish relatively standardized care; the various programs offered temporary shelter, meals, clothing, and medical treatment. Some locations also provided limited casework services, in an effort to remedy other problems the migrants might have.[9]

The Roosevelt administration struggled to balance national and local program management in the Transient Program. Across the board in New Deal programs, many local and state officials objected to what they perceived as usurpation of their authority, although federal administration of FERA programs remained remarkably limited. Local administrators continued to establish policies for the FTP camps that reflected diverse philosophies of rehabilitation and management. For example, some of the 250 transient centers and 190 camps were racially segregated, while others were integrated. As was the case with the Civilian Conservation Corps, the Roosevelt administration prioritized political compromise and coalition building over challenges to the racial status quo.[10]

From the outset, the FTP had the relatively modest goal of ending transiency, not supporting migrants indefinitely. When possible, individuals were to be returned to their community of origin or to a location where they had a job or family network. Administrators hoped to aid selected homeless people, then enact strict prohibitions on vagrancy to discourage travel. The system would be bolstered by planned work programs, which would generate local jobs and further discourage migration. Designed to assist temporarily homeless individuals who were willing to work, the program did not support the unmotivated and chronically unemployed. FERA representatives assured the public that the program would assist the deserving, newly poor victims of the Depression rather than the unemployed migrant poor of prior years. In the words of FERA staffer William J. Plunkert, "I believe that the American public is beginning to realize that our job is not with professional hoboes and bums, but with a group of men and families with something very real to sell in the lines of skilled trades and professions; but for whom there is no market available."[11]

Commentators on the era's homelessness situation repeatedly used this distinction between "bums" and worthy homeless to craft an image of an especially sympathetic population. One characterized the era's homeless as "not hobos but pioneers," crediting many with energy, education, and stable backgrounds. He further described them as "socially valuable and enterprising people willing and anxious to work." By contrast, officials caricatured the turn-of-the-century homeless as having actively avoided labor. The Committee on Care of Transient and Homeless even connected contemporary homelessness to the fabled closing of the American frontier: "The wealth of the land—the mines, the forests, and the great water power—is now vested in the hands of property-holding individuals or corporations, and is not 'there for the taking' by men whose only resources are initiative, courage, and an adventurous spirit." Enterprising individuals, once cultural icons of independence and ambition, this logic asserted, had been reduced to the ranks of wandering beggars, and thus deserved assistance.[12]

Focused on stabilizing a migrant population, the FTP provided lodging and generally ample food, but meager additional services. Most centers offered no religious services or educational programs, although limited vocational training was available in Arizona and California. Administrators hoped to find employment for their residents, but funding limitations and opposition from trade unions posed obstacles, as did the persistent consensus that local recipients of direct relief should receive any available jobs before transients. Some officials devised remarkably creative employment opportunities. In one Colorado camp in an abandoned coal town, according to special investigator Lorena Hickok, "They give them the rudiments of mineral mining, grubstake them, and let them go out into the hills to prospect for gold." Kansas facilities included work camps, family treatment centers, and a hospital for transients; by December 1934, the state's FTP assisted over 1,400 families and over 11,500 unattached individuals. Florida's transients underwent a medical evaluation and were screened for positions in work camps, while Georgia residents in some facilities had the opportunity to take courses in business math, typing, plumbing, and electrical skills.[13]

Camp administrators disagreed over the role social workers should play in the program. The director of North Carolina's Camp Weaver, for example, was skeptical about the usefulness of casework for residents: "I have had five caseworkers coming to this camp, two women and three men. In my opinion they do more harm than good. These boys won't stand being questioned; either they become frightened and vanish, or else they tell glib stories and then return to barracks and hilariously entertain their barrack mates by repeating their biggest lies." Many social workers saw such attitudes as inhibiting the potential effectiveness of the program. Large-scale programs might prove inexpensive through economies of scale, they argued, but more individualized care would be needed to help return individuals to the workforce.[14]

Part of the resistance to casework stemmed from the unusual background of the era's homeless. Since the newly homeless resembled the population at large, many wondered why they would need reform programs at all. Nationwide, most transients aided by the FTP were white, American-born, unskilled and semi-skilled male workers with at least an elementary school education. They were relatively young, 20 percent under twenty and two-thirds under forty-five. Significantly, most were transients only temporarily. The program technically excluded migrant workers, but few applied anyway, most continuing to endure the Depression by eking out an existence similar to what they had previously.[15]

Most fascinating to the American public, though, were the homeless women. Although unattached women made up less than 3 percent of the nation's transient population, popular magazines entertained readers with sordid tales of female hobos. Enduring occasional assaults with stoic grace, in print they appeared to enjoy the bulk of their adventures. Other period commentators speculated about the psychological effects of abject poverty on women. In a 1934 *American Mercury* essay, radical journalist Meridel Le Sueur characterized women's relationship to poverty as "more personal" than that of men. Driven to the brink of their resources, she told readers, women struggled to keep up appearances even as hunger and unemployment ravaged their families. Denied the masculine outlets of public camaraderie through alcohol, and even publicly sanctioned food distribution, women suffered

Figure 15. The Depression-era migrant homeless included large numbers of women and children. Dorothea Lange, "On U.S. 99. Near Brawley, Imperial County," February 1939. Farm Security Administration—Office of War Information Photograph Collection, Prints & Photographs Division, Library of Congress.

more profoundly. She painted as especially bleak the plight of impoverished women dwelling in rented rooms; her female character remarked, "There are four pregnant women in this attic. If they knew. . . . If they knew . . . they would cut their children out with a butcher knife."[16]

Images of morally compromised homeless and impoverished women sold magazines, in part, because they depicted the tragic results of the breakdown of the nuclear family. As men abandoned their families and women survived alone, many feared the erosion of family connections would prove the lasting legacy of the Depression. One Salvationist spoke openly of such fears, seeing in unattached homeless men "a form of disintegration of family life that leads to social instability and final decadence." If American men were unable or unwilling to serve as breadwinners, some argued, surely the American family was in crisis. In response to such concerns, public officials designed some relief programs specifically to accommodate nuclear families, who accounted for approximately 40 percent of state and federal transients. Yet relief programs often failed immigrant and African American households, which often included extended family members and did not fit standardized models.[17]

The migrant labor camps established by the Resettlement Administration also reflected the federal government's commitment to the American family. Immortalized in John Steinbeck's 1939 novel *The Grapes of Wrath*, the camps offered residential facilities to laborers working nearby. Steinbeck and John Ford, who directed the 1940 film adaptation of the novel, emphasized the stark contrast between the clean, democratically administered camps and the squalid Hoovervilles and authoritarian worker housing sponsored by commercial farms. Within the rational, modern government program described by Steinbeck, families could remain together. Perhaps more important, even while subsisting on public aid, they could retain their dignity and standards of decency and hygiene.[18]

Youth languished on the margins of the program as administrators struggled to develop meaningful solutions to their problems. Special investigator Hickok traveled the country, documenting the ravages of the Depression and the federal relief efforts to combat them. In one of her dispatches to Washington, she evaluated the Federal Transient Program. Hickok hoped homeless boys would be separated from the men wherever possible: "I hate the idea of youngsters, some of them in their early teens, mixing with the older men, getting their bitter, hopeless slant on life." Through education and training programs, she hoped homeless youth could avoid the fate of "becoming professional tramps." Although dispirited by the era's adult homeless, Hickok retained optimism for the young: "About all we can do for those adults is to keep them off the road for a little while. Perhaps work a few of them back into some kind of normal life. But here—why we're making honest-to-God citizens out of those kids!" In Los Angeles, 10,000 boys under twenty-one registered with the FTP in less than one year. By early 1935, some social service providers renewed their call for transient youth camps modeled after the Civilian Conservation Corps.[19]

Hickok's fear of programs integrating men and youth undoubtedly stemmed in part from the long established tradition of homosexual practices in transient culture. The migrant poor often traveled in pairs; usually, such pairings included an older man (commonly known as "husband," "wolf," or "jocker") and a younger man or boy (known as "punk," "lamb," or "kid"). Not all such couples maintained a sexual relationship, but some did, the older man often providing protection and support in exchange for companionship. Historians of sexuality connect the remarkable acceptance of same-sex couples to the era's fluid sexual identities. In many working-class American cultures of the time, engaging in sexual relations with another man did not define a man as homosexual, especially if he adopted the more "masculine" role in the relationship. During the 1930s, as record numbers of youth found themselves among the homeless, welfare administrators thus struggled to keep them separated from potential older partners.[20]

In establishing the FTP, the Roosevelt administration had overturned the nation's traditional approach to poor relief. No longer would the policy of localities and states to prioritize their own residents for relief funding mean that the homeless were abandoned. Instead, transients had been foregrounded through a separate, dedicated program of their own. As the FTP began, some believed it might provide a permanent solution to homelessness.

By 1934, the program appeared almost too successful for its own good. "The chief trouble with our transient care, as I see it, may be that it's too good," Hickok speculated after an unsettling visit to the program's Phoenix facilities, "Transients on relief get better care than residents on relief. Especially is this true of single, unattached men. Women, too." She concluded that "any unattached person 'in the know' would be a damned fool NOT to go transient." After visiting a shelter outside Phoenix, where families received food, milk, clothing, and medical care, she informed Harry Hopkins that the camp represented, "what we'd LIKE to do for the great masses of our clients who live in these towns. It's the ideal—which we have never reached in most places."[21]

The FTP in New York

By 1933, New York's homeless facilities were notoriously overcrowded. A *New Republic* author described the city's muni as "like being in a hospital," and compared the South Ferry lodging annex to "steerage quarters." But he reserved the bulk of his criticism for the "Dock" annex that had been established at the foot of East Twenty-Fifth Street:

> it is like nothing else under the sun, save perhaps a scene from
> Dante. One reposes in the "world's biggest bedroom," made of a
> covered pier-shed which extends 800 feet over the East River and
> houses 1,724 idle citizens. Truly a man need no longer feel himself
> alone or "forgotten." Here he is in the bosom of an immense
> family of his fellows who will be coughing and snoring all night:
> hundreds upon hundreds of them in their rumpled nightshirts,
> now sitting up in bed, or climbing.[22]

By the end of the year, the city was lodging almost 7,000 homeless individuals.[23]

The FTP sponsored relatively few urban facilities. In 1933, however, the TERA State Transient Division assumed the operation of Hartford House, a four-story building in Midtown Manhattan. Established by the YMCA in 1931, the program reserved its services for the educational and professional elites among the state's homeless population; only 2 percent of registered transients qualified. Of the 227 men participating one day, over half had attended college and one held a doctorate. At one time, the program included eight accountants, a pilot, a portrait painter, an interior decorator, a metallurgist, and a naval architect.[24]

Hartford House participants resided nearby in furnished rooms, but gathered at the facility for meals and activities. Administrators emphasized job placement, admitting only employable men age twenty to fifty, as well as offering psychological and aptitude testing, employment counseling, and temporary employment placement. After the termination of TERA, the remarkable program folded. In three and one-half years of operation, it helped over 3,000 men find work.

The majority of FTP facilities were rural work camps. Although financed through an innovative, modern federal structure, the camps themselves were a variant of a solution common in the nineteenth century. As recently as 1932, New York City's Welfare Council had proposed that the city adopt a system comparable to European industrial farm colonies that housed and employed the homeless. The planned colony would have accepted men with two years of New York residency who were mentally and physically healthy, and "not chronic alcoholics, drug addicts, or homosexuals." Agricultural labor or road construction and maintenance would occupy the men's time, pay their expenses, and contribute to their savings. By rendering some homeless men economically independent, the colony would lessen the burden on the city's lodging facilities, end panhandling and breadlines, and encourage other cities and states to develop similar programs.[25]

Approximating this model, the New York State TERA launched an experimental program in 1933. Camp Bluefield's initial twenty-five residents were chosen from clients of the muni and area commercial hotels; eventually the population increased to 260. Located in the Blauvelt section of Palisades Interstate Park, several miles north of New York City, the program for single, homeless, unemployed men complemented the park's existing work programs. Jobs and shelter were provided by the park administration, while the U.S. War Department offered discounted surplus clothing. Conditions were spartan; camp residents stuffed rags into oversized shoes in storage since World War I. They earned fifty cents per hour clearing brush, chopping firewood, felling trees, and performing road construction and maintenance. After spending $3 weekly on meals, residents kept additional earnings for use on their return to the city.[26]

A similar program opened in April 1934 at Camp Greycourt, in Chester, northwest of the city. Within months it housed over 600 former muni residents. Approximately 70 percent of participants were city natives, most with only an elementary school education. Labor was integral to the camp's agenda; the men were expected to work approximately thirty hours per week. Winter projects included road construction and maintenance, while summers were spent working on the camp's farm. Each man earned approximately one dollar per day, of which he received less than half. Leisure activities included baseball, horseshoes, soccer, checkers, chess, and a drama club. The camp administrators tried to provide residents with limited casework, hoping to solve the long-term problems they believed had sent residents there. Despite the camp's limitations, nearly a third of the approximately 1,800 men lodged there during its first year found employment, most on nearby farms. Residential programs along the lines of the New York men's camps opened nationwide; by July 1934, the FTP operated 189 camps, many of them rural work facilities for employable homeless men. In New York State, by September 1935, over 3,000 men were lodged in New York camps, in locations from Port Jervis to Saratoga Springs.[27]

The era's programs for homeless women rarely resembled those for men, reflecting instead society's discomfort with women in the public sphere. Most female applicants at the Central Registration Bureau were young and had previously been employed as domestic and industrial workers, or in offices.

While officials determined that homeless men required some combination of labor camps and casework, they initially offered homeless and impoverished women something closer to a vacation. In summer 1933, Camp TERA opened in Bear Mountain Park to accommodate up to 200 homeless white-collar New York City women under thirty. Administrators required campers to perform daily tasks, but explicitly rejected the work camp model offered by other New Deal programs such as the highly popular Civilian Conservation Corps. They sought instead to provide residents an opportunity for rest and rejuvenation outside the urban environment. Activities ranged from art, drama, and woodcrafts to nature walks.[28]

During the winter months, the facility operated as "TERA Lodge," housing up to one hundred homeless or unattached women for four-week stays. A limited work program was instituted requiring campers to earn money knitting sweaters for the men in the CCC camps. Winter residents chose from classes in typing and filing, English, current events, crafts, choir, or amateur dramatics. Since few women wanted to leave the city during the winter, administrators expanded the program to admit more financially stable women as well, including those working at low-wage jobs, mothers, and older daughters.[29]

Federal funding also facilitated other remarkably innovative programs for the homeless. In New York State, young men aged sixteen to thirty benefited from an "experimental academy" launched by the TERA Transient Division in March 1935. Housed at Hartwick School, a former seminary near Cooperstown in upstate New York, the program offered courses in dairy and poultry farming, agriculture, plumbing, and business math, in addition to standard secondary school coursework.[30]

Similarly, some homeless benefited from the Civil Works Education Service, which included bold efforts to educate men in an array of nontraditional programs. On Chicago's West Side, instructors in a "Reclassification Shelter" struggled in oppressive conditions to engage their students, a diverse group of immigrants, African Americans, American-born whites, military veterans, and workers from a variety of trades. At times, four to five hundred men perched on backless benches in a long, dark basement room, equipped with an open urinal along one wall. Blaming in part their "starvation diet," a teacher categorized his students as "dull," "bewildered," "inactive," and "unprotesting." In his words,

I became increasingly doubtful of the physical foundation for an academic life in the shelters. I talked to groups sitting in dark bull-pens or on slum curbs; talked about unemployment insurance and

relief, about the business cycle and surplus value, about politics
and strikes and war. Sometimes they were interested. But it was
always a flagging interest; it died as I left and would not stir again
for weeks perhaps. They were too tired to be excited. Even the
Communists lacked stamina.

Without adequate food, rest, shelter, and incentive, many Depression-era
homeless proved inappropriate candidates for such ambitious educational
programs.[31]

Federal funding thus shaped the approach to homelessness taken by New
York and other cities during the operation of the FTP. Between 1932 and 1935,
New York's resident and transient homeless male population doubled, from less
than 9,000 to over 18,000. The homeless female population followed a similar
pattern, but on a much smaller scale. Camp TERA, in particular, provided a
major source of lodging, accommodating nearly one-fourth of the city's homeless women at its peak. As public expenditures on homeless services rose, private funding dropped from more than half the expenses of resident transient
men to less than five percent.[32]

Public spending on homelessness was growing, at a time when many
types of public aid were increasing. Even at its height, funding of homeless
programs and support to homeless individuals comprised less than 2 percent
of the state's overall relief distribution. In 1935, mayor Fiorello LaGuardia estimated that 400,000 city families subsisted solely on public relief. The federal
government at that time paid half the city's $20 million monthly relief budget,
while the state and the city shared the remainder.[33]

In New York City, increased public relief funding was accompanied by
more behavior regulation. Panhandling, in particular, continued to draw
moralistic criticism. Dr. Ellen C. Potter, medical director of New Jersey's
Department of Institutions and Agencies, cautioned in 1933 that "John Citizen" must refer transients to official service centers, "where all real need
can be met at Uncle Sam's expense." Her appeal echoed earlier campaigns
urging individuals to donate to organized charities. Now, however, the federal government played the role of preferred assistance provider. Bowery
YMCA administrator Elmer Galloway similarly insisted that donating to
panhandlers harmed both recipients and society at large. Instead, he urged
New Yorkers: "Stop giving like that and give to us, and let's stop making
paupers here."[34]

Those caught panhandling faced prosecution. In 1933, the administrators of the BMT subway lines banned beggars from the trains. That winter, the Welfare Council proposed to rid the city of its "professional panhandlers." Interviewers and investigators appointed to the magistrates' courts would refer first offenders to appropriate agencies for social services, while repeat offenders would be prosecuted as professional beggars. Walter Wile, the chairman of the Council's mendicancy committee, assured the public that the program would not penalize the worthy poor: "No man needs to beg today on the streets of New York. The public and private welfare agencies are equipped to provide the necessities of life for any homeless and unattached man who may apply." Charity administrators used the era's increased assistance to the homeless to justify cracking down on beggars.[35]

The following year, the Council plan went into effect in the Night Court. The Civil Works Administration funded an interviewer, psychiatrist, and social worker to work with convicted men, reviewing their criminal records and making sentencing recommendations. Those from outside New York were returned to their community of origin at federal expense. The investigators found many of the homeless ill, and worse, contagious; the first 210 panhandling cases that came before the court involved 90 infected with contagious diseases as well as many who were mentally or otherwise ill. Administrators categorized approximately one-third of the individuals investigated as chronic alcoholics and nearly two hundred as drug addicts. By April 1935, in fourteen months of operation, the program had worked with over 5,000 men. Wile informed the public that less than one-sixth of arrested panhandlers merited the ranking "apparently normal." He used these statistics to justify further regulation of the homeless: "It naturally follows that the abnormality of mendicants makes it obligatory upon the city to control and supervise their activities."[36]

Despite such efforts, panhandling continued. In 1934, the Emergency Relief Bureau estimated that 6,500 New York City beggars had been arrested. That summer, the Welfare Department and the Welfare Council teamed up to distribute cards listing twenty locations throughout the city where the poor might apply for assistance, urging individuals to distribute the cards to panhandlers in lieu of cash.[37]

Few dissented from the mounting choir of voices insisting that panhandling was inappropriate, morally and socially corrupting, as well as unnecessary. One objection came from Dan O'Brien, self-titled "King of the Hoboes." O'Brien, who chafed at the Salvation Army's focus on select needy individuals, squared off against Brigadier John Allan in a 1934 WABC radio debate.

O'Brien insisted that donations to panhandlers were both charitable and humane. In his words, "The human race is a race of beggars. All are born broke,
but some are born luckier than others."[38]

The explosion of transiency in the city during the years of the FTP took
homelessness far beyond the confines of skid row. The large-scale, warehouse lodging facilities established in other neighborhoods, as well as transient camps and work programs located outside skid row, took in many
younger, employable men. Meanwhile, sick and contagious homeless men
were routinely released from hospitals, but barred from entry to many lodging facilities. Desperate, many of the ill slept outdoors or in poorly regulated establishments.[39]

The sick joined older, unemployable men to form the core of a skid-row
population. Too feeble for work programs, they were referred by the FTP to
Bowery lodging houses and restaurants. Federally funded housing and meal
vouchers enabled many homeless individuals to secure temporary accommodations and supported the local economy. Distributing such tickets, the
federal government participated in the city's subsidy of skid row.

Chicago undertook a similar program. A teenager who visited during the
Depression later recalled, "The Transient Bureau gave you a card good for four
nights at a flophouse hotel. Another card entitled you to three meals at a Skid
Row restaurant. If you didn't find employment in four days, you were supposed
to move on to another town." These referral systems allowed officials to assist
area and transient homeless without building additional facilities.[40]

As the federally sponsored camps and facilities reduced New York's skid-
row population, Bowery boosters hoped the neighborhood would shed its association with homelessness. Some optimistically predicted that New York's
skid row was on the verge of drastic change. One enthusiastic local merchant
observed, "The Bowery doesn't have to look back to fame. It's doing as much
business as any other street in New York right now, and just as soon as the 'L'
comes down this will be the Broadway of the east side." His vision proved pre-
mature; the elevated train built in the 1870s would remain in place until the
1950s. But with so many New Yorkers now destitute, the Bowery seemed less
aberrant than it had in the past. The area surrounding the Bowery had improved in recent decades, as well. Five Points and Mulberry Bend, once notoriously dangerous neighborhoods, now housed children's playgrounds. "No,
the Bowery is not 'classy,'" one author concluded, "but it is almost respectable."
The area increasingly attracted commercial interests, especially restaurant
suppliers and jewelry stores. As early as January 1934, headlines proclaimed

reduced breadlines, fewer homeless, and generally improving conditions in the Bowery district.[41]

Even as the FTP had pulled many homeless outside the city, the institutions of skid row remained, as restaurants, bars, flophouses and barbershops catering to the homeless stayed on the Bowery. As the crisis of homelessness rose and fell, the Bowery remained the only home known by thousands of homeless men and some women. The system of subsidizing area hotels and restaurants would continue for decades, affording the city a flexible means of caring for its poor. Especially for the older, sick, and unemployable male population, the Bowery and other skid rows would continue to be home in the coming years.

The FTP had provided vital services not only to homeless individuals, but also to families, offering lodgings, meals, educational programming, and limited casework for those lacking the state residency rendering them eligible for the era's other relief programs. Many had found the program flawed since its inception, however, criticizing the philosophy undergirding its structure, its method of operations, and the political ramifications of its existence. For all these reasons, the program would not survive the 1935 redefinition of the New Deal by the Roosevelt administration, nor would it serve as a model in the postwar era.

Ending the FTP

The structure of the FTP had troubled some observers all along. Many social workers and service providers worried that the program's narrow parameters would skew perceptions of homelessness. They cautioned administrators to resist the temptation to categorize transients as a distinct group, a practice they deemed ill-advised and counterproductive. In *The Transient*, published by the National Association for Travelers Aid and Transient Service, a writer asked dramatically on behalf of the homeless, "Why isolate us as a group and call us 'transients'? Are we not citizens of the United States?" Others rejected even the term "homeless" and the category it constructed, fearing its power to frame them less as needy individuals than as an aberrant population.[42] A 1935 editorial in *The Transient* lobbied for replacing the term "homeless" with the more neutral "unattached":

> "Homeless" has been, very frequently, a misnomer or a piece of
> verbal juggling to rationalize and conceal our own failures to

> provide adequate forms of care for these people, . . . we must get
> away from our opinion that this group of people is, as a whole,
> "homeless" or "non-family." And since words are signposts to
> attitudes and prejudices, we help ourselves and others to better
> attitudes by adopting the word "unattached." [43]

New terms, the authors hoped, would minimize some of the negative connotations surrounding homelessness by emphasizing the similarities between
the homeless and other impoverished Americans.

The Roosevelt administration's efforts to cultivate political alliances had
led to many southern towns refusing assistance to transient African Americans or offering only inferior facilities. Critics called for the development of
better, more comprehensive care that might address the needs of the African
American population more specifically. There was also a problematic, wide
disparity in the types of services that were provided by the various participating states. Arizona, for example, offered no transient shelters and only two-
week camp stays. Its neighboring states maintained shelters and also provided
gasoline tickets and other amenities, prompting many homeless individuals
and families to travel over state lines in search of better conditions.[44]

Despite these criticisms, the FTP had provided unprecedented levels of assistance for the nation's homeless, and had dramatically reduced transiency.
Many assumed the federal government would remain involved with transient
care. In 1933, Ellen Potter of the New Jersey State Department of Institutions
and Agencies had gone so far as to predict, "Whatever may be the outcome
of all the responsibilities assumed by the federal government in this time of
distress one at least seems likely to remain a continuing obligation. Unless all
signs fail, the transient, the homeless destitute American citizen of nowhere
will henceforth to the extent that he persists be the concern of his Uncle Sam."[45]

By late 1934, the Roosevelt administration New Deal programs were un-
der attack from both the political right and the left. Many business interests
objected to the price controls and production regulation enacted through the
National Industrial Recovery Act. Forming the powerful American Liberty
League, corporate leaders called for scaling back governmental intervention
into the nation's economy. That year's congressional elections saw increased
Democratic majorities, reflecting the partisan mood of the electorate. The
American people were supporting the New Deal, and in some cases calling
for it to move farther to the left. Louisiana Senator Huey Long had turned
critical of the New Deal, and was promoting his popular "Share Our Wealth

Plan," which would have guaranteed American families an annual income. Along with other radical politicians, some of whom promoted Communism, Long posed a political threat to Roosevelt in the upcoming election.[46]

In the Second New Deal, the administration would address the concerns of those on the left calling for greater social protections for American workers. Despite resistance from corporate interests, the policies enacted in 1935 would abandon politically volatile direct relief programs in favor of structural interventions in the economy, to reconcile competing visions of relief, recovery, and reform. To maintain political credibility, the administration's pioneering federally funded relief programs were scheduled for termination. In his January State of the Union address, Roosevelt emphasized the connection between "reform" and "recovery," arguing that pursuing one without the other was akin to treating a patient's symptoms without addressing his disease. He painted a disturbing picture of prolonged relief. Continued assistance, he argued, would prompt "a spiritual and moral disintegration fundamentally destructive to the national fibre." In his estimation, such direct relief served as "a narcotic, a subtle destroyer of the human spirit." In truth, Roosevelt and his advisers had never envisioned such programs as ongoing features of the American economy; they had been stopgap measures designed to carry the nation along until it was back on its feet.[47]

Against this backdrop of demonized relief, Roosevelt mapped a two-pronged plan to address the needs of the five million unemployed individuals receiving assistance. The federal government would establish a social security program that would include old-age pensions for qualified workers. This system would enable the elderly to retire, opening more jobs for the young. The simultaneous launch of a dramatic, large-scale program of public works would ensure jobs for the 3.5 million employable, ablebodied individuals then receiving relief. Labor served as the lynchpin of both initiatives, each offering a measure of economic stability to individuals performing specific types of work.

For the 1.5 million "unemployables" receiving relief, Roosevelt proposed another alternative. "Such people, in the days before the great depression, were cared for by local efforts—by States, by counties, by towns, by cities, by churches and by private welfare agencies," he explained. "It is my thought that in the future they must be cared for as they were before." The system of public and private, locally administered aid that was in place through the 1920s would be resurrected. This return to the earlier system defined homelessness and general relief as local concerns. The Social Security program excluded millions of "unemployables," including many homeless, from the scope of federal protection. This exclusion was by design, limiting the program's beneficiaries to the "worthy," steadily working body of Americans.[48]

The age of many homeless further complicated their integration into the Social Security plan. By 1933, nearly 40 percent of homeless men were at least forty-five. Even if the economy rebounded, older men would remain physically unable to pursue new job opportunities. Well aware of their predicament, some older homeless men expressed frustration with age discrimination in employment. In one man's words, "You can't get no job. They won't hire anybody after he's 45. They cut down the compensation law. Who won the war? It was Pershing, and Foch, and Hindenberg, old men. Where in hell would the army be if they didn't have them for leaders, old men?" Considering the future of the elderly, the Committee on Care of Transient and Homeless urged FERA head Hopkins to support complete federal funding of state old age expenses for transients.[49]

The president's pronouncement sparked criticism from social service providers. The following month, Russell Kurtz of the Russell Sage Foundation wondered, once the federal government, in Roosevelt's famous expression, "quit this business of relief, . . . who, then, will carry it on?" The plan to use public works to lighten the relief rolls struck Kurtz as overly optimistic, simplistic, and shortsighted. He voiced particular concern for the "unemployables," whom he predicted would remain unable to find work, despite their desperate need. By August, with FERA's planned November 1 end date fast approaching, some observers doubted the federal government would follow through on its plan to end the program and transfer relief recipients to work projects. Referring to "the residual load that will remain," Kurtz asserted, "It is inconceivable that New Deal America will be indifferent to the fate of this residual group."[50]

In light of the limited roles available to the homeless and transients in the new federal programs, many service providers and social workers pressed for continued national transient assistance. Speaking before relief administrators, William J. Ellis, commissioner of the Department of Institutions and Agencies of New Jersey, referred to "the absurdity of local administration of public assistance," and urged "consciousness of the fact that the traditional concept of the poor law is really dead." Yet the return of residence laws and local hostility would render the mobile poor again vulnerable and stigmatized.[51]

During the FTP's operation, the residents and staff of some camps published newsletters documenting their experience. The publications featured reports on residents' sports competitions, updates on camp work assignments, as well as a range of cartoons, short fiction, and editorials. The humor often poked safe fun at the era's poverty, as in this entry from the "Jest Fun" column of the *Elks Park Digest*:

> Windham: "A fellow can eat dirt cheap in this country."
> Steward: "Yeah, but who wants to eat dirt?"

As the closing date of the FTP approached, some camp residents expressed enthusiasm about their pending opportunities. In the poem "Help Help," one resident wrote, "I want to be put on relief / For tho I have food and employment, / I want a relief from the grief, / Which lessens my sense of enjoyment, / So put me on some sort of roll, / Some new Alphabetical muster, / Affording Relief to my soul, / From ballyhoo, bunkum, and bluster." Some columns offered ironic parodies of the stereotyped vision of the "Okie" columnist. The "Josiah Simpkins" columns in the Washington, D.C. newsletter *Contact* appeared as stylized letters to "Dear Mariah," written in the folksy prose of the imagined transient. By October 1935, "Simpkins" wrote, "This hear buro is a gittin ready to shut up. Most of the fellows has gone and them what haint is a wonderin what they is a gwine to do. A lot of them has got their congressman to git them jobs in the government department, but the poor devils what aininit got no backing will haddar take picks and shovels and work on W.P.A. Projects."[52]

Editorialists in the camp newsletters disagreed about the impending closure of the program. The Asheville, North Carolina, *Highlander* reported, "We still hope that the transient will get an even break with others on the relief rolls but we don't believe they will. There is a very good reason for this belief. Human nature and politics don't change much, so why should we expect an even break with the people on the home relief rolls?" One *Contact* editorial from October 1935 reflected criticism of the FTP:

> Most of the transients throughout the country will be thrown
> on their own resources within a short while. Candidly, that may
> be a good thing for many of us. It has been very comfortable
> to have Uncle Sam to lean on. While it was no Waldorf Astoria
> accommodations, it assured three meals a day and a clean bed on
> which to sleep, and enough spending money to buy tobacco. Some

of us might have gotten out and found work, had we been forced to
do so.[53]

The experimental FTP had emerged from the new perception of homelessness and poverty as temporary conditions caused by the economic disrup-
tion of the Depression. It had offered stopgap measures to assist individuals
and families until they became financially self-sufficient. As indicated by the
newsletter comments, Roosevelt retreated from his plan because it had become a political liability.

Some worried that the structure of the nation's Social Security program
neglected the homeless. One author asked: "What effect will this have upon
transiency? . . . Will transients be considered an integral part of the whole social
life of communities, and will they be eligible, as others, for participation in the
benefits of this new program? Where, in this scheme of unemployment insurance, health insurance, old age security, will people away from home fit in?"
"'Social Security,'" New Jersey Medical Director of Institutions and Agencies
and Transient Bureau head Ellen Potter explained, "is predicated upon a definite duration of residence within a given jurisdiction. How are the homeless to
recover their status of eligibility after these years on the road? Where does the
migratory worker get his 'security number?'" Even those homeless individuals
who worked regularly, either as migrant laborers or other day laborers, would
remain outside the system without special provisions.[54]

Federal administrators vehemently defended the 1935 transformation
of federal policy as one from degrading relief to dignified labor. The Roosevelt administration was committed to creating what sociologist Edwin
Amenta has described as a "work and relief" state. Unemployment insurance and retirement pensions offered greater economic security to many
workers, promising to soften the blow of subsequent economic fluctuations.
The WPA, in its earliest incarnation, held the possibility of near full employment. With jobs for all who wanted them and security measures for
workers, the government would create a significantly more stable economic
system. Full employment never materialized, however, and even the WPA
would prove impermanent.[55]

The termination of the FTP reflected the Roosevelt administration's
primary goal of stabilizing the American economy and labor market while
avoiding a permanent relief system. Many shared this logic; observers worried that young men raised on relief during the Depression had learned no
work ethic, and thus would prefer to "cheat and chisel and lie and steal." A

Newark businessman wrote to the Charity Organization Society, expressing his frustration with the Transient Program, and his approval of its termination:

> Transcient [sic] Training Camps have been a misnomer from the beginning. They never went anywhere and the training has been a great big joke at the expense of a hoodwinked public. A Transient Training Corps going places and doing things adventuresome and constructive for the hundreds of thousands truly homeless would be something worthwhile and worthy of public recognition. . . . The Knights of the Road have had their break—now let the men that foots the bill have a hearing.[56]

Parallel debates over direct relief emerged around other programs. The Civil Works Administration (CWA), launched by executive order, drew two million workers from the relief rolls along with two million others and assigned them to wage jobs. A complex compromise between direct and work relief, the program paid relief recipients cash wages at market rates. Over 15,000 job seekers flooded the program's registration offices on their first day of operation. Desperate to legitimize the CWA in the eyes of the public, administrators employed hyberbolic, overzealous language. Politicians promoted the program with slogans including "real work at real wages" and "an end to the dole," caricaturing and denigrating direct relief, adding to its stigma. Russell Kurtz immediately wondered about the plight of needy, unemployed men not chosen for jobs. With direct relief increasingly understood as a negative force, those individuals excluded from work relief programs faced an uncertain future.[57]

Harry Hopkins also posed work relief programs as preferable to direct relief, arguing that "America has a tradition that a man should work." After drawing direct relief for too long, he continued, a man "becomes a public charge, not only for the present, but for all time." In his view, work relief would keep individuals from becoming permanently homeless. While Hopkins expressed faith in the planned Social Security system, he also envisioned a continued role for work relief: "we are always going to have some relief. I hope and believe it will be work relief—roads and so on, things that private industry will never do, things that would never get done otherwise, things that are crying to be done." Hopkins predicted that work would remain central to the nation's public welfare system.[58]

Not everyone shared this enthusiasm for the incredible power of work relief. A 1933 *New Republic* essay noted, "But the morale of men who earn $54 a month for the total support of their families, one observes, is not much better than the purchasing power. They, as well as the almost equally fortunate groups who have home relief ranging from $2 to $6.60 a week, seem as yet only bewildered and stupefied at being thrust back toward an abysmally low standard of living—the New American standard." Neither charitable relief nor employment in the private sector, work relief programs occupied a vague, new position in American culture.[59]

Religious charities were divided over the significance of labor in offering relief. In 1933, Hopkins had limited the number of private organizations drawing public funds, ensuring more rigorous government administration of relief programs. The Salvation Army and the YMCA continued work programs where possible, but a new separate strand of religious philanthropy sought neither the government's funding nor its validation. Radical Catholics, horrified by the era's dramatic poverty, launched programs offering the direct assistance so maligned in official and public discourse. Some Catholics, including those who followed radio sensation Father Coughlin as he turned against the New Deal by 1935, rejected such efforts. Most Catholics remained committed to Roosevelt's vision of the modern, liberal state. But the new, controversial programs enjoyed the support of some Catholics, as well as other radicals.[60]

In a dramatic example of the power of radical Catholicism, Father James Cox of Pittsburgh led a crowd of 25,000 men, mostly Catholic, in a 1932 march on Washington. Frustrated by the mounting evictions of the poor, Cox was inspired by the example of Jacob Coxey's 1894 march on Washington to protest high unemployment rates. Although new to large-scale political activism, Cox was an experienced service provider. He had operated a soup kitchen since 1930 and had allowed 250 men to build temporary homes adjoining the church, earning the affectionate nickname, "mayor of shantytown."[61]

Similarly inspired by the era's dramatic suffering, Dorothy Day, a radical journalist and Catholic convert, joined French poet and lay theologian Peter Maurin to establish the *Catholic Worker*. The newspaper allowed them to spread their religious and political vision. Day and Maurin eschewed formal administrative procedures, preferring to build a small New York movement in the hope that like-minded individuals in other cities would be inspired to follow suit. They sold penny copies of the paper in Union Square alongside the *Daily Worker* vendors.[62]

The Catholic Worker movement evolved out of idealistic plans and concrete criticisms of existing private and public relief programs. Maurin envisioned a system in which the homeless would support themselves through farming. He and Day optimistically established a Staten Island tomato farm, but found few urban poor interested in agricultural labor. Surveying the work of religious missions, Day criticized the Salvation Army's reported lack of respect for the needs of Catholic guests. But she reserved her sharpest attacks for public officials. The *Catholic Worker* published several dramatic, sympathetic accounts of the eviction of impoverished, deserving individuals and families at the mercy of landlords and the police.[63]

Day and Maurin also rejected the muni's model of homeless assistance. Two 1934 *Catholic Worker* articles included an author's description of visits to the muni. He likened the experience to "tales of prison life," and noted the institution's "application of the eighteenth century poor law." He criticized both the food and the way it was served: "Line up once more at the lunch counter; grab a tray; keep in step with the man ahead of you; get hold of a tin bowl half-filled with what is technically designated as 'Irish Stew' but is more akin to slumgullion in looks and taste; a tin cup of coffee without sugar; three slices of white bread; a spoon partly washed; and another round is completed." He also alleged fraud: "The Muni is filled with endless corruption, special privilege and discrimination. 'Give me a nickel once in a while, or a couple of cigarette butts or a late newspaper,' says the attendant in the flop, 'and I will see that you get a bit of meat in your soup, or see to it that your pockets will not be rifled during the night.'"[64]

Opposed to the moralistic and regimented relief provided by the missions and the muni, Day and Maurin expanded their services from a breadline to taking in lodgers. Their "house of hospitality" would lodge both area poor and group members committed to living as "religious without vows." Sharing the life of poverty, as had earlier settlement house workers, they would provide assistance without judgment.[65]

Day and Maurin refused to accept public funding or even to register the Catholic Worker as a tax-exempt nonprofit organization. Day criticized the government's expanding relief system, calling instead for individuals and families to take up such work:

> The city, the state—we have nicknamed them Holy Mother
> the City, Holy Mother the State—have taken on a large role in
> sheltering the homeless. But the ideal is for every family to have a
> Christ room, as the early fathers of the Church called it. It seems

to me that in the future the family—the ideal family—will always
try to care for one more. If every family that professed to follow
Scriptural teaching, whether Jew, Protestant, or Catholic, were to
do this, there would be no need for huge institutions, houses of
dead storage where human beings waste away in loneliness and
despair. Responsibility must return to the parish with a hospice
and a center for mutual aid, to the group, to the family, to the
individual.[66]

Day referred to the homeless as "Ambassadors of Christ," and encouraged
movement members and others to greet and care for them accordingly.
Drawing on the principles of the Catholic Works of Mercy, she encouraged
members to perform not only the spiritual but also the corporal works,
which included feeding the hungry, giving drink to the thirsty, clothing the
naked, and sheltering the homeless. Day criticized society's hypocrisy toward
its homeless, ridiculing the era's arguments against direct relief: "It is easy for
people to see Jesus in the children of the slums. . . . But these abandoned men
are looked upon as hopeless. 'No good will come of it.' We are contributing
to their laziness. We are feeding people who won't work. These are the accusations made. God help us, we give them so little: bread and coffee in the
morning, soup and bread at noon. Two scant meals."[67]

Day and Maurin struggled to build a lasting movement whose members
lived among the poor as near equals. Their pacifism and controversial opposition to government power led to a decline in membership during and after
World War II. But their religious radicalism drew volunteers throughout the
century, offering an alternative analysis of both poverty and its remedies.[68]

Radical Catholics protested the assumption that the poor must earn
simple assistance, but this remained the minority position. It was thought
by most that if direct relief was a narcotic, then work relief and earned assistance must be preferable. This logic shaped the liberal plans for the emerging
welfare state, and met with approval from many. During its years of operation, the FTP's discrete structure had guaranteed support for the homeless.
By the same token, however, the program's isolation of transiency rendered
the homeless extremely vulnerable to funding cuts.

Ultimately, the FTP lasted only twenty-eight months. On September 10,
1935, FERA representatives instructed state transient directors to stop accept-
ing new clients within ten days. They were directed to return any remaining
program participants to their respective hometowns. The National Commit-

tee for Transients and Homeless asked dramatically, "What happens to transients after September 20? Are we going back to a shrug of the shoulders and
'passing on'?"[69]

Many service providers worried that New York City, where nearly 10,000
transients had migrated during a single year, as well as popular warm weather
destinations like California and Florida, would bear the brunt of the post-FTP
transient crush. New York agencies, including the Welfare Council, urged
Hopkins to delay dismantling the FTP, and called for a specific plan ensuring
the integration of transient workers into the WPA. The general director of the
COS implored Hopkins to revoke the closing. Citing an estimated 13,000 city
homeless, he tried to rally support for the cause. The Welfare Council's Coordinating Committee on Unemployment hosted a hearing on the program's
end, then issued a statement publicizing its findings in bold terms: "We are
in danger of reverting to the old order of the earliest days of the depression
when there was no adequate care for homeless and transients, when the city
was dotted with breadlines and when there was real danger of death from
starvation or exposure to cold." But the protests proved ineffective.[70]

After the termination of the FTP, local governmental and private agencies resumed their roles as the primary service providers to the homeless.
The Salvation Army, for instance, continued to operate its Gold Dust Lodge
and Memorial Hotel, while also serving nearly 20,000 meals in 1936 at its
Working Women's Home, almost 37,000 at the Emergency Lodge, and over
131,000 at the Women's Canteen. In Harlem, the organization distributed over
234,000 meals.[71]

Administrators of the WPA, the second branch of the Roosevelt administration's initiative, agreed to employ transient men who proved acceptable to
local authorities. But many social workers worried that regional and local fa-
voritism of area residents would prevent any significant employment of transients. As the WPA began, such concerns over integration of local homeless
and transient workers proved well founded. In New York City, parks commissioner Robert Moses blocked the homeless from participating in the projects under his direction. Publicly objecting to the presence of "Bowery bums"
among the workers, he branded over 1,000 of the 9,000 men assigned to the
parks "riff-raff picked up by the police as vagrants." Moses argued the men
were both unqualified and unsuited to any work that might involve contact
with children. The city WPA administrator replied that half the 18,000 transients and homeless men on the city's relief rolls were city residents worthy
of opportunities, noting, "The mere fact that these homeless men are living

in lodging houses is no reason for casting aspersions upon them." But Moses insisted that "hundreds of men have been lying around in the parks, doing absolutely nothing excepting jeering at workers, shooting craps, drinking and generally creating a nuisance and a menace to the public." Mayor Fiorello LaGuardia also strongly opposed Moses's stance:

> I resent any slander or slur on hundreds or thousands of men
> who, through no fault of their own, can't wear a tuxedo when
> they go to work for Mr. Moses. The very purpose of relief work
> is rehabilitation of people who have not only been out of work
> months and months but years and years. I believe it is the highest
> form of relief to put these men to work in the open air, where they
> can be rehabilitated morally as well as physically.[72]

The future role of the homeless in work and relief programs remained unclear, as their qualifications, conduct, and character came under renewed scrutiny. Men who had been homeless for years, especially those weakened by age, malnutrition, or substance use, appeared unsuited for labor-intensive projects. At the same time, residence requirements were reinstated by some localities and used to deny assistance to the transient homeless. As a distinct population not integrated into the work or residential patterns of many communities, the transient homeless slipped from view. New Yorkers and Americans at large remained ambivalent about supporting "unemployables" or providing social security to marginal workers.[73]

For the urban homeless, the end of the FTP marked their return to the care of local and private organizations. By 1936, their plight no longer captured headlines or the political spotlight. Worried about the fading attention to homelessness, Bowery fixture Urbain Ledoux resurfaced and resumed his personal media campaign. For the first time since 1932, he accompanied a group of homeless men, many of them disabled, in the Easter parade, marching with empty sugar sacks slung over their shoulders. Ledoux urged onlookers to donate used clothing to the muni and also urged Bellevue Hospital to assist such men. Some observers were moved by the procession, others simply perplexed. One inquired, "Are they supposed to be ironical?"[74]

The FTP had been the first federal intervention into the problem of homelessness. Three trends had made the program possible. For one, the mobility of the era's homeless individuals and families had threatened the nation's stability, prompting a dramatic response. Also, the demographics of the homeless had more resembled those of average Americans than it had in earlier eras, encouraging in many observers a deeper level of empathy. Finally, the extent of the financial crisis had created a political environment in which urban liberals could expand the purview of the federal government with relatively little resistance. The economic upheaval of the Depression had led briefly to a new understanding of the homeless, not as lazy or immoral but worthy of federal assistance.

In creating the FTP, the Roosevelt administration had addressed a fundamental challenge plaguing the homeless. Lacking a legal residence, even geographically stable homeless people had struggled to establish the level of state and local residency required for relief recipients. By encompassing the transient homeless, FTP administrators had experimented with a major expansion of the federal safety net. Such a program would find no place in the world of postwar American cities. As the New Deal shifted its focus from emergency relief to regulatory reform, the homeless were systematically excluded from many federal benefit programs. Urban day laborers, including many homeless, were like domestic laborers and rural migrant workers in that they remained outside the scope of the Social Security program and many WPA projects. Their return to the private and local agencies that had previously sustained them marked the end of federal involvement in homelessness.[75]

The postwar homeless population would be far less mobile than their Depression-era counterparts, thus posing less of a threat to the nation's order. While their socioeconomic backgrounds resembled those of the working classes, the relatively large proportion of women and children who had attracted such attention during the 1930s were lacking. Most important, the postwar political climate would not support generous federal assistance to the homeless. As the homeless once more turned to the state and local levels for assistance, they fell outside even the expanding protection of the federal welfare state. After its abrupt closure in 1935, the FTP receded from the national memory, a relic of the experimental years of the early New Deal.

CHAPTER 3

SKID ROW IN AN ERA OF PLENTY

DURING the early 1950s, author and activist Michael Harrington lived near the Bowery as a member of the Catholic Worker, the group founded by Dorothy Day to help the area's poor. Harrington characterized skid row and its residents as "the bitterest, most physical and obvious poverty that can be seen in an American city." He described Bowery residents as suffering from disease, exposure, and neglect. They spent day after listless day walking, resting, procuring food, and making conversation, expressing few goals and little hope. He marveled at the lack of compassion felt by other city residents at the plight of those he termed the "alcoholic poor": "Though all this takes place in the middle of New York City, it is hardly noticed. It is a form of poverty, of social disintegration, that does not attract sympathy. People get moral when they talk about alcoholics, and the very language is loaded against such unfortunates. (I have not used the word "bum" since I went to the Catholic Worker; it is part of the vocabulary of not caring.)," Harrington concluded, "But of course, nothing is being done, really."[1]

In part, the callousness Harrington observed stemmed from the relative economic prosperity of the era. Whereas approximately 40 percent of Americans had lived in poverty at the turn of the century, and between 30 and 40 percent during the Depression, the rate had dropped to 25 percent by the mid-1950s. Economic vitality would come to define postwar America; by the 1970s, the poverty rate would fall to between 6 and 15 percent. If the clear majority of Americans were enjoying economic success, those who remained in poverty, many reasoned, must be broken. Postwar politicians, social service providers, and the media frequently traced poverty's roots to individual pathology. Poor people in general, and homeless people in particular, would come to be viewed as individuals whose flawed characters required rehabilitation.[2]

This framing of poverty as an individual problem was reinforced by the era's politics. Many wanted to believe theirs was a "classless" society, and that the plethora of opportunities it offered was intrinsically American. In the context of the widespread anti-Communism of the late 1940s, urban liberals refrained from challenging the fundamental structure of the American economy, calling instead on an expanding welfare state to accommodate the needs of society's most vulnerable members. The Cold War climate left politicians honing their credentials as reformers carefully guarding the public coffers, wary of providing overly generous assistance to the poor.[3]

The shifting meaning of alcohol and its consumption further shaped the development of skid rows. Historically, those who drank excessive amounts of alcohol had been judged morally or spiritually bankrupt and were encouraged to find more personal discipline. But during the postwar era, alcoholism was understood as a disease, albeit a complex and hotly debated one. Could homeless alcoholics be rehabilitated and returned to mainstream society? Skid-row drinkers tested the limits of the legal system, the generosity of the missions, the patience of the public, and the political will of urban liberals committed to economic and social justice.

The Cold War Politics of Relief

As the postwar era dawned, American political debate increasingly centered on Communism. Committing itself to a policy of containment, the United States vowed to prevent the spread of Communism wherever it might appear, abroad or at home. As the nation enjoyed a wave of patriotism celebrating American ideals of capitalism and democracy, the poor stood in marked contrast to the increasing prosperity enjoyed by many. Even liberal politicians resisted fully committing to poor relief programs, fearful of appearing to support Communist, socialist, or other radical ideas. Rather than viewing the poor as structural victims of an economic system, they sought to alleviate their suffering in a hostile political climate.

The postwar years saw fewer homeless men living on skid row. Contrary to much public opinion, the homeless were not a uniquely aberrant group of individuals. Instead, as the poorest of a city's poor population, their numbers shifted according to the area's broader economic trends. During the depths

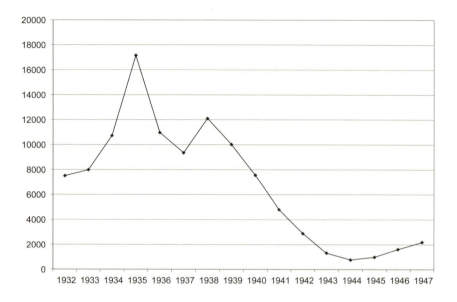

Figure 16. The tabulation of data from public and private agencies revealed that homeless men sought lodging in patterns that paralleled the health of the local and national economy. Data from Homeless Men in New York City: Report of the Project Committee on Homeless Men of the Welfare Council of New York City (New York: Welfare Council of New York City, 1949), 23.

of the Depression, New York City's public assistance rolls had peaked at over 1.5 million, while 17,000 homeless men had sought temporary lodgings. America's entry into World War II invigorated the city's economy; by 1945, well under 200,000 city residents drew public assistance. Mayor Fiorello La-Guardia enforced the Selective Service Act on the Bowery, sending a squad to check the draft registration cards of homeless men, jailing those not in compliance, and sending hundreds of those appearing for skid-row infractions before the Magistrate's Court to jobs in war plants, hospitals, restaurants, and railroads. These forces combined to reduce the number of homeless men receiving lodging to below 2,000 from 1943 to 1946. In August 1945, 2 percent of the city's population received public assistance, while by May 1950 that proportion had more than doubled to 5 percent as returning soldiers and war workers displaced women, ethnic minorities, older men, and other nontraditional workers.[4]

The men on the Bowery at mid-century did not differ vastly from

Figure 17. During and after World War II, life continued largely unchanged on the nation's skid rows. Marjory Collins, "Bowery Hotel About Midnight," September 1942. Farm Security Administration Office of War Information Photograph Collection, Prints & Photographs Division, Library of Congress.

non-homeless New Yorkers.[5] They were overwhelmingly literate, but had somewhat less formal education than other city residents; one-fourth had attended at least some high school, but over two-thirds had not gone on to secondary education.[6] Largely between forty and sixty, most had been last employed as unskilled laborers, the category of workers most vulnerable to layoff. The profile of the Bowery man was that of a somewhat educated, older, dislocated worker who had fallen on hard times through unemployment, traumatic life events, or substance abuse problems. Prisoners serving drunkenness sentences in other cities shared the broad profile of the Bowery population, representing less educated, less skilled members of the workforce.[7]

By 1946, the Department of Welfare controlled too few beds to house even the relatively few homeless individuals seeking assistance. They housed 900 men in the six-story muni on East 25th Street. An additional 600 could be lodged at Bowery flophouses through vouchers issued by the Department. Cage hotels, which offered small cubicles topped with chicken wire, proved especially dangerous. Regulations on such hotels had intensified after a Times Square cage hotel fire three years earlier, in which at least eighteen men died. Subsequent changes to the Multiple Dwelling Law required sprinkler systems, an expense many owners were unwilling to bear. Facing a shortage of beds, up to 200 men slept on the floor of the muni. Welfare commissioner Edward Rhatigan lobbied mayor William O'Dwyer to acquire additional buildings to increase the Department's housing capacity.[8]

The city responded by purchasing the Bowery YMCA for $250,000. Built in 1912, the building contained a cafeteria, dormitory housing for 450 men, and 153 private rooms. Rhatigan hoped these supplemental lodgings would allow the city to house its entire homeless population, but his vision went unrealized; he had not foreseen the use of the block housing the muni as the site of the new Veterans Hospital. As the winter months of highest demand for shelter approached, Rhatigan called on the mayor to take action. If O'Dwyer would not intervene with the Hotel and Rooming House Association to assist the Department of Welfare in securing larger, affordable blocks of rooms, Rhatigan cautioned, he should plan to use the armories as "temporary barracks."[9]

Faced with this impending crisis, and feeling pressure from East Side business interests to remove the homeless from the Bowery, city officials proposed to send them away from Manhattan by reopening Camp LaGuardia, in Chester, where the Department of Welfare had maintained an annex of the muni from 1934 to 1943. The camp reopened in autumn 1947, with one hundred men in residence. Younger men were sent to Camp LaGuardia for shorter, reform-oriented stays away from the corrupting environment of the Bowery. But Camp LaGuardia's principal role was to provide long-term housing for elderly homeless men no longer likely to find employment. These clients were sent to the 323-acre facility for extended stays. Camp programming revolved around diversions to pass the time, including film screenings, a library, and a craft shop, where residents were encouraged to make toys for children in the Family Shelter. The Department of Welfare gradually transferred additional men to the camp until, by the mid-1950s, over 800 were in residence.[10]

Moving the older homeless men to Camp LaGuardia alleviated some of the political pressures on the mayor's office, but many homeless remained on the Bowery, much to the dismay of other area residents. A July 1949 survey of East Side residents' attitudes toward the nearby homeless population found respondents complaining of "gross behavior" (defined as public urination, indecent exposure, abusive language, intoxication, and inappropriate contact with children). Several wanted to move away from the neighborhood altogether to escape the encroaching homeless population. One resident of the 200 block of East 17th Street remarked, "The Bowery is moving further and further up Third Avenue."[11]

The situation showed no sign of abating, as the number of homeless people seeking public lodging only increased. As winter 1949 approached, officials predicted that the Department of Welfare would not be able to meet the rising need. Mayor O'Dwyer appointed a Committee on Homeless Men, consisting of representatives of the city's major charitable organizations dealing with the homeless population, to assess the situation more fully. The committee found that demand for the city's homeless services had, indeed, exceeded the supply. In addition to the suffering of the men left sleeping on the muni floor, such cramped conditions in public facilities posed health risks. A 1948 outbreak of scarlet fever and streptococcus throat infection had led to the swift quarantine of 143 residents of the Third Street family shelter. Crowded conditions at the muni left court officials reluctant to send people to a facility so "repellent."[12]

The Welfare Department also struggled to meet the needs of homeless women, who risked not only sexual assault on skid row, but also severe moral judgment anywhere they went. From 1936 to 1943, the public women's shelter on East Sixth Street had welcomed clients referred through the Welfare or Police Departments. When the wartime drop in homelessness left few women at the shelter, it was closed, the remaining clients sent to the second floor of the muni on East 25th Street. By 1947, this arrangement no longer accommodated the city's homeless women, prompting the Welfare Department to propose a separate women's shelter on Rivington Street, abutting the University Settlement on Eldridge Street.[13]

Advocates for the settlement, which had been active in the neighborhood since 1886, were quick to argue that the local youth served should not be exposed to homeless women. Their letters poured into Mayor O'Dwyer's office, labeling the plan "ill conceived and inadvisable," "socially unhealthful," and sure to attract "undesired characters." Members of the Friends of the University Settlement, the Tompkins Square Mothers Club, the Church of All Nations and Neighborhood House, and the Manhattan Chapter of the American Veterans Committee came together to oppose the plan. Over 400 area residents signed a petition opposing the proposed shelter, fearing it would burden the neighborhood with an additional "negative influence." In his letter to the mayor, attorney Harry Levine articulated the feelings of many area residents:

> The term "homeless women" is a euphemism. The house is
> meant to be used for women off the Bowery. I do not wish to be
> understood as lacking sympathy for these women. I do say that
> their influence would be bad on the young people in an adjoining
> settlement house. These young people are underprivileged in
> many ways and they should not be subjected to the humiliating
> sight of the most unfortunate women in the city.[14]

Welfare Commissioner Rhatigan acknowledged the legitimacy of some of the protesters' concerns, but urged a wider perspective. The women needed to be housed, and no neighborhood was going to welcome them with open arms. They could not continue to be lodged with the men in mixed-sex accommodations. Visions of the public outcry that would greet allegations of the rape of homeless women by homeless men, or publicly funded sexual activity among the homeless, prompted him to warn O'Dwyer: "The establishment of a separate women's shelter becomes more urgent daily because of the fact that the conditions at the Lodging House are so overcrowded and desperate that disaster is ever pending. . . . We have been highly successful in avoiding the unpleasantest kind of publicity because of the conditions there," he went on, "How long this luck can hold out, I do not know but I, for one, should hate to risk it."[15]

Rhatigan's fear of negative publicity proved valid when a major scandal erupted later that year. Instead of single women, though, the lodging of families would spark the controversy. On 9 May, the *New York World-Telegram* and *New York Sun* reported that a homeless Bronx family of six had been housed by the Department of Welfare in a West Side hotel at a cost of $500 per month. Ten days later, another shocker hit the front pages—a hotel-dwelling family of seven had received $640 per month since December. Approximately forty families were being housed in hotels. Department of Welfare representatives argued that the city's housing shortage had prevented them from securing vacant apartments for all homeless families. According to the public assistance director, the only alternative to the hotels would have been to split up the families, sending the children to a shelter and their parents to the muni.[16]

However reasonable the Welfare Department's logic, the tabloid press stoked public ire with headline descriptions of "lavish" and "ritzy" relief. The *World-Telegram* went on to editorialize: "No wonder Welfare Commissioner Edward E. Rhatigan wanted $163,000,000 for his department in the new billion-dollar city budget, instead of the mere $142,000,000 he got. Rhatigan relief-de-luxe comes high!" Not surprisingly, the red-baiting *New York Sun* offered the most outrageous rendition of the story, reporting that hotel stays were only part of the Welfare Department's gross generosity, which provided some relief recipients with babysitters in the evenings, maid service, taxi rides, college educations, and winters in Florida, all at the taxpayers' expense. The *Sun* repeatedly speculated that blame for such largesse should be placed on the presence of Communists in the Welfare Department and the influx of Puerto Ricans moving to the city to apply for relief. Puerto Ricans arriving without such plans, the paper had been informed, were quickly encouraged by U.S. Representative Vito Marcantonio of East Harlem and other Communist sympathizers to register for welfare benefits. In reality, some of those housed in hotels by the Welfare Department were displaced persons and repatriated Americans arriving from Europe, whose expenses would ultimately be reimbursed by the federal government. But as the media hysteria mounted and political forces mobilized, the original hotel cases would be eclipsed by larger agendas.[17]

As the State Board of Social Welfare prepared to launch an inquiry into city relief activities, Rhatigan appealed to the media in his own defense. Releasing copies of correspondence from the State Board urging a client to accept the hotel lodgings arranged for him by the city Department of Welfare, he argued that the state had not only known of his hotel housing policy, but endorsed it. Rhatigan also scrambled to make highly visible changes in department operations, streamlining administrative procedures, requiring relief recipients to offer weekly proof that they were actively seeking employment, and instituting a new auditing process for any relief case surpassing the standard financial cap.[18]

After initially supporting the work of Rhatigan and the Welfare Department publicly, the mayor launched an investigation of his own. His committee condemned the department for lacking sufficient staff training and failing to establish "standards of morality for relief recipients." Unwed mothers receiving public assistance, the committee argued, should be monitored, both individually and statistically. The committee also wanted to ensure that poor residents of other regions would not be drawn to New York City by the prospect of relief.[19]

In part, the scandal reflected the shifting politics of relief funding. Throughout the 1940s and 1950s, the bureaucracies of the city and state struggled to negotiate a formula for the funding breakdown of local welfare spending. In 1946, the "Moore formula" placed 80 percent of the financial burden on the city and state, and 20 percent on the federal government. Over time, as national welfare programs became more centralized, the federal government gradually increased its share of the responsibility, while the state absorbed the gain. By 1954, the federal government financed over 30 percent of the local relief budget, while the city and state each supplied 35 percent. With the state so heavily vested in the city's welfare activities, tensions between the city Department of Welfare and the state Board of Social Welfare erupted into squabbles over programming.[20]

But partisan politics also fueled the attacks on the city Department of Welfare, whose dominant union, the United Public Workers, maintained strong ties to the Communist Party. The CIO had expelled Communist-led local unions by 1947, as part of a broad purge of Communists. Anti-Communist sentiments sharply limited the growth of public welfare programs, purging administrations of many committed social activists and leaving others frightened into silence. In this context, O'Dwyer saw in the scandal an opportunity to weaken the powerful union. The *Daily Worker* chastised the city's tabloid press for using relief recipients as "political pawns" in a controversy instigated by the ambitious governor Thomas Dewey and a coalition of reactionary politicians. Instead, the paper framed the story as one of "starvation amidst opulence," calling attention to the scapegoating of relief recipients for political gain.[21]

From the early days of the State Board's investigation, when reporters asked if membership in the Communist Party provided sufficient grounds for dismissing a provisional employee, O'Dwyer deflected the responsibility back to Rhatigan, saying, "No, but he should have known if he was hiring Commies." Before the State hearings even began, O'Dwyer called for Rhatigan's resignation. Declaring publicly that he had "no apologies nor regrets," the

Welfare Commissioner contended that O'Dwyer knew well the limitations of the city's relief programs. Rhatigan called destitution and poverty the city's "number one municipal headache," arguing that the O'Dwyer administration had failed to make public welfare a priority. The hotel scandal, he argued, was merely an attempt to distract attention from the city's broader housing crisis. Rhatigan admitted, however, that a large percentage of the Department of Welfare employees were, in fact, Communists. He urged officials to identify Communist workers, and to fire them if their politics interfered with their job performance.[22]

As the hearings dragged on and details of individual relief cases were scrutinized in the media, Justine Wise Polier of the Children's Court likened the climate to a "public lynching" of welfare recipients. Edward S. Lewis, executive director of the New York Urban League, called the hearings "a political inquisition for headline stories." Rhatigan, too, worried about the potential effects of such highly publicized investigations. The "man on the street," he argued, already held three major misconceptions of public welfare. First, he suspected welfare recipients lived in luxury. Second, he was sure they refused to work for a living. Third, he doubted the necessity of large welfare rolls, given the overall economic growth.[23]

Rhatigan's fears were realistic. Public opinion of social welfare programs in the 1940s and 1950s was marked by ambivalence. As the number of welfare recipients dropped, and fewer Americans merited the classification "poor," those who did faced increasing suspicion. Public opinion polls on the subject of poverty revealed mixed sentiments. When asked if they supported "welfare," respondents reacted negatively. But when inquiring if people endorsed assistance for the "needy," pollsters received a more positive response. More than a question of simple semantics, the disparity reflected public discomfort with defining the deserving poor and specifying the assistance they deserved. The bifurcated public welfare system forged by the New Deal balanced this ambiguity by keeping Social Security and other supports to the working and middle classes distinct in the popular imagination from the stigmatized welfare programs aiding the poor.[24]

The Department of Welfare's struggle to find a feasible alternative to the muni added to a broader reconceptualization of assistance programs. In July 1950, the Department reinstated its broader work relief program, requiring ablebodied relief recipients to complete assigned jobs. Hailed in public discourse as a way to reduce the number of "chiselers" and "loafers" receiving public benefits, the program required recipients, including many homeless people, to clean vacant lots, work as playground assistants, and provide messenger service for city offices. These reforms resonated with observers who saw the poor and homeless as in need of supervision and discipline. Requiring labor of relief recipients harkened back to the popular New Deal work programs, which had placated public fears of fostering a nation dependent on charitable assistance. Indeed, some postwar observers described even skid row as suffering not from a lack of public assistance, but its overabundance. Arnold J. Vander Meulen, head of the Haven of Rest Rescue Mission in Grand Rapids, Michigan, cited the veteran's pensions awarded to soldiers after the First and Second World Wars as major causes of homelessness. In his view, such programs encouraged laziness, dependence on assistance, and even alcoholism.[25]

Public resentment increased further as African Americans moved in large numbers to the urban North and racist stereotypes permeated discussions of public welfare policies. During the 1940s, New York City's African American population increased by over 60 percent. Across the nation, welfare debates increasingly focused on issues of race and ethnicity by the early 1950s, although only one-third of the nation's welfare recipients were African American. Homeless African Americans found lodgings in public facilities and many religious ones, including the Salvation Army and the Bowery Mission, but many commercial lodging houses remained segregated. Historically, smaller skid-row areas had frequently formed on the outskirts of African American neighborhoods. Homeless black men in New York were younger than their white counterparts, but their overall health and educational backgrounds were indistinguishable from that of the city's broader African American population. Many were recent migrants to the area, as impoverished African Americans migrating from the South joined Bowery whites on skid row. Prior to the early 1960s, little systematic research was conducted on postwar poverty, and even less on homelessness. The rare commentators and analysts who did visit the nation's skid rows often ignored the presence of African Americans, leaving a profound silence in the institutional records.[26]

The homeless also drew a great deal of resentment from politicians, their constituents, and the media. Skid-row residents ranked among the least sympathetic recipients of public assistance, as they were generally perceived as lazy, dangerous, immoral—violent men and women no longer serving a useful function in the local economy. As a result, many Americans were comfortable with aiding the homeless only in a very minimal fashion. As the city debated "luxury relief," some journalists framed the municipal lodging houses as an acceptable method of aiding the poor. *New York Times* editorials emphasized the starkly minimal accommodations at the muni. Articles like "City Lodging House Offers No Luxury" offered readers a rare glimpse of life in the facility. Relishing the mundane details, the author included a lengthy description of the daily menu, with breakfast consisting of coffee, cereal, fruit, and bread, lunch of soup, an orange, and a fortified milk drink, and dinner of stew, bread, and the milk drink again. In bed by 9 p.m. and allowed no more than a single dollar in cash, the homeless man in the city shelter enjoyed no luxuries. Readers could take satisfaction in the knowledge that some of the city's poor lived appropriately spartan lives. Because of the minimal services provided through the city shelters, as well as the economies of scale made possible by the large facility, the Department of Welfare spent, on average, twice as much on individuals receiving public assistance as it did on those in the shelter system.[27]

The gritty, grim environment of the muni, Rhatigan had argued, was especially inappropriate for children. He justified the scandal, arguing: "one would rather pay the price of adverse publicity to high grade cases in hotels, than to think of those families and children in places like the Bowery Lodging House." The following May, the city announced the opening of a new shelter housing women and children on Fifth Street, in the former P.S. 25. The facility's programs emphasized building moral character and included a "Mother's Work Program" designed to ensure that women handled their own laundry, ironing, and child care, while also performing light building maintenance. The program foreshadowed the debates over the "morality" of women receiving welfare benefits that would shape the development of social welfare programs in the 1960s.[28]

Soon after Rhatigan's departure, to the accompaniment of public relations fanfare, O'Dwyer appointed Raymond Hilliard to head the Department of Welfare. Rhatigan had been trained as a social worker, Hilliard as a lawyer. Previously the executive secretary of Chicago's Public Aid Commission, he arrived with a reputation for running a tightly controlled administration and ousting Communists. He set about reducing the power of the UPW, further streamlining department operations, and reclaiming $1.5 million the Department had lost through "fraudulent" relief claims. These highly touted changes did not render the Department immune to public reprimands from the state. A state study of the Department's 1950 operations found one-quarter of the relief cases handled lacking in sufficient documentation. The report went on to call for the city's return of the funds contributed toward such fraudulent expenditures to the state and federal governments. Rhatigan supporters read in the report a vindication of the former commissioner's efforts.[29]

The piecemeal homeless programs that had been sustaining the Department of Welfare were no longer able to meet clients' needs while appeasing an increasingly suspicious electorate. The hotel scandal reflected a city plagued by a housing shortage and no viable system for housing families and children, not one in the grips of a Communist plot. Although the homeless were never central to the Social Security system, they did draw some direct federal assistance monies in the postwar years, primarily through veterans' benefits and Social Security checks. Many, however, lacked the consistent work history necessary to receive substantial benefits. As marginal workers, such men and women were also routinely excluded from the generous "hidden welfare state" of the postwar era, made up of employer-sponsored pension and health insurance plans encouraged by federal tax incentives. Liberal politicians increasingly focused on programs that purported to repair the broken homeless.[30]

Alcoholism and the Individualization of Relief

In 1955, a trio of documentary filmmakers recorded daily life among New York's homeless in *On the Bowery*. Lionel Rogosin, Richard Bagley, and Mark Sufrin coaxed life stories out of the area's normally taciturn men and gradually earned their trust during the production. In the black-and-white film's opening montage of morning on the street of "forgotten men," two drunken men struggled to lift a friend too inebriated to stand on his own, a five-man bottle gang stationed on the curb passed liquor among themselves, and a man read a magazine while reclining in the pushcart he used for daily salvage work. Rogosin and his crew captured the image of skid row in the popular imagination, a procession of stumbling drunks whose lives were either tragic or comic, depending on one's perspective.[31]

Many skid-row residents drank heavily; therefore, many assumed, it was alcohol that rendered one homeless. Why would someone drink to the point of losing job, friends, family, and health? Was alcoholism a disease or simply a habit? The debate over the nature of alcoholism preoccupied researchers for decades, prompting new understandings of both substance abuse and homelessness. The resulting model, although compelling, remained incomplete, offering the public an overly simplified vision of skid row and the people who lived there.

Combating alcohol on skid row was nothing new for urban religious missions. From the Salvation Army's earliest days in nineteenth-century London, founder General William Booth and his followers had searched for "effectual deliverance for the drunkard." The Army advocated total abstinence, viewing social drinking as a preventable sin, even if later, excessive drinking was unavoidable. During its initial decades in New York City, the Army had been plagued by ridicule, criticism, and even physical attacks. But by the postwar years Salvationists were a widely accepted Christian denomination; their work with the city's down and out earned them a place in the hearts of New Yorkers, who were willing to overlook their unfamiliar customs and insistence on pseudo-militaristic ranks and uniforms. Salvationists appeared in popular culture as eager, fresh-scrubbed workers in crisp uniforms reaching out to the wretched masses. "Blade Winters," a comic strip created by writer Ed Jurist and cartoonist Ed Mann, featured this storyline for ten weeks in 1953, following the actions of Hope Lowell, a young, attractive blonde staff member of the Army's Bowery Corps. Skid-row habitué characters like "Go-Away Gorrogan," "Potato Pete," "Gentleman Johnson," and "John 'Footlight' Fornsworth" dubbed the singing, uplifting woman the "Angel of Skid Row."[32]

The real Bowery Salvationists were Luella Larder and Olive McKeown, who directed the Army's work on skid row for over fifteen years. After working abroad with the USO during World War II, the pair had requested to be stationed on the Bowery. More than simply carrying out daily operations, Larder and McKeown also actively shaped program development. McKeown began lobbying Army administrators in 1947 for the construction of a facility specifically dedicated to the rehabilitation of excessive drinkers: "To make any kind of a come-back his actual needs are a bed, a chance to wash and shave, a place to launder his clothing, a few square meals in his stomach, and Christian friends to help revive hope and confidence. This is where we are stymied." The Army Bowery Memorial Hotel officially refused entry to any man "with the slightest odor of liquor on him." McKeown hoped a "drying-out" center located near but not on the Bowery would allow clients to maintain a respectable address to use when registering with employment agencies, thus avoiding some of the taint of skid row.[33]

McKeown's efforts were largely successful; in 1951, the Salvation Army held a cornerstone-laying ceremony to launch a half-million dollar renovation, adding an Alcoholic Rehabilitation Center to the Bowery Corps. Sergeant-major Jack Cleveland, the most famous Bowery Corps worker and one of the few Bowery converts to enter the Army, addressed the crowd: "I look back to

Figure 18. During the postwar era, the Salvation Army Bowery Corps renewed its commitment to assisting the homeless through construction of a modern Alcoholic Rehabilitation Center. Cornerstone-Laying Ceremony, October 1951. Front (left to right): Jack Cleveland, Red Lynn (convert), Donald McMillan; Back: Olive McKeown, Addy Olley, Luella Larder, Mrs. Captain Cannuti, Esther Oliver. Courtesy of Salvation Army Archives and Research Center.

long ago when I used to flop in a scratch-house (hotel, that is). I remember this very spot, used to be a horse-market (restaurant, that is) and above it was a place where we used to drink our smoke (half water and half denatured alcohol, that is). When I knelt to pray at the Bowery Corps, I had cardboard on my feet, and rags on my body, but I found God. I haven't touched a drop of drink since." Cleveland had been born to a pious Christian New Hampshire farm family, but had gradually lost control of his social drinking and landed on skid row. After three years of homeless drifting along the Lower East Side, Cleveland found religion and a new beginning through the Salvation Army in 1929. As the Alcoholic Rehabilitation Center opened, many Army officers held high hopes that others would soon follow in Cleveland's footsteps.[34]

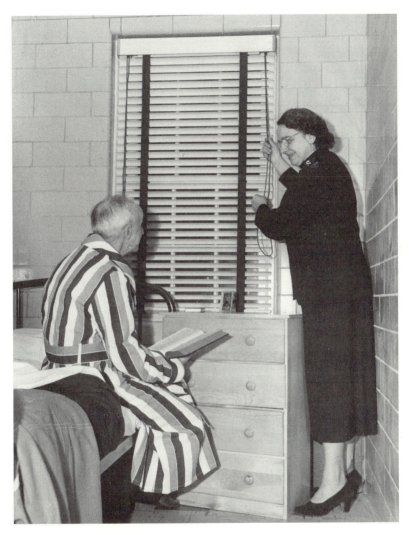

Figure 19. Inside the new Alcoholic Rehabilitation Center, Senior-Captain Luella Larder posed in a client's private room, 1952. Courtesy of Salvation Army Archives and Research Center.

The three-story center was impressive, modern, and well-equipped to serve both residential and daily clients. The man visiting for the day would participate in meetings, nightly open-air religious services, counseling, and an employment referral service. If not dependent for support on the Department of Welfare, he could also apply for membership to the Red Shield Clubroom. Once issued a membership card, he would be entitled to use the clubroom's books, magazines, ping-pong table, television, radio, and snack bar.[35]

Those men admitted for residential treatment were assigned to one of the nine private or three semi-private rooms upstairs. Each room was furnished with a bed with a waterproof mattress, wardrobe, chair, and chest of drawers. An isolation room equipped with a tiled draining floor was available to those men who entered the program in distress from alcohol use. Initially isolated from the rest of the center's clientele, men who were "drying out" spent time in a separate dining room and lounge. Clients obeyed a strict curfew—the front door was locked at 11 p.m. and lights were out by 11:30. As they grew physically and emotionally stronger, they performed small tasks throughout the building, which could include standing on the corner of Third Street distributing religious tracts. Finally, the recovered man would be assigned to various paid jobs outside the facility. Stays ranged from four weeks to six months, depending on the man's condition when admitted and his responsiveness to treatment.[36]

As an evangelistic organization, the Salvation Army's core tenets were religious. A man could be admitted to the center, "regardless of color or creed . . . provided he is sincerely interested in a spiritual approach to his alcoholic problem." Participants also needed to be both physically and mentally qualified for employment. Those applicants requiring more intensive treatment were referred either to other Salvation Army facilities or to the muni. Most program enrollees entered after participating in the daily religious services; others applied directly at the program's office, or were referred by family, friends, or area churches. As the Salvation Army began its new program of alcoholic rehabilitation, it remained critical of the emerging treatment philosophies espousing psychotherapy. While such programs might be effective for clients of "normal intelligence," Army officials argued, surrender to the will of God would be attainable for even the "skid row habitué," the "person of low intelligence," and the "jail drunk." Salvationists also saw their ultimate goals as distinct from those of more secular programs: "Our job is not merely to make sober men; our job is to teach them to be Christians."[37]

Other religious groups also used charismatic skid-row converts to reach countless homeless people seeking a spiritual path to sobriety. George Bolton, the high-profile minister of the Bowery Mission for seventeen years, frequently shared the story of his own religious conversion and struggle with alcohol. A native Englishman, he had spent several years as a professional gambler, ultimately abandoning his wife for life on the road. After experiencing religious conversion in the 1920s at Jerry McAuley's Cremorne Mission in Times Square, he had pursued religious training and taken over the leadership of the Bowery Mission. Bolton's engaging preaching style was legendary; he closed each sermon with the signature line, "You've tried the rest, now try the best."[38]

Such religious approaches had been commonly used for over one hundred years, reflecting the persistent commitment of churches and missions to helping the homeless. The nineteenth century had also witnessed other efforts to end excessive drinking, including the temperance movement, which called for a national ban on the production and consumption of alcohol on largely moralistic and religious grounds. During the Progressive era, as Americans called for public solutions to social problems, investigative researchers exposed the living conditions of the poor and homeless in conjunction with their use of alcohol. Sociologist Nels Anderson's 1923 study divided the homeless into three groups—hobos, tramps, and "bums"—who often drank heavily without working or traveling. Anderson described the conflicted reactions such men received from the public, who found them simultaneously "pitiable" and "repulsive." Some medical reformers during this era had also targeted excessive alcohol consumption as a disease. The American Association for the Cure of Inebriates, a group of medical and business professionals, called for a system of public asylums to house chronic drinkers separately from the institutionalized insane.[39]

The 1920 implementation of Prohibition under the Eighteenth Amendment transformed the nation's relationship with alcohol. Now illicit, alcohol production and consumption became part of a rapidly developing underground culture. Reacting against the rural, Protestant, middle-class, reactionary tide of anti-drinking sentiment, urban, working-class Catholics and other immigrants continued to imbibe, as did the nation's elites. Alcoholic beverages became less mainstream, and part of a criminalized subculture.[40]

When the Roosevelt administration repealed Prohibition in 1933, regulating the legal production and sale of alcohol fell to the states and counties. On an individual level, Americans began to redefine their relationship with alcohol, through the framework of compulsive drinking. Just two years after Repeal, Alcoholics Anonymous (AA) was founded in Akron, Ohio, by New

York stock speculator Bill Wilson and Ohio surgeon Robert Holbrook. The group popularized a mutual aid ethos to assist members on the road to sobriety. The founders of Alcoholics Anonymous argued that some individuals had an "allergy" to alcohol, and could never control their drinking once they began. Rooted in the concept that sobriety was attainable only by facing "one day at a time," AA's program centered on its "Twelve Steps" of rehabilitation, which included taking a moral inventory of one's life and making amends to people one had harmed. Central to the group's philosophy was complete renunciation of alcohol; even social drinking was barred.[41]

As AA became popular and influential, its approach was strengthened by the emergence of the alcoholism movement. Movement pioneer Elvin M. Jellinek, a Yale professor of applied physiology, published influential descriptions of the "phases of alcoholism." Tracing the periods in an alcoholic's life through the lens of alcohol consumption, he charted the descent of many individuals who lost control of their lives.

Jellinek's own explanations of the nature of alcoholism were far more nuanced than some streamlined versions imply.[42] He divided alcoholics into five categories, not all of whom were "addicted to alcohol," carefully distinguishing between addictive drinkers and "non-addictive alcoholics." Those not vulnerable to alcohol addiction would never "lose control" of their drinking, leading them to the "crucial" phase of alcohol addiction. Jellinek described the crucial phase as one in which an addict became aggressive, punctuated by persistent remorse and bouts of abstinence. He would set rules for his drinking, limiting it to specific settings, even as he began to lose friends, in part due to his rising self-pity, and sometimes leave jobs or see family ties erode as alcohol came to dominate his life. He would fail to eat properly, lose interest in sexual relationships, and begin to need a drink on waking each morning. He might be intermittently hospitalized for issues related to his drinking. Now drinking in the morning, he had entered the chronic phase of alcoholism. He might now go on "benders" of extended drinking, see his judgment clouded, and be plagued by vague fears. A gradual loss of alcohol tolerance could leave him just as intoxicated as in previous years, but through the consumption of far less alcohol. Ultimately, obsessed with drinking, he might long for the comfort of religion, and could admit defeat, leaving himself open to intervention and treatment.[43]

Jellinek directed the Yale University Section of Alcohol Studies, established in 1943, and the Summer School of Alcohol Studies. The school generated little new research, but proved highly effective in communicating its findings to the medical community as well as the broader public. This success was due in part to the assistance of public relations professionals who were hired to ensure that the Yale school significantly influenced American culture. Following that advice, they emphasized a simple, coherent narrative explaining that alcoholism was a disease. Repeatedly, the school informed the public that problem drinkers were sick, could be helped, and were worthy of assistance.[44]

Heavy drinkers who never lost control of their drinking were not, in Jellinek's analysis, addicted to alcohol. This aspect of his explanation was rarely reported, leaving Americans to fixate on the powerful concept that alcoholism was a disease. Jellinek's model also paralleled the "bottoming out" described by AA, making it easy for many to understand. Researchers and social service providers looked to the skid-row homeless as a population comprised largely of chronic alcoholics. The heavy drinking of many skid-row homeless was not news to researchers. Anderson's 1914 study of clients of New York City's muni had found 44 percent drinking excessively and 43 percent drinking moderately.[45]

Precisely how much alcohol did the postwar residents of skid row consume? Many researchers did not employ a quantitative analysis of alcohol consumption due to the varying effects drinking could have on individuals. Instead, many projects defined "excessive" as any amount of drinking that led to problems in one's life. Another barrier to adequate data was the fact that homeless men, accustomed to skid row's heavy drinking culture, did not perceive their alcohol consumption in the terms used by researchers. Nearly one-fourth of skid-row men classified themselves as "spree" drinkers, who periodically indulged in a drinking binge, but researchers suspected many of those respondents were actually heavy, steady drinkers.[46]

Several large research projects, however, revealed consistent findings. A study conducted on Detroit's skid row found 72 percent of a clinic's clients self-identifying as alcoholics. Researchers in Chicago found 20 percent of skid-row residents drinking less than the equivalent of a half pint of whiskey each week, 33 percent between .5 and 1.9 pints 25 percent from 2 to 4.9 pints, and 22 percent five or more pints. Overall, 32 percent classified themselves as light drinkers, 26 percent as moderate, 23 percent as periodic, and 19 percent as heavy. Precise tabulations were impossible, given the fluid nature of the category "alcoholism." While all sources agreed that many homeless individuals drank heavily, no evidence proved that a significant number of the homeless would merit the clinical definition of an "alcoholic."[47]

Qualitative research depicted the daily lives of many hard drinking skid-row residents. Asked to describe his life, a sixty-five-year-old man receiving a railroad pension said: "Well, if I got money, I get up in the morning and have two or three drinks for breakfast and go to work if I have a job. In the evening, I have a few more drinks and watch TV and go to bed. That's in the summertime. Now I get up about 8, start drinking, and drink all day. Mostly beer." Some men surveyed described their relationship to alcohol as one of compulsion and addiction. A twenty-nine-year-old commented, "If I start drinkin', then you know what happens. If I'm workin', I just go to work. If I want to try to save some money, I try to stay around the lobby here, maybe go to a show. If not, I start drinkin'. I spend quite a bit of time in the lobby here—all the time, when I'm not drinkin'. As a rule I don't talk to no one. I hang by myself unless I get with a bottle gang. To be truthful I spend most of my time drinkin'." Even though research showed that not all homeless people were alcoholics, the precise use of terms became blurred. While acknowledging that not all homeless alcoholics followed the same path, the author of a 1962 article neatly conflated the two themes: "It is not unusual, however, to find that, as they have reached the status of homelessness gradually, passing through the various phases of alcoholism on the way, they represent the later stages of the disease."[48]

Beginning in the late 1940s, some specialists had questioned the model of alcoholic progression, often as it applied to skid row. Robert Straus, a researcher in the Laboratory of Applied Physiology at the School of Studies on Alcohol, had noted that individuals sometimes began drinking heavily before they became homeless, while others accelerated their drinking rapidly only after arriving on skid row. But the model of decline proved attractive, not only to those dedicated to working with alcoholics, but also to the broader medical community.[49]

The medicalized view of the heavy drinker that emerged during the 1940s and 1950s yielded both positive and negative results. Straus predicted that the framing of alcohol as a disease would improve the relationships between doctors and their patients, leading to more effective medical care. Also, the medicalized view lessened the stigma surrounding heavy drinking, leading to more opportunities for assistance.[50]

By the 1970s, though, Jellinek's model of disease had yielded to the "public health perspective," which took a broader approach. Critics of the theory argued that it had been overly simplistic, especially in the form conveyed to the public. Much of the research that had supported the alcoholism movement, they noted, had taken extremely heavy drinkers as a subject. Beginning from that perspective, they argued, it was no surprise that alcoholism looked like a progressive disease. By focusing so closely on the heaviest drinkers, some lamented, researchers had lost opportunities to analyze the drinking habits of other Americans. Perhaps most problematic, the disease theory had left many Americans with the impression that heavy drinking was only a problem for those especially vulnerable to alcohol's effects.[51]

Some of the era's smaller alcohol treatment programs rejected the disease theory. The director of Bridge House, Edward J. McGoldrick, Jr., through a program sponsored by the Department of Welfare, scorned the characterization of the alcoholic as sick, arguing instead that he suffered from "improper, destructive, or ignorant thinking." Working with patients referred from the muni, Magistrate's Court, Rikers Island, and Bellevue Hospital, he argued for complete abstinence for problem drinkers. A recovered alcoholic and "lay therapist," McGoldrick asserted that the problem drinker needed "information not reformation." The program, operating by the 1950s out of a three-story building near Bronx Park, accommodated up to eighteen participants. McGoldrick boasted that approximately 50 percent went on to abstain from liquor for a year and continued to attend scheduled therapy sessions. The Department of Welfare supported this claim with statistics indicating that one-third of the men referred to Bridge House from the muni did not return to the shelter after completing the program, though their actual whereabouts remained unknown. By 1959, Bridge House was treating almost 350 "students" per year.[52]

The skid-row homeless often seemed poor candidates for rehabilitation programs, refusing offers of treatment altogether or, if they did accept, failing to complete the programs. The centrality of alcohol in the social life of skid row posed additional barriers to treatment. Although skid rows did not exhibit the typical markers of community that one would find in other neighborhoods, communal activities often centered on procuring and consuming alcohol. Bars provided rare sites for entertaining, talking, sharing stories, and laughing. Similarly, groups of men coming together in a "bottle gang" to share a bottle of wine or liquor worked together toward a common goal. Many skid-row men who drank heavily seemed more socially integrated into the area's limited community than nondrinkers. This model of heavy social drinking did not reflect that of mainstream society, where many heavy drinkers found themselves relatively isolated, and challenged therapeutic rehabilitation techniques.[53]

Jellinek's model was influential, however, in shaping not just the ways in which alcohol use was understood, but also the ways in which it was treated.

The school established Yale Plan Clinics in New Haven and Hartford in 1944. These clinics did not provide direct treatment, but focused on offering guidance and referrals to programs such as those given by Alcoholics Anonymous, the Salvation Army, and other groups. Jellinek's medicalized interpretation also inspired an array of programs across the country.[54]

Perhaps the clearest example of the evolving nature of the dominant perception of alcohol problems is found in the history of Willmar State Hospital in Minnesota. The hospital had been established as a home for inebriates during the Progressive era; funded by a tax on liquor, it opened in 1912. For heavy drinkers, the facility was primarily used as a "jag farm," where a man on a drinking binge could be sent for a short stay to get sober. Soon it also treated those deemed chronically insane. By the 1950s, over 1,400 of its 1,500 beds were occupied by mentally ill patients. Although occupying only a 75-bed ward, the treatment program for alcoholics became more medically sophisticated. Men first underwent physical and neurological exams, before settling in for a longer stay of five to six weeks. While hospitalized, patients were informed about the nature and treatment of alcoholism, and were introduced to the philosophy of AA. After release, patients were offered counseling by a recovering alcoholic as well as access to an outpatient clinic.[55]

Pioneer House, another Minnesota institution, was also influenced by the era's changing model of alcohol treatment. The facility was established in 1940 by the Division of Public Assistance of the Board of Public Welfare in Minneapolis, with the explicit goal of lowering the city's public assistance rolls. By investing relief funds in a rehabilitation facility, officials hoped to remove any families living in poverty because of alcoholism from the welfare rolls. Located at Mission Farms, twelve miles outside the city, the program was grounded in the AA therapy program, coupled with vigorous activity and nutritional support. During the summer months, clients fished, gardened, and performed maintenance tasks; in the winter, they did woodworking projects. The program boasted that over three years and 716 clients, 63 percent had emerged economically self-sufficient.[56]

Wide-ranging services were offered by a Washington, D.C., alcoholic outpatient clinic opened in 1950. Clients participated in a physical intake exam followed by individual and group therapy, as well as intelligence and aptitude tests. The facility was well staffed by psychiatrists, nurses, doctors, clinical psychologists, and recreation leaders. Program administrators urged expanded outpatient services to those heavy drinkers not yet homeless: "the early alcoholics of today are the destitute, skid row figures of tomorrow." They called for a new system of flexible hospital commitment terms for alcoholics.[57]

Boston's Long Island Hospital established an innovative residential work program through which patients lived at the hospital for up to six months, participated in weekly AA meetings, and took Antabuse, the drug that made a person who drank alcohol ill. During this time, patients worked offsite during the day, gradually reintegrating themselves into mainstream society. The program was remarkably successful at helping participants learn to work steadily and live a mostly sober life as a member of a family. Administrators analyzed the variables between successful and unsuccessful patients, finding the key factors of success to be marriage, youth, being more highly educated and more occupationally skilled, and coming from a family of origin that had not been financially dependent on the community. They also found that 65 percent of patients had been arrested for drinking or a similar offense before age twenty-five. They joined the era's other researchers, calling for interventions earlier in the drinking lives of individuals. Similar research in Detroit had found that successful rehabilitation was more likely if the clients were skilled workers who attended church and admitted they were alcoholics. They argued that these traits were actually far more critical to determining the probability of successful rehabilitation than the length of time an individual had been drinking heavily.[58]

In the early 1950s, New York trailed these other states in adopting innovative techniques. The state's only outpatient alcoholic programs by 1952 were in Buffalo and Rochester. New York State's leaders seemed less concerned about the impact of alcoholism on the welfare system than their counterparts in Minnesota, perhaps due to research showing that only 0.5 percent of New York City welfare recipient families had an alcoholic member.[59]

Camp LaGuardia had epitomized the old-fashioned model based on sheltering the homeless without an active attempt to rehabilitate them. Officials took a more ambitious approach when opening a rehabilitation facility on Hart Island, easily the bleakest property in the five boroughs. Located near City Island, only a mile long and varying in width from an eighth to a third of a mile, the island had served as the city's potter's field since 1869. Generations of the city's unclaimed dead lay buried in the plot occupying a quarter of the tiny island, while the remaining grounds had served as a workhouse, a boys' reformatory, and, most recently, a wartime naval prison.[60]

During ten-week stays, men participated in occupational therapy and AA meetings. Welfare Commissioner Hilliard employed dramatic tactics of social control to ensure the participation of homeless alcoholics. The program was posed as an alternative to a jail term. Those who refused to participate or left the island for "an invalid reason" were threatened with the loss of their public assistance benefits, and the return ferry to City Island was available only twice a week.[61]

The announcement of plans to establish a homeless shelter on Hart Island had triggered protests from City Island residents. The quasi-voluntary nature of men's enrollment in the program alarmed area residents, who feared bands of homeless men terrorizing their neighborhoods. A representative of the City Island Board of Trade spoke for many locals when he criticized the O'Dwyer administration's prioritization of the interests of Manhattan residents over those of Bronx residents: "The authorities . . . choose to forget the fact that what they actually will do will be to bring the Bowery to City Island." Over seven hundred City Island residents petitioned the mayor to block the plan, while East Side interests, including Cooper Union and the East Side Chamber of Commerce, predictably endorsed it. Moving forward with the project, O'Dwyer and Police Commissioner William O'Brien assuaged hostile City Island residents by offering them a "guarantee" that they would suffer no harm at the hands of the incoming homeless men.[62]

The Hart Island program began operations in August with nineteen participants, transfers from the muni. The program quickly expanded, housing 250 men by the end of the year; during 1953 approximately 2,000 men were admitted for an average stay of ten weeks. The isolated location was deemed ideal for rehabilitative efforts, as the men would be "free from the difficulties and temptations which otherwise 'overpower' them." The director, Joseph Mannix, spoke optimistically of the program's ability to end some homeless men's migration from court to prison to the streets. He envisioned the Hart Island program making a real difference in participants' lives. Mannix publicized the success story of a client who had spent over seven hundred days between 1937 and 1950 in jail or in a Welfare Department shelter. After arriving at Hart Island in 1950, the fifty-three-year-old man was quickly and successfully "rehabilitated"; by December he was employed in a job he had obtained through the employment referral service.[63]

Judging the Hart Island program a success, the Welfare and Health Council Committee on Alcoholism noted that nearly half its graduates had not requested further help from the Department of Welfare. By early 1954, the facility's capacity had been increased to 800, and plans were underway to build a new center housing up to 2,000 men at a time. Beginning 1 January, the state funded half of the shelter's expenses. Mannix, who had run the muni, Camp LaGuardia, Hart Island, and the East Fifth Street family shelter, noted changing public attitudes toward homelessness by the mid-1950s: "It used to be that, if they spent more than three nights in a shelter, they'd be arrested as vagrants. Now they're no longer regarded as bums. They're regarded as men in need of direction."[64]

Whatever Hart Island's rehabilitative potential, it was cut short in 1954, when the Police Department's crackdown on crime led to a shortage of prisoner housing, and the Department of Correction regained control of Hart Island. The primary program dealing with the city's alcoholic vagrants in the coming years was no longer a Welfare Department-sponsored rehabilitation center, but a traditional workhouse run by the Corrections Department on Hart Island. Three months after the Corrections Department had taken over the facility, 1,700 men were lodged in the workhouse, most serving short terms for public drunkenness. Any man arrested in New York City on such charges was transported to Hart Island, sobered up, and taken before a judge in the Social Court for Men. Correction Commissioner Anna M. Kross spoke glowingly of the new program: "New York City should have begun this experiment in social rehabilitation long ago. Ninety-five percent of the men here are not criminal at all; many have not even committed a misdemeanor in the true sense. They just could not hold their liquor."[65]

Caroline K. Simon, Republican candidate for city council president, later argued that the Wagner administration had dropped a vital program when it let go of the Hart Island rehabilitation center. "Granted that it was not the best rehabilitation center in the world," she said, "But it was a center. It had a capacity of 1,000 men and it was abundantly used. The alcoholics it served were skid-row bums who wanted to get well." Such criticism was echoed by the Public Health Committee of the New York State Bar Association, which argued that the city's new policies did little more than "keep alcoholics off the street and out of public view." In 1957, the committee described the city's efforts to rehabilitate its homeless alcoholics as movements "backward."[66]

After losing the large facility on Hart Island, the Department of Welfare was faced with the dilemma of housing its remaining homeless men. The commissioner decided to transfer many of the Hart Island residents to the shelter at Camp LaGuardia. No longer imprisoned on the island, several of the younger men broke free from the Department's constraints. Seven were quickly arrested for alleged misconduct in the surrounding communities. Three immediately left the area for parts unknown, and two were killed while walking along the nearby railroad tracks. The relatively open atmosphere of Camp LaGuardia remained effective for lodging older men, but lacked the restrictive qualities upon which the Department relied to control the behavior of younger men.[67]

By the early 1960s, alcoholic researchers proposed an array of programs designed to help those in various states of need: hospital-based programs for those requiring medical care, outpatient clinics for those able to work and live on their own, foster homes for those who could not maintain an independent home, halfway houses for those needing closer supervision, rehabilitation centers for those needing lengthy commitment, permanent supervision for those unresponsive to other treatments, and state mental hospital commitments for those who were psychotic. The medicalization of heavy drinking had focused the attention of not only doctors, but also social workers, politicians, and the media on the skid-row population, leading to new possibilities for their care.[68]

During the postwar years, urban homelessness came to be understood in new ways, as a result of the shifting political landscape surrounding both poverty and alcohol use. Reform-oriented politicians wanted assurances that the homeless were receiving minimal support, fearing accusations of generosity might brand them Communist sympathizers. Alcoholics, meanwhile, were being perceived as ill people in need of treatment. These trends coalesced on skid row, where the homeless were increasingly viewed as an aberrant population whose primary problem was its pervasive alcoholism. Service providers earnestly tried to cure the homeless of their drinking, in an effort to fix the broken men of the Bowery. Although this approach brought many positive results to the skid-row population, including new and sometimes innovative programs, it also limited the ways homelessness was understood. Educational and job training programs were not emphasized, as alcohol use was presumed to be the central problem of skid row. Even alcoholism experts did not unanimously support the creation of programs focusing so tightly on alcohol use; some argued instead for the increased funding of broader public health systems, such as mental institutions and medical hospitals, which would be better able to deal with the varied problems faced by alcoholics.[69]

Viewing the homeless as a group of sick individuals also drew attention away from serious structural analysis of poverty. During the Depression, the American public had been highly concerned with poverty and the economy in general, because the victims of the economic collapse included broad swaths of the middle and working classes. Postwar poverty, in contrast, affected

fewer people, and those it did affect were seen as flawed and in need of rehabilitation. Throughout the postwar era, American liberals hoping to aid the
homeless focused on ways to change them rather than ways to modify the
broader economic structure.

These perceptions of the homeless also shaped the ways in which politicians and urban planners approached skid rows. The population of migrant workers that had occupied skid rows during the late nineteenth and
early twentieth centuries had been disappearing prior to the Great Depression. When national prosperity returned, the booming economy employed
large numbers of marginal workers while the burgeoning postwar welfare
state shielded many Americans from life on the streets. Skid rows became the
holding area for many city residents who were too elderly, ill, or otherwise
weak to work steadily, and others who did not meet the criteria for assistance
elsewhere. The Bowery's population shrank from an estimated 14,000 in 1949
to less than 8,000 in 1964, as Chicago's West Madison Street skid row population dropped from 30,000 in the 1930s to 21,000 in 1950, and 13,000 in 1958.
With lower population density on the nation's skid rows, these areas began to
look like potentially valuable urban real estate opportunities. There would be
little opposition to bulldozing decrepit skid-row areas, especially if those men
who called them home were widely perceived as alcoholics.[70]

CHAPTER 4

URBAN RENEWAL AND THE CHALLENGE OF HOMELESSNESS

B Y the late 1950s, America's skid rows were sparsely populated slum districts. Surveying the Bowery, the New York City Planning Commission observed "a mixture of old tenements, commercial and industrial structures and cheap hotels . . . in poor, run-down condition, with narrow, dark halls." Amid these dilapidated buildings were small clusters of homeless men. In the late 1940s, approximately 1,800 men had stayed in commercial lodging houses; a decade later barely 500 remained. Eying skid rows as valuable, underutilized real estate, enterprising urban planners launched ambitious redevelopment projects fueled by federal spending.[1]

Razing skid rows seemed at first a straightforward proposal. Who would argue against the prospect of encouraging investment in urban centers, eradicating blight, and ushering in a modern city marked by gleaming, sanitary, mixed-income developments? But destroying skid rows sparked debate, as did other postwar urban renewal projects. Increasingly, observers questioned whether or not the poor and homeless had a right to live in the city. By the 1960s, changes in the law and its enforcement meant that homelessness itself was not a crime in New York and other cities. Liberal legal decisions affirmed the rights of the homeless to exist in the nation's cities, even as their environs were being destroyed.

Acknowledging that the poorest of the poor had to live somewhere, urban officials had accepted skid rows and their residents as necessary elements of city life since the late nineteenth century. By attempting to disperse the homeless across the urban landscape, urban renewal posed the first real challenge to skid rows. The debate around such projects set the tone for the coming decades in urban policy, as many began to wonder whose interests were really served by urban planning decisions.

Clearing the Slums

By the mid-twentieth century, the Bowery's lodging houses lingered in a shabby state of disrepair. For decades, their small rooms and dense occupancies had posed fire hazards, triggering periodic calls for renewed industry regulation and more rigorous enforcement of building and fire codes. More careful maintenance of facilities and establishment of reasonable minimum hygienic standards for commercial hotels might have ensured that temporary accommodations remained available to the homeless. But instead of working to improve conditions of Bowery flophouses, 1950s urban planners and politicians hoped to see them simply disappear.[2]

The postwar federal urban renewal program funded redevelopment projects that attempted to revitalize downtown districts, which often dislocated low-income residents. Relying on public-private partnerships, it encouraged business interests to invest in and reap profits from urban projects. Ironically, the program, which would ultimately displace many poor and working-class Americans, had originated in New Deal efforts to develop low-income public housing.

Diverse voices representing a variety of political perspectives had called for an expanded role of the federal government in the nation's housing market as early as the 1920s. The first major piece of legislation that shaped the contours of postwar housing development emerged from the New Deal, when members of the Labor Housing Conference worked with Senator Robert Wagner to revise the public housing bill he had introduced in Congress in 1935. The addition of increased federal sponsorship of cooperative housing developments targeting middle-income citizens enticed the support of the American Federation of Labor, which saw an opportunity to ensure the development of decent housing for families earning union wages. The unions wanted a feasible alternative to the Federal Housing Authority's emerging agenda of providing funds to guarantee mortgages, a practice they saw benefiting lending institutions. The forces of commercial real estate—including the National Association of Real Estate Boards, U.S. League of Buildings and Loans, and National Retail Lumber Dealers Association—lobbied against the legislation. The struggle over the bill was between New Deal liberal "public housers" and their conservative foes. After being debated in three Congresses, the Wagner bill was passed in 1937 as the United States Housing Act. But compromises struck along the way erased many of the bill's most progressive features, including support of nonprofit and cooperative housing. The legislation linked construction of public housing with clearance of existing slums.[3]

New Deal-era patterns of legislative support were repeated in the debates around the Housing Act of 1949, which was endorsed by the AFL, CIO, American Association of Social Workers, YWCA, and U.S. Conference of Mayors, and opposed by rural Congressmen, the Chamber of Commerce, and the National Association of Manufacturers. Title I of the Act established the protocol for approval and implementation of federally sponsored urban renewal projects. First, the local governing body was to designate the renewal area, and authorize an application for federal planning funds. After a public hearing, the body would formally adopt the plan and submit it to the Department of Housing and Urban Development. The local public agency would next acquire the property to be cleared, whether through purchase or power of eminent domain. The tenants would be relocated, the land cleared, and the site sold to private developers. The Housing and Home Finance Administration would provide temporary loans to cover costs of land acquisition and a portion of the planning expenses. Federal capital grants would be available to absorb up to two-thirds of the loss on the project (called a "writedown"), while the other third would be financed by the local public body or government.[4]

By the 1950s, Eisenhower moderates were far more interested in urban renewal programs than public housing. Eisenhower's Advisory Committee on Government Housing Policies and Programs recommendations formed the basis of the 1954 omnibus housing bill, which revised Title I legislation and expanded the program's agenda. Title I projects could now consist solely of redevelopment, rehabilitation, or a mix of both. Significantly, the legislation also dropped the requirement that the projects be entirely residential. As much as 10 percent of the federal funding could now be devoted to areas destined for use in commerce and industry.[5]

The 1954 Housing Act, unlike its predecessors, received strong bipartisan support. New Deal liberal mayors had struggled against the interests of the business community, but their 1950s counterparts actively formed coalitions with business leaders, hoping for partnerships that would change the future of the nation's urban centers. The New Deal urban liberal coalition had fractured over the housing issue. Groups that had formerly endorsed public housing, including the Conference of Mayors and American Municipal Association, now endorsed urban renewal programs. These shifting alignments left public housing few allies; some progressives continued to support independent public housing initiatives, but moderates swung to urban renewal.[6]

The highly publicized "decline" of the nation's cities during the late 1950s and early 1960s offers a partial explanation for this shift in political alignments, as urban politicians competed against representatives of the burgeoning suburbs for limited federal funds. Overall population decreases were noted in the 1960 Census in Boston, St. Louis, Pittsburgh, Detroit, Buffalo, Minneapolis, Cleveland, Philadelphia, Chicago, Cincinnati, Baltimore, and New York City. As largely white, middle-class families moved to the suburbs in increasing numbers, low-income ethnic minorities flocked to the cities, changing both the cultural and economic makeup of urban areas. Manufacturing was leaving the city as well, taking with it both revenues and employment. During the 1950s, New York City lost one hundred thousand manufacturing jobs. Such jobs fell by 6 percent in the city between 1958 and 1963, while rising by 14 percent in the surrounding counties.[7]

Numerous pieces of federal legislation passed during the 1940s and 1950s encouraged the nation's rapid suburbanization. Ranging from Veteran's Administration loans, to returning veterans to the 1954 Internal Revenue Code subsidization of suburban strip malls, to the 1956 Interstate Highway Act, such programs underwrote a large portion of the costs of development and maintenance of suburban communities populated largely by middle-class white Americans.[8]

Within America's cities, Congress authorized $5.4 billion for urban renewal between 1949 and 1966. The program effectively demolished many of the nation's slums, replacing them with a variety of residential, commercial, and industrial developments. But, contrary to the program's popular reputation, it had never been intended to create a great deal of low-income housing. From the adoption of the 1937 legislation, the ultimate effect of pairing of public housing and slum clearance was to limit the funds available for construction of low-income public housing, and to ensure that any net increase in total number of housing units in the cities would be minimal.[9]

In this context of demographic decline, America's skid rows were shrinking in both population and geographic size during the 1950s and 1960s.

Sociologist Howard M. Bahr's influential 1967 study found that twenty-four American cities had witnessed a decreasing skid row population in recent years. Similarly, a later study of the demographic changes occurring in the skid row areas of forty-one U.S. cities found that the population of each had dropped by an average of 58 percent between 1950 and 1970. There was no clear consensus on the specific reasons driving this trend. Bahr cautioned that this decline did not necessarily indicate that fewer homeless people were residing in a given city, merely that they were no longer gathered in a single district.[10]

Urban renewal programs were a major cause of the end of America's skid-row era. Armed with federal funds for slum clearance, city planners across the nation embarked on campaigns to uproot the homeless and reassign skid row areas to commercial interests, defining central city areas as profit-generating business territories. As skid rows fell, homeless residents scattered to various new locations, changing the landscape of many cities.

Located in a potentially desirable neighborhood, Philadelphia's skid row proved an early target of urban renewal. The city's homeless population congregated near popular tourist attractions including Independence Hall and the Liberty Bell, offering an ironic juxtaposition of suffering and fabled freedoms. The Health and Welfare Council found it "inconceivable that the public will be able to stand the sight of a beautiful park with Independence Hall at one end and utter dependency at the other." In order to create a sanitized, modern area for visitors, some local business interests set out to demolish the district, while others urged caution. One business association, the Greater Philadelphia Movement Skid Row Study Committee, commissioned in 1956, issued a report two years later questioning the logic of urban renewal undertaken without sufficient attention to the needs of the area's homeless population. Such clearance, the report warned, might lead to increased panhandling, vagrancy, and crime in the downtown areas, while also leaving the homeless population at risk of death from exposure. That year, the Philadelphia Redevelopment Authority officially designated the city's skid row for clearance as part of multiple urban renewal projects. The Independence Mall area was to be leveled to make way for office and commercial buildings, while the area near the bridge would house light industry. The Independence Mall Urban Renewal Project ultimately razed the core of the skid-row area. After the neighborhood renovation, fewer local facilities for the homeless remained; in 1952 the area housed twenty-two flophouses, but only thirteen by 1963.[11]

In Minneapolis in 1945, Robert Cerny's "Civic Center plan" proposed to route a four-lane expressway through the skid-row Gateway district, while adding a veterans' center, federal courthouse, and library. His ideas inspired aspects of the Minneapolis City Planning Department's mid-1950s vision for the area, "Beautiful Entrance to a Beautiful City," which advocated clearing forty blocks of skid row and warehouse district over the next twenty years. Seventy-five percent of the old skid-row buildings were to be demolished, and a public housing facility built to accommodate the formerly homeless population. An area resident asked about his plans replied, "If they tear this building down I suppose I'll have to move. But I hope they put up a new Skid Row before they move us out. We can't live in a vacant lot."[12]

The Minneapolis Housing and Redevelopment Authority developed a rival vision with federal funding in 1955, the Lower Loop Redevelopment Plan. The city implemented the plan, which designated a smaller area for clearance, but demolished a higher percentage of the neighborhood's buildings. The plan omitted the expressway and pushed industry out of the district in favor of offices and public buildings. Northwestern National Life Insurance Company agreed to fund a portion of the development, including a $6.5 million Northwestern National Life Building, $12 million Northern States Power office building, $1.5 million Pure Food and Drug Building, $2.5 million IBM building, and $11 million Sheraton-Ritz Hotel. For the previous denizens of skid row, the Housing and Redevelopment Authority planned a housing project containing many single-occupancy rooms. But public outcry from area residents opposing the housing project blocked that aspect of the proposal. Many area homeless received $5 and relocation advice on their dislocation, others nothing at all. Some homeless individuals moved in with relatives, others entered convalescent facilities, a few found small apartments, but many simply disappeared from the official record.[13]

Chicago's urban renewal program called for the destruction of one of three downtown skid rows. The three hosted 451 residential facilities, including almost 12,000 sleeping spaces, most of them cubicles. Housed in dilapidated buildings over seventy years old, many transient hotels were classified as "unsafe, unhealthful and socially undesirable." Vacancy rates ran high; even during the winter peak occupancy period, the cubicle hotels had a vacancy rate over 20 percent. Sociologist Ronald Vander Kooi opposed relocating the current residents. Instead, he proposed the construction of modern skid-row community facilities, including churches, restaurants, lodging facilities, and employment offices. But the city ignored his vision and demolished West

Madison Street single residence occupancy (SRO) hotels with almost 3,000 beds. In other cities, too, urban renewal brought the end of skid row. Detroit's Michigan Avenue was demolished in the 1960s. In St. Louis, the Great Arch project renovated much of that city's skid-row neighborhood.[14]

Boston's longtime skid row, Scollay Square, was razed in the $185 million urban renewal project to build Government Center. Home to legendary movie theaters, tattoo parlors, burlesque houses, and bars, the area had acquired the patina of a historic district, prompting some to call for its preservation. Such gritty districts, they argued, were a vital part of the fabric of real cities, and should not be covered over in the name of progress. Officials, however, saw the district as out of step with Boston's future. They pushed for the destruction of the dirty, dangerous, old-fashioned area for symbolic reasons, as well as practical ones. Government Center embodied the forward-looking orientation of a modern, sophisticated city.[15]

Urban renewal leveled several of the nation's largest skid rows, leaving in their wake revitalized downtown business districts. In most cities, the homeless proved a relatively easy group to displace, as they lacked the formal organization and financial resources necessary to mount a substantial protest. The plans put forth in Minneapolis and Chicago to build lodging facilities for use by the homeless were rejected because city officials and their constituents feared recreating skid-row conditions. The Minneapolis plan did not include the seedy bars and religious missions of skid row; planners hoped to create a new, modern housing project that would allow the homeless to maintain their sense of community. This concept was anathema to the trends in urban planning, however, as well as the desires of the public. Throughout the twentieth century, urban residents by and large did not want homeless people living in their neighborhoods, nor did they wish to fund residential programs designed to offer continued housing assistance. The homeless were to be returned to "normal" life rather than being placed in supported living situations.

By the late 1980s, more low-income housing units were being destroyed than being built. In Chicago, between 1973 and the mid-1980s, 18,000 SRO units were destroyed or redeveloped into market rate condominiums. The lack of new homeless facilities and foresight on the part of city planners and community groups led to the migration of homeless individuals to the streets of many urban neighborhoods in the coming decades. By blocking the construction of residential facilities, city residents effectively paved the way for later homeless street dwellers.[16]

Urban Renewal and the Changing Nature of
Homelessness in New York

Postwar liberalism fueled the strength of the urban renewal program. New York City, a bastion of urban liberalism, embraced it in pursuit of a metropolis characterized by efficiency and an array of mixed-use arenas that would bring the city's various socioeconomic classes together in planned settings. Through business interests cooperating with the public sector, the modern city would be rebuilt. This heavy-handed, interventionist approach to urban planning reflected a deep desire to reshape the city quickly, with little consideration for community dialogue and consensus building. New York's urban renewal projects were dramatically shaped by the influence of Robert Moses, who embraced liberal values of social uplift through government intervention. Moses hoped the working classes would benefit from many of the broader changes he would make, but saw no place for the skid-row homeless in his sanitized version of the city and attempted to erase them from the urban landscape.[17]

Unlike the situation in other cities, Robert Moses exerted a great deal of single-handed control over the urban renewal process in New York. A public servant since the 1910s, Moses had come to power in 1924 when governor Alfred Smith appointed him president of the Long Island State Park Commission, a springboard to the chairmanship of the State Council of Parks. Mayor LaGuardia appointed him New York City Parks Commissioner in 1934, a post he held until 1960. He led the Triborough Bridge and New York City Tunnel Authority from 1946 to 1968. By age seventy, Moses was also city construction coordinator, City Planning Commission member, chairman of the Mayor's Committee on Slum Clearance, and Youth Board member, among other titles. At the state level, he chaired the Power Authority.[18]

Moses used his positions to alter the landscape of New York City and its environs dramatically. Between 1924 and 1968, he directed $27 billion in public works projects. From his 1920s creation of the nation's most extensive system of state parks, through his staging of the 1964 World's Fair in Flushing Meadows, Moses participated in every major New York development project. He was responsible for building fourteen city expressways, including the Bronx-Queens, Van Wyck, and Major Deegan, seven bridges, including the Triborough, Verrazano, and Bronx-Whitestone, and major urban centers, including Shea Stadium, United Nations Headquarters, and Lincoln Center for the Performing Arts.[19]

As chairman of the Slum Clearance Committee, Moses directed the city's

Title I urban renewal projects. Mayor O'Dwyer had established the Committee in December 1948, in anticipation of the passage of the 1949 Housing Act. The Board of Estimate approved his initial report in early 1950, giving him the green light to proceed with Title I slum clearance. Due in part to Moses's power in the city's political structure, he enjoyed a greater amount of freedom in planning and executing the city's urban renewal program than did his counterparts in other cities. The committee worked out of his Randall's Island Triborough Bridge and Tunnel Authority office, supported by his own staff. This particular system increased Moses control over the information released both to other city agencies and to the public.[20]

In other cities, the redevelopment agency chose the sites to be cleared, drew up the plans, and took responsibility for relocating current tenants. The agency would then demolish the existing buildings, selling only the cleared land to the developer. In New York, Moses invited pre-selected developers to bid on the property, rather than holding a public auction. The city was also distinctive in selling the land to the developer with tenants still in residence, leaving it to the sponsor to relocate them and clear the land. This practice effectively rendered the developers city-sanctioned slumlords, who collected rents from residents until the land was cleared.[21]

Moses defended these "preliminary negotiations" with potential project sponsors, arguing that the large-scale risks involved in Title I work would otherwise prevent the city from attracting viable private investors. Following the protocols enacted in other cities would have slowed the urban renewal process; instead, New York City's Title I program led the nation. By the end of September 1959, New York had received over $50 million in federal Title I funds, 22.3 percent of the amount disbursed nationwide. The twenty-four slum clearance projects then completed and in planning would have cleared 314 acres of land, using $174 million in federal and local government subsidies and $739 million in private investments. While taxes on the properties had previously been worth only $4.3 million, after development they would have totaled almost $14 million. When the list is broadened to include "future" and "deferred" projects, New York City would have cleared 900 acres of land, utilizing a total of $1.5 billion in private, federal, state, and city funds.[22]

The urban renewal projects undertaken in New York displaced thousands of residents. Planners understood the dislocation of residents as part of the cost of completing massive projects, such as Manhattan's Lincoln Center. Although guided by liberal principles, the urban renewal efforts of the 1950s ultimately furthered the city's ethnic and socioeconomic segregation by pushing low income, often minority residents to the less desirable areas of Manhattan and the outer boroughs. Cynical observers referred to urban renewal projects as "Negro removal" or "Puerto Rican removal" projects. Moses disregarded such accusations of bias shaped by class and race, focusing on creating mixed-income neighborhoods by situating middle-income apartment buildings near public housing for low-income families. Mixing the lower and middle classes marked the extent of Moses's vision. As the first step in securing Title I funds, the City Planning Commission had substantially revised the city Master Plan in 1954, designating several areas of Manhattan as "Sections Containing Areas Suitable for Development and Redevelopment"; the east side of the Bowery was included for clearance.[23]

In an effort to jumpstart a project at Cooper Square, Moses tried unsuccessfully to engage the interest of George Meany, president of the American Federation of Labor. He then turned to Abraham Kazan of the United Housing Foundation (UHF), a pioneer who had promoted cooperative housing for the city's middle and working classes as early as World War I. Kazan longed to see the labor movement play a more active role in the city housing market. His Amalgamated Clothing Workers Corporation had operated two major coops, the 1928 six-building Amalgamated Houses in the Bronx and the 1930 Amalgamated Dwellings, a six-story building on Grand Street with eight elevators and a central court housing over 200 apartments. The Lower East Side building quickly earned a reputation in the neighborhood; local children, accustomed to tenement life, enjoyed after-school joyrides in the building's elevators. Through their productive partnership, Moses and Kazan significantly increased the city's supply of middle-income housing.[24]

The Cooper Square project developed by Moses and Kazan would have eliminated nearly 4,000 beds used by the city's homeless. They planned to demolish the entire east side of twelve Bowery blocks, from Ninth to Delancey Streets. The project would raze the Kenton and Liberty Hotels above Houston Street, as well as several below Houston, including the Sunshine Hotel, built in 1922, 200-bed Alabama House, 200-bed Andrews Hotel, and Houston Hotel.[25]

Cooper Square would have been one of the city's most ambitious urban renewal projects, second only to Lincoln Square in both gross project cost and planned area. As was the case at Lincoln Square, the project would have resulted in a net loss of housing stock; Cooper Square would have created almost 500 fewer apartments than the site contained previously. In addition to the homeless, the project would displace a large population of low-income tenants. The area was popular with service industry workers whose earnings, below Manhattan median wages, drew them to the area's relatively inexpensive rents. Surveys found the area home to many long-term residents, as well as many who wished to remain if possible.[26]

The 4,000 beds for use by the homeless destroyed by the project were not to be replaced. Moses denied the Salvation Army request to continue operating its Bowery Corps as a community center, arguing that such an organization would be out of place in the new development. The new Bowery would be a modern, clean testament to the success of urban liberalism. It would highlight the achievements of cooperative investments, the powerful expanded scope of the federal and municipal governments, and the ability of visionary planning to create successful urban environments. The homeless denizens of skid row played no role in this modern vision and symbolized the old urban order of tenements, slums, and SRO hotels. Moses did not set out to house the Bowery's populations in better conditions. Instead, he planned to replace an undesirable population with a different, more desirable one.[27]

In place of the homeless facilities, Moses and Kazan planned to erect the Robert Owen Cooperative Houses. United Housing Foundation architect Herman Jessor designed five cross-shaped apartment buildings that would house a total of over 1,700 units, amid small parks, a market, and a garage. At the northern end of the site near Astor Place, he planned an expanded campus for Cooper Union and a facility for the Lexington School for deaf children.[28]

The Bowery seemed ripe for clearance. Area buildings were less sound than those in Manhattan overall or the outer boroughs. Yet, the area demonstrated potential for growth and vitality. It was near transit facilities and the ample working-class labor supply of the Lower East Side, rendering it potentially useful for light industry as well as residential buildings. By 1956, the Planning Commission recommended Moses apply for advance planning funds for the area.[29]

By late 1958, the city's plans for Cooper Square touched off a storm of controversy, some of it caused by the potential problems of displacing the Bowery's homeless population. Proprietors of local businesses catering to the area's homeless population expressed understandable distress at the revelation that the homeless would be absent from the "renewed" neighborhood. Frank Gatto, a Bowery hotel operator, cautioned, "If they can't flop here, they'll flop at City Hall. Wait and see. . . . Just wait and see. They say that during the winter there are more than 10,000 homeless men on the Bowery. Where will they go? Will they start invading other parts of the city?" Major Olive McKeown, head of the Salvation Army's Bowery Corps, wrote to Colonel Albert Pepper, "The statement in the Relocation Report that these men will 'probably disappear' is ridiculous! These unfortunates will have to relocate and The Salvation Army will have to relocate with them." Army staff contemplated the loss of their recently opened Alcohol Rehabilitation Center, as both commercial and charitable agencies faced expulsion from the area. Owners of other businesses also objected to the city's plans. Harry Kirwan, proprietor of McSorley's Old Ale House, the city's oldest saloon, referred to the Marble Cemetery when he quipped, "So they're going to keep the cemetery and it has a wall around it. Maybe that's what I'll do. I'll build a wall around McSorley's and we'll keep it right here and just continue serving ale in the face of progress."[30]

By proposing to destroy 4,000 beds and offering no feasible alternative accommodations for the homeless, Moses was attempting to rid the city of most of its skid row. His plan implied that buildings somehow created their occupants, as if including enough modern architecture in the downtown district could eliminate dire poverty. Pragmatically, the assumption was that the homeless would leave the city and migrate to the outer boroughs or other cities altogether if it did not offer reasonably priced accommodations.

The Cooper Square project ultimately failed, due in part to the efforts of savvy protestors who had studied carefully the tactics used in other cities and across town. By the late 1950s, organized protest groups across the country were effectively calling attention to the problematic nature of many projects. Tenants in the path of urban renewal projects in Philadelphia and Boston began to protest by 1957, and similar movements arose in other cities over the next six years. The reasons for the protests varied due to the program's intense localism. In Cincinnati, for instance, white residents opposed the building of a low-income housing project for African Americans dislocated by urban renewal. Other protestors wanted to protect public areas from privatization.[31]

In New York Jane Jacobs co-chaired the Committee to Save the West Village, which launched a 1961 campaign to block the city's urban renewal plans for their neighborhood. Arguing that the City Planning Commission had not held a community hearing on the proposed project, Jacobs and her colleagues rejected the compromise offered by Mayor Wagner's office and pressured the administration until Wagner stopped supporting the plan. This was the most high-profile victory against an urban renewal project. The radical nature of the movement stemmed from its core position that the neighborhood was indeed old but not "blighted."[32]

On the Bowery, conflicting visions for the neighborhood's future soon emerged. The liberal proponents of the planned union-sponsored housing cooperatives emphatically touted their plan's benefits for the city's expanding middle class. Other interest groups, including social service providers, artists, and ethnic minorities, found representation through efforts of area activists. Following the release of the controversial Relocation Report, Thelma Burdick, Esther Rand and Frances Goldin joined others to form the Cooper Square Committee, representing area business owners and tenants opposing the city's renewal plan. Rallying the community, Burdick distributed flyers reading, "We need low cost housing and low middle income housing, with no down payment, in our neighborhood for ourselves." After holding a series of community meetings, the group's representatives spoke on behalf of site tenants embittered by "the inference that they are not fit to live with because they are poor, that they must get out of their community because middle-income housing is so important to the future of the City of New York, that they are expendable pawns in the housing experiments of the intelligentsia."[33]

Some business owners joined the protests against urban renewal. Operators of skid-row facilities and related enterprises argued that the renewal project would put them out of work. In the bigger picture, though, large corporate interests sided with the forces of renewal. Moses had worked closely with investors like Metropolitan Life to overcome the earlier squeamishness of groups—including the U.S. Chamber of Commerce, National Association of Real Estate Boards, and U.S. League of Building and Loans—that had opposed any public housing projects as early as the 1930s. Rather than reflecting any unified coalition of "business interests," large and small enterprises represented a range of motivations and positions.[34]

The Cooper Square Committee (CSC) went beyond protesting the city plan by commissioning city planner Walter Thabit to design a complete rival plan for the area. In its Alternate Plan for Cooper Square, the CSC scaled down the clearance plans. While the city had slated twelve blocks for clearance, the CSC called for only six to be cleared and three others "reconditioned." In contrast to the bulldozer strategies planned by the Slum Clearance Committee (SCC), the CSC proposed a program of gradual renewal to take place in carefully planned phases. It also called for the inclusion of accommodations for displaced tenants among a mix of low-rent, moderate rental, and middle-income housing.[35]

The CSC furiously objected to the city's callous disregard for both the area's Puerto Rican and homeless populations. As Thabit later recalled, "Because they made light of it, we made much of it." The group accused the city of minimizing the Puerto Rican presence to shield its plan from criticism, as it had done in the course of previous urban renewal projects. The CSC research documented a substantially larger Puerto Rican population than that report-ed by the city. The group hoped that tabulating and publicizing the size of the area's ethnic minority population would mobilize opposition to the plan.[36]

Burdick also expressed alarm at the lack of a relocation program for the area's homeless population in the city's plan. Rather than "disappearing," the homeless would "simply move out to down-grade the surrounding area un-less adequate provision is made for them." Like Moses, the group envisioned an ultimate end to the neighborhood's function as a skid row. Thabit's plan described the Bowery homeless as "a constant depressant in the area" who had "worn out whatever small welcome they once possessed."[37]

The CSC plan for the Bowery nonetheless proved more sensitive to the needs of the homeless than Moses's brusque clearance program. It proposed deferring clearance of the area from Stanton to Delancey Streets until provi-sions could be made for the homeless men occupying that area's 2,000 beds. The CSC also lobbied to keep the Salvation Army's Alcoholic Rehabilitation Center in its current location, but wanted the Welfare Department's muni replaced by a reception center and cafeteria south of Delancey Street. The group suggested expanding the facilities at Camp LaGuardia to accommo-date an additional 500 homeless men and proposed relocating another 500 to furnished rooms elsewhere in the city. The CSC also described a daily work program that might provide employment opportunities for approximately one thousand Bowery men. Instead of simply demolishing the buildings used by the homeless, the city should focus on developing programs for rehousing and rehabilitating the Bowery population, with the ultimate goal of reduc-ing the demand for flophouses and other skid-row establishments. Offering advice not merely on structural clearance and construction but also on social services, the CSC proposed a gradual, humane, and therapeutic approach to ending the city's need for a skid row.[38]

As criticism of the Cooper Square project mounted, the city's broader slum clearance program gradually ground to a halt. Feuds between Moses and federal officials had caused significant project delays as early as 1957, leaving him requesting land acquisition funds for Cooper Square from the City Planning Commission in 1959, far behind his original timeline. In May that year, the UHF accepted applications and deposits for apartments in the proposed Robert Owen Houses, Inc. By October, the critics of Moses's pro-

gram grew increasingly vocal; the Metropolitan Council on Housing distributed 100,000 leaflets that cried, "For New York to grow, Moses must go." City
officials urged the mayor to restructure the SCC, reducing or eliminating Moses's role, as calls for an investigation of the city's Title I practice led to the for-
mation of a House subcommittee to probe the program on the national level,
with special emphasis on the city. Even the *New York Times*, long supportive
of Moses's work, launched attacks. The New York method of urban renewal
haunted Moses and tainted the program's reputation. These articles described
site sponsors collecting years of rent monies from tenants without beginning construction, then reselling the land, leaving the city to pay the back
taxes. Moses bitterly insisted such attacks would render prospective sponsors
unwilling to invest in upcoming projects. Other than those projects already
in planning and those sponsored by the labor unions, Moses predicted the
program's demise: "From now on . . . no full tax-paying speculative sponsors will be found and to that extent Title I is a dead duck." Moses's decline
heralded the end of the UHF large-scale clearance and construction projects.
The International Ladies Garment Workers Union 1963 Penn Station South
project proved the final large cooperative building opened by the organization in the central city; its remaining developments in the outer boroughs
involved far less intensive clearance programs.[39]

On the Bowery, Moses's departure meant a reprieve for the lodging
houses and other establishments patronized by the homeless. The Cooper
Square project was put on hold, leaving the area largely untouched for years
as bureaucratic processes were developed to take the place of the centralized
power Moses had wielded. Successor city planners considered renewal of the
Bowery, but to far less dramatic ends. Wagner appointee J. Anthony Panuch
urged the creation of a Housing and Redevelopment Board (HRB) that would
function as a proper city department. By May 1960, the HRB had dropped the
Cooper Square project.[40]

In 1962, the City Planning Commission's Community Renewal Program
evaluated Cooper Square, identifying rehabilitation potential in many of the
area's buildings. The city's new plan resembled the one initially advanced by
the CSC, but enlarged the project's boundaries. The city now avoided the Moses approach of simply ignoring the homeless population in hopes it might
disappear. Instead, officials agreed to leave the major facilities including the
muni, the Bowery Mission, and the Salvation Army's Memorial Hotel intact
until other arrangements could be made for their clients. The city hoped to
avoid sudden dispersal of the homeless, preferring to facilitate a gradual tran-

sition of the population away from skid row. As the project remained stalled, the CSC continued to lobby for the execution of its original plan throughout the decade, gradually winning supporters. A compromise plan developed in 1969 called for spot clearance on a smaller site. Tenant activists hailed the plan's 1970 approval by the Board of Estimate as a landmark victory for grass-roots community planning. An independent group had not only blocked an urban renewal project, but also successfully persuaded the city to adopt its alternative plan. But the fiscal crisis facing the city in the 1970s left even this less ambitious plan stalled, and none of the Cooper Square plans was executed.[41]

As he lost power, Moses continued to defend the liberal principles that had sparked the federal slum clearance program and ridiculed those tenant activists and other protest groups arguing for less radical destruction of neighborhoods:

> The greatest obstacle today is opposition to moving people, even those in the worst rookeries and rabbit warrens. . . . The social workers, local politicians, yellow journalists with their lurid exaggerations of occasional hardship cases for years screamed for slum clearance. Now they demand that it be slowed up until every last resident has been moved to a better place to his complete liking.[42]

The spot rehabilitation favored by many community groups, too, struck him as a "phoney compromise" committed only to "patching up a few buildings here and there." Blindly devoted to his vision of middle-income housing as the core of Manhattan real estate, Moses stubbornly defended the principles of slum clearance followed by construction of large-scale coops. He continued to demonstrate little compassion for low-income residents who stood in the path of his projects, and none for the homeless.[43]

Critics have characterized the era's urban renewal programs as fundamentally misguided. In her influential 1961 critique of city planning and urban renewal, *The Death and Life of Great American Cities*, Jane Jacobs called the nation's Title I projects "not the rebuilding of cities" but "the sacking of cities." She argued that slum clearance projects avoided solving the core problems of the urban environment, focusing instead on altering the physical manifestations of those problems. Jacobs described such programs as "the dishonest mask of pretended order." Rather than fighting to bring the middle classes back to the cities, she advocated placing emphasis on nurturing and develop-

ing the lower-income communities to ensure that their residents would become members of the middle class. Jacobs's concerns were echoed by sociologist Herbert J. Gans and others who argued that the urban renewal program
of the 1950s and 1960s had been doomed from its inception by attempting to
rid the cities of slums, rather than provide the poor with decent housing.[44]

Jacobs cautioned against making sweeping generalizations about the effects of the homeless on an urban area. She characterized the homeless as
neither inherently dangerous nor peaceful, observing that some responsible
and respectful homeless individuals flocked to one area, while others prone
to drunken public sleeping congregated in another. She called for sensitivity
to the unique features of a neighborhood when making planning decisions,
noting that no single design would function in the same way if transported to
a different area. She reminded readers that even parks, often hailed as vital to
a neighborhood's property values, might attract different visitors, or none at
all, depending on the specific location.[45]

People's impressions of urban neighborhoods often fused their physical
terrain with the habits of their residents. Such analyses conflating space and
character typified, for instance, late nineteenth-century housing reformers'
criticism of not only the physical conditions of the city's "slums," but also
their residents' behavior. Similarly, the discourse surrounding mid-twentieth-
century public housing projects frequently collapsed perceived moral failings,
including high crime rates, into discussions of architecture and neighborhood planning without examining those connections. Observers of skid row
often embraced similar logic when confronting dilapidated physical structures housing extremely impoverished individuals who displayed behavior
prohibited in other neighborhoods. The prevalence of outdoor sleeping and
public intoxication, in particular, distinguished skid row from more genteel
and even working-class neighborhoods. Rather than addressing the concerns
of the city's impoverished citizens, urban renewal advocates hoped to replace
them with less problematic, higher income individuals and profitable businesses. Jacobs and other critics envisioned alternatives to the extremes of
both suburban living and slum clearance, detailing examples of sustainable,
mixed-use zones at the heart of cities. Such noble endeavors often proved in-
credibly complex and nearly impossible to execute in the treacherous terrain
of urban politics.[46]

Like Jacobs's prototypical urban neighborhood, New York's skid row had
evolved in response to the needs of the homeless, welfare administrators, law
enforcement, local business interests, and social service providers. By mid-

century, the interests of those groups were largely overlooked by city officials intent on maximizing the profitability of the urban center. The plans for Cooper Square advanced by Moses and the CSC offered opposing visions of the neighborhood, yet both sought ultimately to rid the city of its historic skid row.

As urban planners and theorists battled over the physical space of skid row, lawyers, advocates, and law enforcement officials redefined the areas and facilities to which the homeless would be allowed access, as well as the behavior that would be permitted. The shifting legal climate of the 1960s brought traditional policing practices and the criminality of homelessness under increased scrutiny. While urban planners might not have wanted the homeless in the city, the justice system ultimately ruled that they had a legal right to exist there.

Decriminalizing Homelessness

In the early 1960s, the legal community reconsidered several of the laws traditionally used to regulate the behavior of the homeless. In a 1962 *Atlantic Monthly* article, chief justice of the Court of Special Sessions John Murtagh, involved in establishing both the Hart Island program and the Homeless Men's Court in the late 1940s and early 1950s, called for reform of the legal system's treatment of the homeless. He praised New York's policy of arresting homeless men not for public intoxication, a practice he characterized as "inhumane" and even "unchristian," but for disorderly conduct. Still, he argued, penal solutions in general would remain ineffective toward problems fundamentally "social, medical, and spiritual in nature." Murtagh located the root of urban homelessness not solely in economic inequality, but in a society guilty of producing too many "misfits," and "inadequate human beings." Citing the "hostile public" as the impetus for continued unfair policing and social policies toward the homeless, he urged officials to "stop dignifying its thirst for vengeance and instinct for hate."[47]

The vagrancy and public intoxication ordinances Murtagh criticized had deep roots in American legal history. Modeled on medieval English precedents, the nation's vagrancy laws dated to colonial statutes. In the modern era, they rested largely on the 1837 *City of New York v. Miln* decision, in which the Supreme Court endorsed banishment of vagrants from the city to protect other residents. Employing the metaphor of "an infectious disease," Justice Barbour argued that such "precautionary measures" were justifiable, in order to prevent the spread of "the moral pestilence of paupers, vagabonds, and possibly convicts." The Depression prompted renewed debate on the topic, when popular destination states like California proposed "Okie laws" to prevent the entry of vagrants. In 1941, President Roosevelt vetoed a bill that would have classified "any person leading an idle life . . . and not giving a good account of himself" as a vagrant, on the grounds that it afforded the police inappropriate discretion. Still, by the late 1940s, the courts maintained that the status of vagrancy remained sufficient grounds for prosecution. In *District of Columbia v. Hunt*, for example, the court held that "A vagrant is a probable criminal; and the purpose of the statute is to prevent crimes which may likely flow from his mode of life." By 1958, police executed almost ninety thousand vagrancy arrests annually, most often punishing an individual for his economic status, with no requisite pretext of the commission of an otherwise criminal act. Homeless men echoed Roosevelt's sentiments concerning the uneven and unfair enforcement of vagrancy laws. In the 1960s, some homeless individuals complained of being profiled for arrest based on their physical appearance. One man observed, "If you dress well, they won't pick you up unless you are falling-down drunk on the sidewalk. If you dress poorly and look beat, you don't even have to be drinking to get picked up." Or in the words of another, "I ain't never been arrested by the police, I'm proud to say. That's because I kept myself clean-looking all the way down to the gutter."[48]

After World War II, legal scholars increasingly criticized vagrancy statutes. Caleb Foote's work on Philadelphia argued that such laws provided the police with the means to prosecute individuals on the basis of mere suspicion. By the late 1960s, a series of state and federal decisions began to erode the strength of such laws. In *Fenster v. Leary*, New York's Court of Appeals noted that such statutes furthered isolation of the homeless by prosecuting those guilty primarily of "leaving the environs of skid row and disturbing by their presence the sensibilities of residents of the nicer parts of the community." In the 1970s, the Supreme Court struck down vagrancy laws, finding them in violation of the Fourteenth Amendment. The decision effectively decriminalized homelessness by making the state of being without financial resources insufficient grounds for arrest. The homeless attained, on one legal front, the right to exist.[49]

The 1960s witnessed a similar shift in the legal consequences of public intoxication. Research completed for President Lyndon Johnson's Commission on Law Enforcement and Administration of Justice found that public intoxication arrests wasted valuable financial resources. While regional variations meant that some cities issued far lighter sentences than others, the overall trend was one of repeat offenders draining vast amounts of law enforcement agency, court, and correctional facility resources. A 1957 study found that six chronic offenders of the Washington, D.C., drunkenness laws had spent between them a total of 125 years incarcerated, on the basis of over 1,400 arrests. The lack of legal counsel for skid-row defendants, coupled with the rushed nature of their court appearances, struck the commission as a shamefully unfair combination. Although disorderly behavior should be prosecuted, the committee concluded that public drunkenness should be decriminalized. The commission called for the development of a more humane approach to the problems of the skid-row alcoholic, in the form of "civil detoxification centers."[50]

Johnson's commission echoed the shifting position of the courts on public drunkenness. In *Robinson v. California*, the Supreme Court ruled drug addiction an illness rather than a crime, due to the Eighth Amendment's prohibition of "cruel and unusual punishment." The decision provided the groundwork for the *Driver v. Hinnant* ruling, which classified a habitual and chronic drinker a diseased person not liable for public drunkenness. Similarly, in *Easter v. District of Columbia*, the courts held that the disease theory of alcoholism provided a valid defense to charges of public intoxication.[51]

Two years later, the case of *Powell v. Texas* challenged many accepted views of alcoholism. Powell, a resident of Austin, had been arrested dozens of times for public drunkenness, and argued the arrests were a violation of his constitutional rights. The Supreme Court did not agree, but was divided five to four over the issue. The Court struggled to determine how far to extend the definition of cruel and unusual punishment, especially if alcoholism was truly a disease. The 1971 Uniform Alcoholism and Intoxication Treatment Act moved toward widespread decriminalization of public intoxication and emphasis on medical treatment.[52]

In New York City, lawyers helped to usher in a new era of law for the homeless, as the Legal Aid Society began providing legal representation to homeless individuals facing routine charges. Due to their intervention, as well as the changing climate of judicial opinion, subsequent conviction rates for such offenses fell from 98 to 2 percent. Homeless individuals were now far less likely to be arrested and jailed for minor infractions.[53]

The judicial decisions at the heart of this trend reflected the nation's broader legal developments, as the liberal courts extended access to education, welfare, and legal representation to historically economically and politically underprivileged groups. At the state level in the 1950s and the national level in the 1960s, through the leadership of U.S. Supreme Court chief justice

Earl Warren, the courts afforded opportunities to those previously excluded on the basis of "race," ethnicity, and class. In so doing, the courts also enacted significant controls on police procedure, including institution of "Miranda" warnings after *Miranda v. Arizona* and provision of legal counsel to indigents after *Gideon v. Wainwright*. The liberalization of legal attitudes toward the homeless formed one lesser-known aspect of this legal trend: vagrancy and public intoxication ordinances, in particular, were seen as unjust persecution of the poor and sick.[54]

Such rulings also called into question traditional national policies on homelessness, examining the many assumptions that had previously been made at their core. The nineteenth-century official stance—positing crime as a likely result of allowing vagrants entry to a community—no longer resonated with popular and judicial opinions seeking to lessen discrimination. On another level, decriminalizing vagrancy acknowledged an impoverished citizen's right to remain in his town of residence, even if it did not mandate the extent of the services the community should provide.

Similarly, the new legal approach to drunkenness laws reflected more than a simple attempt to curtail wasted efforts and funds. The previous system of repeatedly arresting chronic offenders, fueled by the logic that the homeless would either change their behavior or leave the area, proved unfounded. By remaining in place, many homeless convinced officials that due either to illness or personal choice they would not respond to such treatment. The search for innovative detoxification programs began after such traditional approaches proved ineffective.

The liberal courts of the postwar era expanded individual rights in a range of realms, employing the power of the bench to bring about not only legal but also social change. Homeless individuals would now enjoy greater rights to legal representation and even simple existence within the nation's cities. Their citizenship had been fundamentally affirmed by the expansionist vision of the courts. Homeless people would avoid repetitive arrest and police harassment under the new laws. Beginning with the decriminalization of vagrancy and the relaxation of the public drunkenness laws, homeless Americans began to approach legal equality. In New York, the homeless would gain a legal "right to shelter" by the 1980s, necessitating the development of new homeless policies and programs.

Robert Moses's plan to raze the Bowery had centered on the hope that destroying the neighborhood inhabited by the homeless would rid the city of their presence, while rejuvenating a dilapidated area for commercial gain.

Conflating the homeless with their environs, urban renewal advocates considered both the city's most impoverished residents and their dwellings components of urban "blight." Their plan would, indeed, have placed an orderly, middle-class mask atop one of the most visible faces of the city's poverty, as it had in many of the nation's other cities. But the poor and homeless would not have disappeared. Ultimately, Moses's large-scale slum clearance program sputtered to a halt, leaving the Bowery intact and granting its residents a temporary reprieve from relocation.

As skid row staved off attack, New York City's homeless gained implicit permission to remain on skid row. As laws governing the public behavior of the homeless, which had long been used to control their location and activities, drew increasing criticism, the homeless gained explicit permission to occupy space in the city. Legal scholars, practicing attorneys, and judges argued that such statutes essentially criminalized the existence of the indigent poor, framing poverty itself as a crime. The liberal legal community was leading the way to new policies toward homelessness that would offer individuals some official protection from harassment.

Postwar urban liberals embraced the goal of modernizing the nation's cities, which would be clean, safe, profitable, desirable places to live and work. They disagreed over the strategies needed to achieve these goals, perhaps nowhere more dramatically than in the debates over urban poverty. As urban renewal advocates strove to demolish skid rows and other slum districts, they argued among themselves over the role public and subsidized housing should play in accommodating the urban poor. Simultaneous developments in the legal realm were redefining the rights of many minority populations, including the poor. The legal face of liberalism would ultimately affirm the rights of the homeless to occupy urban spaces. In New York, these changes would affect the lives of the homeless more directly than the struggles over urban renewal.

The era's wrangling over spatial politics and legal procedures thus left the Bowery population in place, even as other cities flattened their skid rows. New York City's efforts to rid itself of the symptoms of homelessness through urban planning had stalled. In response, city officials pursued a third, related strategy. In the 1960s, they directed the tools of social science toward the Bowery, as did analysts in other cities, in hopes of better understanding and perhaps reversing the causes of homelessness.

CHAPTER 5

OPERATION BOWERY
AND SOCIAL SCIENTIFIC INQUIRY

THE interviewer seated in the lobby of the Bowery's Uncle Sam Hotel with a homeless man who was lodging there, proceeded to ask a series of questions. "Subject six," he learned, had been born in Elmer, New Jersey, in 1898 to a glassblower and a stay-at-home mother. His family included a stepbrother and a sister. When he was six, the family moved to Virginia, then to New Jersey, then back to Virginia when he was thirteen. He left school at fourteen to go to work, having achieved a third-grade education. At that time, he held no ambitions or plan for his life. By eighteen he had joined the navy. He worked as a merchant seaman, off and on, from thirty to sixty-three.

Never married, he had no present contact with his family, or any close friends in the city. He was amenable to knowing Bowery men, but knew none by name. He had spoken to four or five people the day before the interview. He was not a registered member of a political party and had never voted in an election. Raised Methodist, he had not been to church in several years. He was in fair health, despite an injury to his left knee. He received $174 per month from a veteran's pension and Social Security. He avoided the muni and the missions, read the paper daily, and left the Bowery regularly. Each day he watched approximately two hours of television. He classified himself as a light drinker who drank beer, alone, less than a few times per week.[1]

Why was subject six homeless? Was the answer somewhere in his family background? In what ways was he different from other men who shared his background but did not become homeless? These were the questions teams of social scientists posed during the 1960s, as they ventured into the flophouses and facilities of skid rows to study the homeless. Urban liberals hoping to end the problem of homelessness funded these initiatives to learn the truth about the poorest of the poor. Convinced that the causes of homelessness were to be found in the lives of individuals, they searched for patterns that might explain their curious plight.

In 1970, sociologist and expert on homelessness Theodore Caplow observed,

> Whatever else he may be, the skid row man is not his brother's
> keeper. Nor his brother's opinion-leader, norm-enforcer, or
> action-initiator. That is to say, he is about as different from *Homo
> sociologus* as it is possible to be while still remaining human.
> Therein lies skid row's fascination for the sociologist. For the
> price of a subway ride, he can enter a country where the accepted
> principles of social interaction do not seem to apply.

Sociologists turned to skid row looking for information not only about homelessness, but also about the nature of human relationships and their influence on individual development.[2]

The City Looks at Homelessness

In the weeks leading up to the 1961 mayoral election, local political conflicts predictably intensified. Mayor Robert Wagner had broken from Tammany Hall and the powerful political boss Carmine De Sapio earlier that year. De Sapio, long the leader of Manhattan's Democratic political machine, was facing a backlash against his heavy-handed efforts to control city elections. Wagner now publicly criticized De Sapio's tactics as anachronistic, hoping to deflect the challenge posed by the Republican mayoral candidate, attorney general Louis J. Lefkowitz, with the support of reformers including Eleanor Roosevelt. Homelessness came to the fore when twenty-five New Yorkers gathered days before the election to demonstrate at the 59th Street entrance to Central Park. Wearing sandwich boards reading "Our children must be safe," "Parks are for children, not hobos," and "Lefkowitz will make New York safe," representatives of the United Citizens' Committee protested the presence of the homeless in the city's largest park. Men numbered among the protesters, but the coverage of the event in the next day's *New York World-Telegram and Sun* focused on the role of women. A photograph featuring the female protestors posing with the park's famous carriage horses evoked the sanctity of home, family, and middle-class respectability, contrasting starkly with that of the "sodden bum" sleeping on a park bench featured below.[3]

The "demonstration," an orchestrated publicity event, responded to Wagner's announcement of the launch of Operation Bowery earlier that week. The initiative furthered two distinct yet related goals. First, the twelve thousand homeless men who inhabited the streets, hotels, and missions of the Bowery would somehow be returned to the workforce and to other, more humane living conditions. Second, with the homeless out of the way, the city's plans for urban redevelopment could be advanced, and the neighborhood rendered cleaner and more profitable. Wagner connected these goals in his remarks: "As we chip away at the concentration of the men who make up Skid Row, we will be lifting the pall that covers the center of the area and obstructs its improvement and rehabilitation." In a departure from the dominant model of urban renewal in the Moses era, Wagner emphasized not the area's architectural redevelopment plans, but the fates of its current residents.[4]

The *World-Telegram* staff quickly labeled Operation Bowery insincere, calling it a "vote-swaying, bum-saving" effort. If Wagner were truly concerned about the plight of the homeless, they asked, why had he ended the innovative Hart Island program in 1954? The Republican paper quoted a Lefkowitz supporter who branded Operation Bowery "an election stunt," arguing that Wagner merely pretended "to become the champion of the homeless and destitute of the Bowery." Lefkowitz, meanwhile, pledged, when elected, to "drive the panhandlers, punks and hoodlums off our streets—so that once again our people can walk streets and parks in safety."[5]

The *World Telegram* went on to publish "A Touch of Terror," a sensational six-part series of articles on homelessness. Featured prominently on the front page of the paper each day of the week leading up to the election, the articles portrayed a city overrun by aggressive homeless men, its citizens held hostage by their frightening advances. The first article, "New Wave of Derelicts Poses Menace in Parks and Streets," cited mission workers' estimates of the city's homeless population at 40,000, nearly triple previous figures. It described a "wave" of young, "alcoholic drifters" who were "hostile," "menacing," "violent," and no longer content to remain on the Bowery, instead "infesting" almost all of Manhattan's neighborhoods, including upscale Park Avenue, Sutton Place, and Gramercy Park. Employing the sensational, urban documentary photography popular since the late nineteenth-century work of Jacob Riis, the paper captured flash-blinded homeless men camped out in a subway station. The accompanying caption assured readers that such men slept in the subway less out of dire need than "to save the price of tomorrow's muscatel." Later articles in the series described an array of frightening homeless men, including a panhandler who tormented diners at a sidewalk café and threatened a young couple with a hammer after they refused his request for money. Armed with broken beer bottles, one homeless man chased passersby, while another warned an East Side doorman, "Leave me alone or I'll cut you up."[6]

Although none went as far as the partisan and sensational *World-Telegram and Sun*, other media outlets also seized the opportunity to portray the Bowery as a neighborhood in crisis, emblematic of a city out of control. The *New York Times* reported complaints about the homeless from representatives of Cooper Union and quoted Father Michael Allen of the Church of St. Mark's in-the-Bowery describing homeless men harassing parishioners and visiting the church to "defecate in the pews." According to some city media, the homeless masses infringed on the rights of all residents, causing them distress and potential harm. Rather than simply reporting such alleged incidents, papers like the *World-Telegram* crafted depictions filled with sordid detail, inviting readers to enjoy the voyeuristic pleasure of observing the fascinating habits of members of a supposedly alien culture.[7]

Mass-market paperbacks offered readers nationwide similar opportunities to revel in urban poverty under the guise of educating themselves about the subject. The cover of *Skid Row, U.S.A.* promised "A shocking true account of the people on Skid Row and how they got there," and author Sara Harris successfully delivered on that claim. Before narrating the "shocking" stories, she indulged the traditional, romantic drifter character, introducing readers to a charismatic sage, Schloime the Troime (Sam the Dreamer), who enjoyed the intellectual freedom the homeless life afforded him, while lamenting the plight of his peers: "Most men ain't here for looking up to stars. They don't even know, poor little people, is stars or not. Many of them is not here because they want but only because what else is?"[8]

A sociologist, Harris argued that a disproportionate number of skid-row residents had been overly doted on by their mothers, and thus grown unaccustomed to a life of work. She described such men as "egoless," characterizing them as individuals who tolerated lives on skid row, in part due to low perceptions of themselves. But the sordid tales of individual suffering promised on the cover formed the bulk of her text. One family she described subsisted entirely on begging. The father, Mackie Chambers, "an amputee who has stubs where his legs should be," had lost his legs either in a construction accident or in World War I, depending on which story one believed. His wife, described by Harris as "feeble-minded," also begged for a living, although less successfully than her husband. "I never made the kind of money Mr. Chambers made, though. He's a pretty lucky fellow," she observed. "All he needs to do is ride around the streets in his cart and show his stumps out." The couple's adult daughter, too, begged for a living, feigning a physical impairment to inspire greater public sympathy. From her parents, Harris assured readers, Lady had learned contempt for those who gave money to panhandlers. "If a sucker wants to give, why shouldn't I be the one to benefit?" Harris quoted her as saying, "I give him something he needs in return for the money—the feeling that he's a pretty great guy." Harris offered readers a blunt, unflattering, often unsympathetic depiction of life among the city's homeless and panhandlers. Scholars branded Harris's work naïve and ill-informed, accusing her of relying upon the testimony of skid-row "tour directors," informants known for specializing in guiding visitors and often relating fictional stories.[9]

Such books derived much of their appeal from their ability to offer readers entry to a foreign world, complete with its own distinctive language. Harris's audience experienced the flavor of Bowery lingo through quotes like one from Gyppie Johnson, a sixty-nine-year-old Brooklyn native: "My flop is fourteen dollars. I get free grub with the 'soul savers.' If I need a benny in the winter, I take a nose dive, so's they'll give me a coat for free. Any bloody bucket'll let me drink on the cuff." Another of the era's paperbacks on the subject included an appended glossary, "The Argot of Skid Row," clarifying definitions of such useful terms as "live one—one who has money and will buy drinks" and "dead one—a retired hobo."[10]

Harris took her readers beyond the realm of language, introducing them to a world of differently abled panhandlers known as "halfies" (those with no legs below the knee), "wingies" (those lacking arms), and "blinkies" (the blind). She also offered glimpses of a secret world of skid-row sexual fetishes: "The sickest among them fantasy while they caress the shoes and stockings and slips and hair and hide them under the itchy blankets on the cots and hold them next to their bare bodies." Such popular media depictions of the homeless reflected their complex role in American culture. At once envied, feared, and reviled, skid-row denizens fascinated economically mainstream Americans.[11]

The homeless appeared as stock characters in cartoons like those in the *New Yorker* magazine and elsewhere, instantly recognizable by their ill-fitting, rumpled clothing, wilted hat, scruffy beard, and amiable demeanor. Such depictions rendered the homeless as nonthreatening elements of the urban landscape, whose poverty and perceived lack of personal and professional ambition contrasted with the pursuits of "businessman" characters.[12]

Similarly, a 1962 Broadway production based loosely on Edmund G. Love's 1958 book, *Subways Are for Sleeping*, depicted middle-class New Yorkers dropping out of mainstream society to live fantastic, escapist lives among the city's homeless. The musical's opening number set the stage for its unlikely premise, playing on the exclusion of many homeless from the expanding system of federal benefits: "You wouldn't think, in this age of Social Security and Unemployment Insurance, that people can get lost / But it's true, they still do / Right under your eyes, all around the city / . . . subways are for sleeping and so are so many other places / lofts and cellars and fire escapes, car lots, museums and excavations . . ." Modern, middle-class New Yorkers, living "in this age of psychoanalysis and modern housing developments," as the play had it, lacked meaningful social connections and values, which could be conveyed through the metaphor of homelessness. Journalists, popular sociologists, and artists marketed the language, habits, attitudes, and values of the urban homeless to their audience as an exotic, exciting, reckless underworld. The realities of life on skid row, as researchers soon learned, often proved far more mundane.[13]

Journalists who wanted to understand the real lives of the urban homeless sometimes continued the tradition of posing among them. Barnard Collier chronicled his nineteen-hour journey into homelessness for *New York* magazine, in one notable effort. Collier registered with some of the skid-row employment agencies, which offered men menial jobs after payment of a placement fee. After being harassed by the police, ignored by passersby, and sent on an overnight dishwashing job, Collier ended the assignment early. His essay emphasized the social gulf that divided the homeless from middle-class New Yorkers, noting that they shared the same geographic space, but lived in different realms.[14]

A controversial, empathetic effort by the *Village Voice* underscored the conflicting views surrounding visual representations of homelessness. Opening a 1968 article, Steve Lerner drew on the visceral language of the counterculture to describe the city's skid row: "The streets of the Bowery are the bowels of America," he observed, "Sticking out like an infected anus at the end of an island, the Bowery lays a fart in the face of New York. The stench carries for blocks, embarrassing the gentle folk who work downtown." Lerner criticized the city's inability to provide adequate assistance to its homeless population, characterizing the Bowery as a site of public shame. A series of photographs by Jay F. Good of Bowery residents accompanied Lerner's sobering depiction of the harsh realities of life on the streets. The pictures depicted a man drinking, an artistic portrait of a seated man smoking while looking directly into the camera and, reminiscent of Margaret Bourke-White's famous Depression-era photograph, an image of three seated men looking into the distance near a large billboard reading "Vote for Javits. He votes for you." Borrowing on the earlier model, Good highlighted the isolated hopelessness of the Bowery men through contrast with the trite optimism of the campaign advertisement.[15]

In a write-in column a few weeks later, David McReynolds criticized the newspaper's inclusion of the portraits. In his view, such photographs endowed Bowery men with a dignity that detracted from the potential power of their story. "I would rather fill four pages of *The Voice* with nothing but shots of men who have passed out," he wrote; "There is no drama to such a picture—certainly not to more than one such picture—but I think it might shock some people if they knew that during the warmer months you can pass 10 or 20 men lying against buildings on each block between Houston and Spring." Instead of focusing on the intense personal, psychological suffering endured by homeless individuals, McReynolds advocated emphasizing the scale of the situation through pictures documenting the number of homeless sleeping outdoors. Similar debates had plagued earlier uses of photography in social reform efforts. Most notably in the work of Jacob Riis and Lewis Hine, and later in that of the Farm Security Administration, photographers had struggled to develop visual vocabularies capable of depicting the plight of the poor without reducing them to simplified types. Staged, posed, or portrait-style photographs allowed a photographer to convey the humanity of an individual, inspiring empathy for his suffering, but notoriously risked neutralizing the "documentary" effect such photographs might exploit. Increasingly savvy about the operations of both images and text, late 1960s journalists committed to social justice remained unsure which type of coverage would further their cause.[16]

New York City officials wanted to add to the limited existing knowledge about urban homelessness. Little current information documented the lives of the homeless and the journeys that had brought them to skid row. The era's popular culture depicted them as carefree and exotic, even as politicians portrayed them as violent criminals. Somewhere between these polarized media images the truth had to lie. In their efforts to generate data, city officials partnered with social scientists operating from an academic culture complete with its own rules and motivations.

The Limits of Welfare and the Power of Social Science

Despite its controversial, media-hyped launch, Operation Bowery would outlast Wagner's election victory, evolving into a significant resource for the city's homeless population. Supervised by Welfare Commissioner James R. Dumpson, the program drew on the expertise of representatives from the Departments of Health, Hospitals, Community Mental Health, Police, Corrections, and the City Administrator's and Budget Office. It functioned primarily as an information and referral service, employing administrators, social workers, a vocational rehabilitation counselor, physicians, and a registered nurse. The staff reached out first to skid row's younger residents and relative newcomers, speculating that they would be the most likely candidates for rehabilitation. Clients participated in a screening interview and a medical examination, as well as psychiatric and vocational evaluations. In its first year of operation, the program screened over four hundred individuals, with repeat clients bringing the total caseload close to 500. The staff referred over one hundred of those individuals to jobs, and others to Camp LaGuardia, Bridge House, and various welfare centers.[17]

Referrals from Operation Bowery helped some homeless people to develop new life skills and habits, as in the case of "J. N.," a thirty-three-year-old man described as a "severe alcoholic." Drinking since age fourteen, he lived on the Bowery for several years before approaching Operation Bowery staff in search of assistance. After a series of counseling sessions, he successfully completed the Basic Emotional Skills Training Program, earning qualification for employment as a maintenance worker.[18]

In addition to outreach work and referral services, the program staff also administered the "Bowery Day Center" on the first three floors of the muni. Advertised as a "wholesome recreation resource for homeless men," the center provided up to 160 men each day with access to a television, radio, reading materials, chess and checkers games, and crafts. After some Operation Bowery participants complained of being insulted by other muni clients, the program moved its office off the Bowery, to the corner of Lafayette and Bleecker Streets, in the hope that more homeless men would feel comfortable accessing services at that location.[19]

Inspired by the program's success, Operation Bowery staff proposed opening a public rehabilitation facility for homeless men on North Brother Island. The project received a favorable reception, earning a $600,000 allocation in the 1966 city budget. But the city dropped the project when the Department of Public Works determined that the requisite renovations would be prohibitively expensive. Shuttling the homeless back to Hart Island surfaced briefly as a possibility when the Department of Corrections announced plans to consolidate its operations on Rikers Island, but Governor Rockefeller proposed using Hart for a drug treatment center instead so officials again dismissed the idea of using the facility for the homeless.[20]

Unable to expand the program, Operation Bowery staff became frustrated by the limitations placed on their work. Longing to develop innovative programs for the homeless, Dumpson and his associates requested a closer examination of their clients' needs. Operation Bowery's clients had been left behind in the rapidly modernizing workplace, the staff observed, due not only to their lack of job skills, but also their personal problems: "These men suffer not just economic poverty, but intellectual, social and emotional impoverishment as well." Overwhelmed by the complex, multiple challenges facing skid-row residents, Operation Bowery staff members hoped that social science might shed light on the core causes of homelessness. Such knowledge might then allow the establishment of appropriate preventive and rehabilitative programs.[21]

Increasingly convinced that changing the lives of the skid-row homeless required the provision of more than food, shelter, or even vocational training, they wondered if an intangible variable, or a set of such variables, might form the root of the population's dramatic problems. They hoped to identify the cause of homelessness through a more detailed understanding of the individual and collective profile of skid-row residents, and thus develop more humane and effective approaches for dealing with the problems. In 1963, Morris Chase, head of Operation Bowery, contracted Columbia University's Bureau of Applied Social Research to conduct a major study of the city's homeless men. The project would provide a detailed portrait of the Bowery neighborhood and its residents, enabling the city finally to eradicate its skid row. During the project's pilot phase, researchers conducted an exhaustive literature review, analyzed individual case records, mapped the region, counted its population, and conducted participant observation. Initially funded by the city, the project was later supported by the federal government, through the National Institute of Mental Health.[22]

In Chicago, Donald Bogue pursued a similar project as part of an urban renewal study conducted by the University of Chicago Social Science Division and funded by the Wieboldt and Ford Foundations and the federal government. Bogue lobbied to remove skid rows from cities across the nation, describing them as not merely "a physical eyesore," but also "sociologically poisonous to neighborhoods in a broad surrounding zone." Bogue emphasized the effects of homelessness on neighboring communities of economically mainstream individuals, largely ignoring the concerns of the indigent themselves.[23]

Caplow, head of the Bowery project, had conducted social science research on homelessness since the Depression. The new project centered on a three-year research program begun in 1964, "Homelessness: Etiology and Consequences." By collecting and analyzing the life histories of a random sample of homeless men, researchers hoped "to extend the knowledge of homelessness as a condition by analyzing homelessness as a process." Compiling and studying the characteristics of homeless men, he hoped, would further both theoretical and applied knowledge of the nature of homelessness while determining ways such men might be assisted earlier in their lives. Significantly, the project diverged from the city's initial goals by not setting out to develop solutions for those individuals who were already homeless. Causes and remedies were sought in the backgrounds of individuals, not in their present lives, in hope of aiding future at-risk populations. The research team attempted to identify those traits, habits, or events that placed an individual on the path to homelessness.[24]

Distinct definitions of "skid row" shaped the approaches taken in the era's various research projects. Some scholars employed spatial definitions, using the term to describe district housing facilities catering to the needs of the homeless, while others applied social ones, viewing skid row as "an isolated and deviant subcultural community expressing the features of a distinct and recognizable way of life." In the Columbia project, Caplow and Bahr sought to fuse the two concepts, defining skid row as both a geographically distinct location and a frame of mind. They defined homeless men as those who did not live with family, were over twenty-one years old, paid "little or no money" for housing, and worked, if at all, in low-level positions.[25]

The Columbia team set out to study not only the Bowery but also the district encompassing its intersecting blocks.[26] The area's thirty-seven commercial lodging houses, combined with the Bowery Mission, Municipal Shelter, Salvation Army Hotel, and Salvation Army Alcoholic Rehabilitation Center, housed almost 5,000 men in 1966. The researchers generated a random sample of 240 men from this group, from whom they collected over two hundred interviews. At Camp LaGuardia, they interviewed almost 200 additional men. The project also set out to employ cross-class analysis. By comparing data on the homeless and men of the lower and middle classes living in the working-class Brooklyn neighborhood of Park Slope and the Park Avenue area of Manhattan, they hoped to discern useful variations.

Employing a survey form over thirty pages long, interviewers covered a wide array of subjects ranging from childhood experiences and educational achievements to parents' occupations and religious practices. Each man supplied detailed information about the places he had lived, various jobs he had held, and specific groups to which he had belonged. Defining homelessness primarily as a state of "disaffiliation" and "a condition of detachment from society characterized by the absence or attenuation of the affiliative bonds that link settled persons to a network of interconnected social structures," the Columbia team considered the homeless to be isolated individuals living on the margins of society. The team hypothesized that a lifelong pattern of similar behavior would emerge. They rejected the stereotypical notion that all skid-row homeless had migrated there due to chronic alcoholism, and sought to profile the diverse individuals on skid row, in part as a corrective to that false image. Significantly, they categorized homelessness as a form of "deviance" on par with alcoholism and downward social mobility, and expected to ascertain its cause. Homelessness was in this formulation a nexus of behaviors, rather than the result of various structural economic and social forces. The homeless were seen fundamentally as individuals who cut themselves off from society through antisocial behaviors, which might be analyzed and corrected in future cases.[27]

Initially worried that the homeless would prove unwilling subjects, researchers were relieved when most of the men they approached cooperated fully; the team completed the Bowery and Camp LaGuardia interviews in only two months. They were unpleasantly surprised to find that those in working-class Park Slope, by contrast, required more than four months of effort. Landlords and building superintendents, suspicious of the interviewers' motives, often refused to allow them entry. Some area residents also actively avoided the interviewers. One African American man who initially eluded his prospective interviewers later confided that he had suspected them emissaries of his racist landlord, sent to evict him. Although the homeless were often regarded as a taciturn, isolated population unwilling to discuss their situation with passersby, service providers, or researchers, the Columbia team found the opposite to be true. Ironically, the working-class men proved more difficult to reach, and less willing to share the intimate details of their lives.[28]

Turning to the skid-row homeless for information about their plight worried some researchers, who remained skeptical about the veracity of responses they received. Sometimes their doubts were justified, as in the case of an eighty-one-year-old Irish immigrant who admitted to drinking steadily since age fifteen. Although he faithfully responded to each question, he experienced predictable difficulty recalling specific dates, names, and other details. But researchers found other respondents decidedly unhelpful. One participant, "Warren," an Italian American from Queens born in 1922, had perhaps embellished his life history for the amusement of his friends looking on when insisting he'd spent his first night on the Bowery at the tender age of twelve. He also kept private some details of his life, mentioning that he'd served nearly ten years in Sing Sing for armed robbery, yet declining to provide additional information about his criminal past. His interviewer was most troubled by Warren's clever reframing of the simplistic survey questions. Asked whether it was more important to fight poverty or Communism, Warren replied, "If you eliminate poverty, then you won't have communism." Asked if there had been problems in his failed marriage, he replied, "I was a no good bastard." And when asked, "What kind of person rates highest around here?" he answered first, "Me," then, "Nobody." While Warren's quick wit and ironic sense of humor probably helped him to survive on skid row, his Columbia University interviewer characterized him merely as "resistant" and "arrogant," noting, "most difficult so far—He wouldn't give me one straight answer." Similarly, a sixty-eight-year-old resident of the Uncle Sam Hotel replied, "I haven't found out what communism is yet." In his notebook, the interviewer recorded, "On attitudinal questions, R was very reflective and much too sophisticated for them. He pointed out to me that terms such as 'most' and 'average' are ambiguous and the question can be answered either way, and also that many of the questions were related to one another." But overall, Bahr concluded that homeless men were no more likely to give false responses than any other "disadvantaged" group studied, although their relatively high rates of mental illness limited their accuracy.[29]

Such interviews with homeless men formed the core of the Columbia

University Homelessness Project. Rather than simply observing skid row from the perspective of an "outsider," as had so many journalists, politicians, city officials, and even social service providers, the Columbia team probed the experiences and lives of the homeless. Their demanding methodology required researchers to spend significant amounts of time on the Bowery, interacting with the homeless and listening to their recollections. The researchers navigated complex social hierarchies as they brought the machinery of social science into the flophouses of the Bowery, and some individuals resented their inquiries. Overall, though, homeless men cooperated with the efforts, sharing information about their life histories and attitudes with researchers.

In developing the methodology for the Bowery project, the Columbia team built on a long tradition of sociological inquiry into poverty and homelessness, expanding and reframing questions first posed forty years earlier. Homeless men had long attracted significant attention from social scientists. Highly visible, easily accessible, and seemingly rejecting the bedrock values of American society, the homeless offered generations of researchers a proving ground for various sociological theories. Although such projects generated useful demographic information, they yielded few cohesive explanations for the behavior of the homeless.[30]

In the 1920s, early social science research into homelessness eroded the dominant, moralistic position maintained by late nineteenth-century reform groups like the Charity Organization Society; they tried to inculcate in vagrants a stronger work ethic by requiring them to perform manual labor prior to receiving assistance. By contrast, more nuanced theories emerged from studies such as Alice Solenberger's *One Thousand Homeless Men* (1911) and Frank Laubach's *Why There Are Vagrants* (1916), which distinguished various "types" of homeless men by identifying multiple and sometimes overlapping causes for their plight.[31]

The discipline of sociology centered on the Chicago School in the 1920s, where Robert Park and Ernest Burgess sought to explain the "urban ecology" of modern cities by mapping Chicago as a series of concentric zones, originating in a core area of decay. An analysis of homelessness by Nels Anderson, a graduate student in the program, *The Hobo: The Sociology of the Homeless Man* (1923), appeared as the first in a series of University of Chicago publications that planned to address the modern urban world, rife with crime, vice, and poverty. Drawing on his own experiences traveling the country, Anderson developed a typology of homelessness that isolated five types of homeless man: the seasonal worker, the occasional worker, the wandering tramp, the bum (who neither worked nor wandered), and the home guard (who remained in the area he defined as "Hobohemia").[32]

Social scientists of the 1950s and 1960s returned to Anderson's typology, expanding and refining it to reflect life in the postwar city. In 1963, based on interviews with social service providers, Donald Bogue developed a twelve-category model structured around a man's disability status, level of alcohol consumption, and age. Bogue's emphasis on alcoholism as a central factor in skid-row life was later criticized for perpetuating stereotyped visions of the homeless. Anthropologist James Spradley developed an even more elaborate typology, grouped around eight central categories.[33]

Postwar homelessness researchers also drew upon traditional sociological theories of human behavior. For Bahr and Caplow, the concept of anomie proved especially influential; on the Bowery, they looked specifically for its effects. French sociologist Émile Durkheim first advanced the concept in the 1890s in his doctoral thesis, *The Division of Labor in Society*. He developed the concept further in *Suicide*, but it did not assume widespread influence among sociologists until the 1940s. Durkheim described modern society as failing to regulate individual behavior while encouraging individuals to achieve ambitious goals without offering reasonable means by which to do accomplish them. This tension placed pressure on individuals, leading to the development of anomie.[34]

In an influential 1938 article, sociologist Robert K. Merton connected Durkheim's anomie theory to deviant behavior. Suffering "strain" induced by the gap between goals and means, individuals in Merton's scheme faced five possible modes of adaptation: conformity, innovation, ritualism, retreatism, or rebellion. Frustrated by this situation, Merton argued, some individuals became "estranged" from society and resorted to deviant behavior. He linked anomie to "open-class societies" such as the United States, whose members were routinely encouraged to aspire for prestige, regardless of their birth status. Anomic theory thus posed a challenge to the era's dominant, mythical "American dream," cautioning that evaluating individuals' accomplishments as if they had enjoyed equal opportunities led to unjust comparisons.[35]

As social scientists explored and expanded the theory of anomie, its meaning shifted in crucial ways. In the 1950s and 1960s, some used the concept to explain the situation of a wide variety of marginalized groups in American society, including the elderly, widows, African Americans, immigrants, the uneducated, the poor, the downwardly mobile, and the divorced. While

Merton described anomie as a characteristic of certain social structures, later scholars, especially psychiatrists, framed the concept as a state of mind held by certain individuals. This key distinction frequently became blurred, clouding the subsequent application of anomie and related theories to the study of poverty and the poor. Merton's theories influenced structuralist approaches to economic inequality. In *An American Dilemma*, for example, Gunnar Myrdal framed the alienation of African Americans in terms of the limited opportunities afforded them by a nation plagued by racism.[36]

Other social scientists, exploring "cultural" explanations of poverty, borrowed on similar theories, but placed greater emphasis on the psychological effects of social alienation on the individual. Anthropologist Oscar Lewis's influential and, ultimately, infamous "culture of poverty" model exemplified both the potential and dangers inherent to this approach. In a style of anthropological writing that he termed "ethnographic realism," Lewis presented detailed portraits of impoverished families in a series of popular books, most notably *The Children of Sanchez* (1961) and *La Vida: A Puerto Rican Family in the Culture of Poverty* (1966).[37]

Lewis identified specific traits he witnessed in people immersed in the culture of poverty. Many of the traits on his list also appeared as categories of analysis in contemporary sociological studies of the urban homeless: unemployment and underemployment, low wages, absence of savings, chronic shortage of cash, pawning, borrowing from local money lenders at usurious rates of interest, spontaneous informal credit devices, constant struggle for survival, use of secondhand clothing, lack of privacy, high incidence of alcoholism, free unions, abandonment of mothers and children, mother-centered families, limited memberships and participation in both formal and informal associations, strong feeling of marginality, strong feeling of helplessness, strong feeling of dependency, feeling of inferiority and personal unworthiness, strong present-time orientation with little ability to defer gratification, resignation and fatalism, high tolerance for psychological pathology, low level of education and literacy, lower life expectancy, and considered marginal to national institutions (social security, labor unions, banks, etc.). The Columbia team, for example, compiled a similar list of the characteristics of homeless men. An eclectic mix of economic and behavioral traits, their list covered a wide span of life areas: "poor work history, heavy drinking, poor marital history, low standard of living, dependency, wanderlust, reckless youth, poor health, and repeated arrests for drinking and more serious crimes." Lewis's poor strongly resembled those under study by Caplow and Bahr, with one key difference: Lewis remained tied to a specific location, a community, and a family, while the Columbia team examined the socially detached, historically mobile poor who had now settled in skid-row neighborhoods.[38]

In Lewis's analysis, the more than seventy traits on his list reflected the ravaging effects of poverty on individual psychology. Faced with bleak prospects for socioeconomic advancement, the poor adopted specific perspectives that differentiated them from their middle-class American counterparts. Lewis (and Michael Harrington, whose *The Other America* further popularized Lewis's theory) used the term "culture of poverty" loosely and often seemingly carelessly, failing to distinguish clearly the causes and effects at play in his model, rendering it ready ammunition in moralistic attacks on public benefits programs and other services to the poor. Later scholars reframed Lewis's "culture of poverty" as a "psychology of oppression," better capturing his sentiments. Yet any individualistic analysis of poverty risked fueling the blame of the poor for their plight.[39]

Not unlike Lewis, Bahr and Caplow located a major cause of homelessness within the individual. Some people, they argued, failed to form the social bonds that would integrate them fully into mainstream society. Pulled by economic need and pushed by alienation from the institutions and processes of formal education, poor people often left school at an early age, rendering them unprepared to perform the remunerative work necessary to achieve social mobility. As this process continued, they became increasingly isolated, residing in a world distinct from that occupied by economically mainstream Americans. The nation's poorest residents, ultimately, alienated both spatially and socially, developed "negative attitudes" toward mainstream society, with whom they felt no sense of community.[40]

Two schools of thought shaped sociological research on homelessness. Social order analysts, in general, examined ways the homeless participated in forms of community on skid row, arguing for less restrictive policies on the part of service providers. Social problem analysts, on the other hand, including Bogue, Caplow, and Bahr, focused on ways to eliminate skid rows. Although Caplow disagreed publicly with aspects of Lewis's culture of poverty theory, the Columbia research on the Bowery shared its politically dangerous focus on the impoverished individual.[41]

Alcohol use and addiction further complicated the study of homelessness. Buoyed by the disease theory of alcoholism, research on the drinking habits of the skid-row homeless expanded in the postwar years. Many researchers sought to determine the extent to which homeless men effectively departed

from society, becoming isolated, independent individuals in their journey to
skid row, or whether they simply left, in fact, one community for another.
If the latter were true, social scientists surmised, social patterns, ties, and
processes of socialization would be discernible, even if different from those
structuring middle- and working-class culture.[42]

When homeless men lacked sufficient money to purchase alcohol individually, they sometimes pooled their resources. This seemingly rare example
of voluntary socializing and entry into group activity proved a popular topic of study. Scholars analyzed the bottle gang on multiple levels, describing
it as a "corporate" group with "leaders" and rules governing memberships,
and as one divided into distinct phases, ranging from "salutation" through
"consumption" to "dispersal." Differences were noted among groups, down to
minute details, including whether the leader drank first or last, and whether
the bottle was passed to the left or the right.[43]

While many scholars devoted a great deal of attention to bottle gangs,
Bahr distanced himself from such research, emphasizing instead the highly
fluid nature of social ties and networks uniting homeless men. While bottle
gangs maintained codes of conduct, he noted, men who violated the rules
were not banished for long and soon returned to the fold. Similarly, most
skid-row men reported feeling no sense of community among each other.
Paralleling research in other cities, Patricia Nash's Columbia pilot study on
the Bowery found two-thirds of respondents unwilling to lend money to fellow homeless people. Likewise, 77 percent of Bowery men surveyed expressed
no desire to know more homeless men by name. Some replied, "I'm sorry that
I know the ones I do." Only a minimal sense of shared experience united the
homeless, lending credibility to the Columbia team's theory of disaffiliation.[44]

In evaluating the drinking habits of homeless men, the Bowery team
struggled to develop a reliable method of measurement. When asked to
describe their alcohol consumption qualitatively, homeless men described
themselves as light to moderate drinkers. But when asked to quantify their
drinking, their responses indicated more were heavy drinkers. Not surprisingly, the definitions of "heavy" and "moderate" drinking proved socially
malleable, carrying one meaning among the homeless and another altogether
among members of the middle class.[45]

The Columbia interview records reveal the ways in which many homeless
men understood "light" and "heavy" drinking. One respondent said he had
started drinking a few times per week at age twenty-one. From 1955 to 1964,
he had consumed two pints of whisky per day. He currently drank four pints

of beer each day. He had been to AA meetings, yet characterized himself as a "very light drinker," explaining that "I never was arrested for drinking or anything like that." An eighty-one-year-old man who defined his drinking as "light" consumed a glass of beer less than a few times per week. Another "light drinker" drank one pint of wine per day. He would have consumed more alcohol, but "it costs money to drink." A hotel clerk drank "heavily," consuming a pint of wine and three pints of beer each day. He also drank whisky, when he could afford it.[46]

Class-based drinking norms shaped the ways homeless men understood their drinking, leading them to describe as "light" levels of alcohol consumption that appeared moderate or heavy by middle-class standards. Some men had accelerated their drinking after arriving on skid row, while others were limited by their lack of funds. Few men described their journey to the Bowery in terms of a simple descent into alcoholism; most cited other precipitating factors.

Bahr used a 1964 survey of men in Bowery lodging houses to evaluate the relationship between alcohol consumption, social interaction, and the identification of homeless men with their neighbors and environment. Among the skid-row homeless, Bahr hypothesized, drinking functioned as an important socializing activity, and heavy drinking men would be the most acculturated. Bahr's survey results bore out his theories, showing that heavy drinkers interacted less with "normals" (non-skid row residents), and more with other homeless men than did their lighter drinking counterparts. Overall, the findings led Bahr to conclude that once a man was fully socialized into skid row, largely through heavy drinking, he came to see himself as a skid-row resident, and continued to do so, even if later in life he became increasingly isolated. While alcohol consumption was found to shape a man's skid-row status and relative "disaffiliation," the level of drinking did not function as it did in the society at large, where an alcoholic might be alienated and secretive; heavy drinkers were frequently more "affiliated" on the Bowery than those men who drank lightly or not at all. The highly social culture of alcoholic consumption among homeless men rendered it one of few activities through which they forged social ties. Such connections further distanced the homeless from mainstream society.[47]

Psychiatrists, too, weighed in on the well-being of the homeless. In 1955, Boris Levinson administered the popular Rorschach test to fifty men lodged at the muni. He found them to be emotionally immature, depressed, lacking in drive and definite goals, suffering from feelings of despair and worthlessness, apathetic, having few interests, insecure, and unable to empathize. Levinson saw life on skid row as a way for such men to "act out" conflicts and relieve guilt. Such traits were inherent to the men, Levinson theorized, but exacerbated by life on skid row.[48]

The era's researchers drew upon the precedent of earlier social science projects on homelessness. Informed by earlier typologies, but not limited to their methods, they documented and analyzed the social connections forged on skid row. The Columbia team began the project associating with the camp of researchers who hoped to see skid rows eliminated. They expected and found little there to change their mind. Far from radical, their project maintained strong connections to core theories of social science, and resonated with the era's other projects. Like Lewis and other contemporaries, they maintained a focus largely on the individual level. Even in studying institutions of skid row, including bars, hotels, and the muni, they emphasized the nature of the connections men found there. They set out to document primarily the isolation of the homeless, finding out how many men had been active in youth groups, churches, and other organizations, as well as the number of conversations they currently had on an average day. This research focus limited their work on the Bowery.

The Limitations of Research

Embarking on its ambitious research program, the Columbia team had first set out to obtain an accurate count of New York's homeless population. U.S. Census takers in 1960 employed special tactics to count the homeless, visiting hotels and missions while sending a separate team to scour parks and doorways. The Columbia staff conducted similar Bowery censuses, venturing out one night each year and combing the streets for homeless men. Researchers knew that fifteen thousand homeless individuals accessed the services of the men's shelter in 1963, twice the number believed to be living on the Bowery, and struggled to tabulate the population. In a creative, yet not statistically sound, effort to ascertain the number of homeless men living throughout the city, they analyzed the death certificates of men buried in Potter's Field. Since Bowery residents made up one-fifth of the men buried there, they extrapolated a total figure, inserting the era's standard estimate of 7,500 Bowery men into the resulting one-to-four ratio, estimating that 30,000 homeless men lived in New York City (38,500, including Camp LaGuardia residents).[49]

Analyzing skid-row institutions, Bahr and Caplow studied the health care available to the homeless, noting that the death rate of Bowery men averaged 50 per 1,000 in 1964, five times the national average. While other men their age died from heart failure and cancer, the skid-row homeless yielded to fatal alcoholism and cirrhosis of the liver. Homeless men comprised a disproportionate number of hospital admissions. Because they did not receive regular or preventive care, their first point of access to the health care system came through hospital doors, most often for serious conditions, leaving them with a higher hospitalization rate.[50]

Bahr and Caplow recognized skid-row bars as another key institution. To better understand bar culture, Columbia's George Nash spent a day at the One Mile Bar at Rivington Street and the Bowery, drinking from early in the morning, beneath pictures of FDR, JFK, and the World War II Japanese surrender. Posing as a patron, he learned that such bars provided services to patrons beyond access to alcohol, offering check cashing, cash loans, use of a mailing address, referrals to odd jobs and a place to sleep, as well as a place to entertain friends.[51]

Striking, poignant insights into the thoughts, feelings, and perspectives of the urban homeless remain the most potent legacy of the era's research projects. Researchers probed homeless men's attitudes toward skid row and ascertained their future plans, revealing many of their motivations and desires. When asked why they chose to live on skid row, most respondents cited the area's affordable meals and lodgings as its most attractive features. Indeed, fully one-quarter were referred to Bowery facilities directly by the Department of Welfare, given tickets for food and lodging that were redeemable only on the Bowery. Only one in six mentioned the traditional, romantic notions of escape from social pressures and the haven of anonymity. Researchers also asked the homeless what factors they perceived to have led them to skid row. Respondents frequently cited their lack of formal education as a precipitating factor. When Bogue asked homeless Chicago men the changes they would make if able to live their lives again, seeking further education topped the list of replies, followed by limiting drinking, learning a better trade, marrying or being more successful in marriage, saving money and preparing for the future, working harder and more steadily, and being more actively religious. But the research done by both the Columbia staff and Bogue found that homeless men possessed levels of formal education comparable to that of their working-class peers. More significant appeared to be the relationship between educational achievement and higher levels of "affiliation." Men who had completed more years of schooling proved more likely to have been married, voted, and at some point, belonged to a formal organization. They were also more likely to associate with a regular group of friends, maintain friendships with people outside the Bowery, and interact with multiple people each day. As with so many of the era's research findings, these results offered little in the way of concrete conclusions.[52]

As urban renewal projects demolished homeless districts across the nation, researchers asked homeless men their plans if their skid row disappeared. Overall, the findings indicated that most homeless men wished to remain in their home cities. Only 14 percent of Philadelphia and 20 percent of Minneapolis respondents planned to leave the area. When asked where they saw themselves in a year, 40 percent of Bowery men planned to remain there, as did one-third of Camp LaGuardia residents. Other men maintained plans and dreams that extended beyond the confines of skid row. Over 25 percent of Bowery men expressed a desire to leave the area, some to reunite with family members, others to relocate to warmer climates such as Florida, California, and Arizona. In both Chicago and New York, 30 to 40 percent expressed a desire to remain on skid row indefinitely, while the rest hoped to leave within a year.[53]

As anticipated, the Columbia team found skid-row residents formulating few realistic plans to improve their lives. Indeed, when asked where they would be in a year, more than 25 percent of Bowery residents mentioned death, in terms such as, "I don't think I'll live that long," "Maybe dead. I've got no idea," "I don't know—maybe in my grave. Here, in NY," and "Hard to say—Don't know where I'll be tomorrow—Won't live here if I can get out." Those who maintained hope of leaving the Bowery often clung to flimsy plans. A man who had not seen any of his family members since 1955, for example, speculated that within a year he would be reunited with his wife and children in Tennessee. Others cherished sadly impractical professional ambitions. A fifty-year-old African American man who had completed two years at Howard University, for instance, but found employment in only low-status positions such as errand boy, catering assistant, and restaurant employee, declared his hope to give music lessons, and to acquire a real estate business and a rooming house in the upcoming year.[54]

Although many of their personal goals remained impractical, homeless men stayed informed and opinionated about electoral politics. A 1964 survey indicated most Bowery men supported President Johnson, whether or not they voted. In 1968, a poll conducted at the Bowery Mission found nearly 80 percent of skid-row men self-proclaimed Democrats, while only 20 percent favored Richard Nixon over Johnson for the coming term. Citing Franklin D. Roosevelt as their favorite recent president, they speculated that the "worst possible choice for president" would be California governor Ronald Reagan. Researchers interpreted such engagement as indicative of an encouraging, wider, continued perception of themselves as citizens.[55]

Contrary to popular perceptions of the homeless as uniformly lazy, many supported themselves through work or received pensions based on prior employment. To learn more about the nature of skid-row jobs, Columbia's Nash joined Ed and Tom, two Bowery residents, on their journey to find work through the Labor-Aides employment agency on Church Street. He was sent out for a day of manual labor moving cardboard and paper. Such temporary employment, involving little responsibility or skill, fit the profile developed by researchers.[56]

Although the Columbia team acknowledged the regular work habits of skid-row men, more intriguing to them were the enigmatic Camp LaGuardia residents, who defied conventional notions of the homeless behavior. Most skid-row denizens seemed to avoid situations in which they might be compelled to take on responsibilities, but camp residents voluntarily participated in a program requiring them to work. The camp offered an example of an outmoded, historically specific approach to the problem of homelessness. As a "total institution," in the manner of prisons, mental hospitals, and tuberculosis clinics, it provided for all a resident's needs. In an era when some prisons and other total institutions were moving away from this model by instituting work-release and other programs to afford residents increased exposure to the outside world, Camp LaGuardia perplexingly continued to prosper, successfully attracting, retaining, and occasionally rehabilitating homeless men. Investigators hoped to determine which aspects of the LaGuardia model might prove applicable to other types of institutions.[57]

Beginning their research at Camp LaGuardia, the Columbia team expected to isolate a "dependent personality" type explaining why some men endured life inside a confining institution. They were surprised to find residents of Camp LaGuardia largely indistinguishable from the rest of the Bowery population. Their hypothesis that many camp residents would have lived and worked in institutional environments that provided for their needs, such as railroad labor, military service and resort hotels, proved untenable. Researchers were unable to locate any specific variables in the camp residents' background that explained their successful use of the facility; they found the men less "dependent" than currently in a position of dire need.[58]

The research team also predicted camp residency would be associated with low self-image, inspiring them to evaluate the facility's reputation among the Bowery homeless. Validating their thesis, most respondents characterized camp residents in negative terms such as "Sick men—down and outers," "Doing bad," "A guy who's had a hard time—to dry up," "Guys that don't want to work," "Old people with no money," and "Lazy bastards!" Young men in particular resented the notion of staying at the camp, yearning instead to earn their own living.[59]

Despite the negative opinions of outsiders, most residents enjoyed camp life, commenting, "I feel better and more contented. . . . Being able to sleep and eat right instead of worrying all the time," and "It's quiet and tranquil. Restful atmosphere. No hullabaloo." Still, some found the environment uninspiring: "You can't get ahead here," one man told surveyors; "It's the same thing over and over." Another portrayed the camp as a dead end: "You ain't got nothing to look forward to—like a vegetable."[60]

Camp residents shared their Bowery counterparts' skepticism toward friendships among the down and out. A man with no close friends in the facility knew a few men by name, but had no desire to know any more. "As far as trying to make friends, I don't go in too much for it because I don't favor the 'doings' of some of the men. I don't want to know them." When another was asked what he found unpleasant about talking to other men at the camp, he replied, "When they start in telling me their troubles. I got my own!"[61]

The Camp's philosophy reflected its Depression-era roots; its founders believed that work would provide the basis of the men's "rehabilitation." Administrators assigned residents jobs, whether in the laundry, kitchen, garage, recreation room, carpentry shop, tailor shop, Social Service department, on the farm crew, coal gang, or as janitors or groundskeepers, and deducted lodging fees from their pay, to simulate employment and the economic structure of the outside world. Not unlike workers lodged in factory housing, their duties, earnings, and spending opportunities were dictated by the management. On alternate weeks, camp residents received two dollars in spending money. Some also received a portion of their Social Security check and additional funds from a "payroll job" as a foreman or department head. Offered a rare amount of autonomy, camp residents were trusted with money and allowed to purchase tobacco, toiletries, newspapers, paperback books, and beer in the tap room, and sometimes to visit the nearby town of Chester, where wine was available.[62]

Somewhat surprisingly, the Columbia team concluded that the camp management did not exert significant social control over camp residents through this system of wage labor. While some men worked hard, most did not invest much energy in their jobs. Writer Elmer Bendiner similarly depicted skid row as a world untarnished by the ambition and stress common to modern urban life. The jobs available to skid-row men also lacked the potential for "responsibility, advancement, or success," Bendiner noted, inspiring little effort in workers. He described the men of the Bowery as "the most retired men in the world." Through their refusal to become deeply invested in the rewards and punishments distributed by administrators, camp residents forged a value system resembling that in place on skid row. Although many of the practical realities of their lives were strictly regulated by outside forces, the homeless were offered little incentive to ascribe to the social values and "work ethic" promoted by officials.[63]

In the end, Camp LaGuardia proved less successful as a rehabilitation center than a retirement home; between one-fourth and one-third of its residents never left. Most camp residents were over fifty, fueling much of this trend. But Bahr and Caplow tried to determine the other factors separating the camp's permanent from its transient residents. They found permanent residents had histories of lower "affiliation" in nearly all categories surveyed; they were less active in formal and informal organizations, both as children and adults, and many had not married. The Columbia team concluded that such men generally "preferred" a residential atmosphere like that of the camp.[64]

The research carried out by Caplow and Bahr, which had drawn on Merton's work with anomie and strain theory, was in keeping with broader trends in sociology during the 1960s. Merton's theories were influential in a range of studies focusing on deviant behavior and delinquency, and shaped much of the era's approach to crime prevention, as researchers connected criminal behavior with frustrated ambitions. But in the realm of homelessness, the work done on skid row received mixed reviews.[65]

Caplow and Bahr circulated their Bowery findings in a series of reports, papers, articles and books, most significantly Bahr's 1973 overview of the project, *Skid Row: An Introduction to Disaffiliation*. *Skid Row* received a tepid reception from social scientists, who appreciated its thoroughness but criticized its failure to extrapolate an understanding of broader sociological trends. A contemporary book, *Skid Row and Its Alternatives*, by Blumberg, Shipley, and Shandler, presented similar material, focused on Philadelphia, drew nearly identical conclusions. Both studies called for strengthening the relationships between the homeless and service providers and establishing more intensive casework-based rehabilitation programs.[66]

Later criticism focused on the researchers' lack of attention to the class-based factors at play on skid row. Most significantly, social scientist Kim Hopper argued that the Columbia team overlooked a core methodological problem. Using formal and informal social memberships to measure an individual's level of affiliation, he noted, researchers disregarded the fact that such social membership was often determined by socioeconomic class, with wealthier and higher status individuals typically joining more organizations than working-class and poor counterparts. Similar criticism could be leveled at much of the research. The era's researchers performed only limited analysis of each of the multiple variables they identified. Education, employment, marital history, and other factors remained in tension, each offering some partial explanation of the plight of the homeless, but synthesized to few broader claims.[67]

While other research projects had tracked the path to success, such as those profiling the traits of wealthy businessmen and other socially lauded individuals, the Bowery project set out to map the opposite road, producing "a study in failure, measured in terms of middle-class standards." But in the end, Caplow and Bahr found no demonstrable connection between anomie and homelessness. Defining the concept for research purposes as the gap between aspirations and achievement, they compiled the dreams and accomplishments of homeless men, but found their aspirations no higher than those of the Park Slope residents, with low aspirations outnumbering high ones. Further, where an "anomic" gap did exist, it did not correspond to men who were more "socially withdrawn." Anomie, as a specific concept, did not explain the condition of homelessness. If its lack of a unifying theoretical orientation rendered the Bowery research of limited use to later generations of sociologists, it still generated detailed and occasionally surprising data on homelessness.[68]

One fascinating result of the era's research into homelessness was the subjective data provided about the key roles played by skid-row institutions in the lives of the homeless. Because they maintained few connections outside the area, residents found health care and social networks on the Bowery, although limited and shabby. Despite the inarguably negative conditions of skid row and the relatively low standard of living its residents enjoyed, many men hoped to remain there for the rest of their days. In part, this attitude stemmed from their lack of resources and connections outside skid row, as well as the pervasive lack of hope offered in the area. But researchers also documented the ways in which skid rows met the basic needs of homeless men, by offering lodgings, meals, alcohol, and acquaintances, if few friends. Consolidated into a single district, the homeless might not have created a close-knit community, but their relationships had meaning. Dispersed across the landscape, later generations of homeless people would often struggle to maintain such connections.

Even though they lived in a world apart from mainstream society, the social science research of the 1960s had documented the continued participation of the homeless in the economic and political life of the city. Many city residents forgot about their presence, since the homeless were concealed on skid row. Many Bowery men, however, did not forget about the rest of the city and considered themselves both Americans and New Yorkers. Working, paying bills, and pursuing entertainment, the skid-row homeless led lives that proved far less exotic or whimsical than the tales circulated in the press and through mass-market paperbacks.

Research into homeless districts revealed richly detailed information about not only the demographics of skid row, but also the outlook and habits of its residents. Focusing tightly on theories about social affiliation, researchers disregarded the significance of many of their findings about the dynamics of race and sexual activity. As they discovered, skid-row society resembled that of the mainstream in some regards, echoing and exaggerating certain attitudes. But in other aspects, it remained a markedly distinct terrain.

Skid-Row Segregation

Prior to Columbia's Bowery project, generations of skid-row researchers had ignored the plight of homeless African Americans. In part this neglect stemmed from a popular notion that the postwar urban homeless were nearly all white. Others have speculated that African Americans provided one another with mutual assistance in times of need, keeping many from reaching the streets. Some homeless individuals also congregated in areas of African American neighborhoods like Harlem, outside the confines of the skid rows studied by social scientists.[69]

Yet even when the era's researchers generated substantial data on homeless people of color, as the Columbia team did, they failed to analyze those findings in light of the effects of racial discrimination. Instead, they focused almost exclusively on demographic trends and levels of alcohol consumption among homeless African Americans. Thus they knew that African American Bowery men were younger than their white counterparts, with a median age of forty-six versus fifty-six. They also confirmed that African Americans landed on skid row at an earlier age than did most whites; only 3 percent were over fifty on arrival on the Bowery, contrasted with nearly 25 percent of Irish, and one in six Northern Europeans. But their findings did not prompt an analysis of the reasons for such trends. African American respondents were not asked to detail their perceptions of how their lives had been shaped by structural and overt racism. Similarly, researchers did not develop a means of studying which social networks useful to whites might be closed to African Americans, if any. Overall, researchers found simply that the ethnic composition of skid-row populations varied widely between locations, but typically paralleled the demographics of each city's overall population. In Minneapolis, whites comprised 95 percent of the homeless population, while African Americans accounted for only 3 percent. By contrast, African Americans made up between one-fourth and one-third of the Bowery population, loosely reflecting their proportion within the population of New York City.[70]

Researchers also demonstrated curiously little interest in the highly segregated nature of the nation's skid rows. Focusing tightly on the individual behavioral traits that might render and keep a man homeless, analysts largely avoided broader questions of race relations, both on and off skid row. But the racism that poisoned American culture in this era permeated skid row as well. Images of African Americans as violent, dangerous criminals proved especially potent on the Bowery, exacerbating the area's racially discriminatory practices. Fearing the "black jackroller" who brutally attacked and robbed his victims, homeless whites justified continued segregation on skid row.[71]

Racial politics defined life in the lodging houses, a core institution of Bowery life. Eighty percent of Bowery residents patronized the area's lodging houses, far more than utilized the services of the missions. More than a place to sleep, many hotels provided homeless men with lobby access, a place to spend the day watching television. They also offered check cashing, mail service, property holding, and sometimes the extension of credit; a man's hotel comprised an important aspect of his life.[72]

Whites and African Americans found very different options in Bowery lodgings. Some hotels, like the Dakota, catered to an all-white clientele of some economic standing. The hotel's management actively refused to accept muni lodging tickets, and while the owner claimed that a sober, well-dressed, nonviolent African American man would be admitted, none appeared. The Dakota's residents enjoyed access not only to check cashing services, but also to soda, candy, and ice cream machines. At the other end of the spectrum, hotels like Victor House excluded no one. Most Victor residents were African Americans holding lodging tickets from the muni. All guests were treated equally, and enjoyed the same privileges. A third type of hotel, such as India House, welcomed a diverse clientele, but afforded some residents preferential treatment. African Americans, whites, muni ticket bearers, and paying residents all utilized the hotel. But men whose expenses were paid by the muni were not permitted to watch the lobby television and were required to leave the building each morning by 7 a.m.[73]

Racial segregation also divided Bowery bars, the cornerstone of the area's social life. Of the area's twenty-two bars, only the Old Landmark and Bar Seven attracted a primarily African American clientele. Most patrons of the other bars were white, though some establishments served African American customers. Important not only as places to drink, but also as sites of access to employment, information, and social networks, the bars' relative segregation merited far more attention than it received from social scientists. Columbia researchers accepted largely at face value the claims of Bowery staff that the homeless voluntarily chose residential and social segregation. Although such "self-sorting" was rumored to be common in a variety of settings, including gospel missions, parks, and drunk court, the topic was not one explored by researchers who did not ask the homeless their opinions on integration.[74]

Some types of racial segregation were inarguably structural. At Camp La-Guardia, where African Americans made up over 25 percent of the resident population, racial segregation had long been an official policy. The staff not only made segregated dormitory assignments, they also routinely delegated the worst jobs to African American residents, such as working on the "coal gang" loading and unloading coal by hand. Such discriminatory practices, as well as accusations of financial misconduct, sparked a scandal resulting in the departure of the camp's executive director. By the time of the Columbia study, new staff had shifted residence and work assignments, and had largely integrated the camp.[75]

On skid row, too, some jobs were racially segregated. In Philadelphia, African Americans were routinely passed over for positions through employment agencies, recruited instead for low-paying agricultural day labor harvesting tomatoes and berries. Working thirteen- or fourteen-hour days for minimal wages, some laborers spent their meager earnings on food and wine.[76]

At Camp LaGuardia, the Columbia team met two African American men whose employment histories reflected the dead-end nature of work in low-skilled, nonunion trades and the services industries. Forty-nine-year-old Harvey, a Camp LaGuardia resident for a year, was the youngest of five children born to a Connecticut factory worker and a housewife. A poor student before leaving school during the Depression, he never realized his childhood dream of becoming a doctor or an undertaker, working instead as a porter, shipping clerk, pinball and slot machine repairman, waiter, sheet metal inspector, and dishwasher. Like many African Americans of his generation, he achieved his highest level of professional responsibility in the armed forces, earning the rank of corporal while serving in the Army from 1942 to 1947. His neighbor, forty-seven-year-old R. Carter, had been to Camp LaGuardia eight times since 1960. Raised in Washington, D.C., the eldest of six children of a Department of Agriculture employee and a housewife, he left school after ninth grade to seek employment. As a young man, he wanted to become a professional boxer. At twenty-one, he fought six matches in the Golden Gloves Amateur Athletic Union, but that ended his involvement in the sport. He worked as a cook in the navy during World War II and later spent five years in prison. He supported himself as a dishwasher, deliveryman, file mover, car loader, freight handler, hospital ward attendant, and just prior to his Columbia interview, numbers runner. Although never arrested for drunkenness, the former boxer was charged with assault twenty-six times. He held no optimism for the future; when asked where he expected to be in a year, he replied, "If luck don't change, in a penitentiary." Possessing only a limited education and few professional skills, such men faced few opportunities to improve their socioeconomic status.[77]

Unfounded assumptions about the character and culture of African Americans led researchers away from the potentially insightful analysis their data might have yielded. Approaching Camp LaGuardia, Columbia researchers predicted that older men and African Americans would make up a substantial portion of the population because "Negroes have lower self-esteem and since there is less premium on self-respect in lower-class Negro culture." During the 1930s, a number of social and mental scientists studied the effects of racism and segregation on the personalities, behavior, and self-esteem of African Americans. John Dollard, a Yale University sociologist, applied Freudian analysis to those with whom he interacted in Mississippi. The Columbia team did not pursue similar strategies, focusing instead on a model of affiliation that did not foreground race. The biases embedded in the research directed toward homelessness foreclosed other, potentially fruitful modes of inquiry.[78]

Although skid row demonstrated more crude racism than some other areas of the city, it remained relatively welcoming toward homosexual activity. Gay prostitution occurred regularly in some Bowery bars, as did friendly homosexual cruising. While conducting participant observation at the One Mile Bar, Columbia's George Nash observed several homosexual advances, characterizing them as "the standard sexual release" for some of the regular patrons.[79]

Some men found male partners useful on the Bowery, as they could provide needed lodging and assistance. As one homeless man told Nash, "They sure have nice rooms; they live by themselves. They will never give you no money but they'll give you a good meal and it's a good place to get cleaned up." Other skid-row men found same-sex relationships acceptable, if less desirable than heterosexual ones. One homeless man admitted to such episodic, pragmatic homosexuality in crude terms: "Sure, I've gone with some fags—when I couldn't afford women."[80]

For other skid-row men, homosexual relationships lasted far longer than a brief encounter; the gay relationships between "jockers" and "punks," common during the hobo era of the late nineteenth and early twentieth century, sometimes played out on postwar skid rows. One mass-market paperback on homelessness detailed the experiences of Jimmy Ferguson, a Kansas native in his early thirties, who ran away from an abusive father at fourteen and spent several weeks tramping. An older man known as "Red Bill" pressured Ferguson into a long-term, abusive homosexual relationship. In the jargon of the road, Ferguson played the "punk" to Bill's "jocker," and Bill kept Ferguson with him for many years through threats and intimidation, ultimately abandoning him for a younger man.[81]

In a similar deviation from the norms of mainstream society, sexual encounters on the Bowery often crossed ethnic and racial lines. Many homeless men sought the company of the area's female prostitutes, most of whom were African American. Homosexual relationships among men, too, were frequently interracial. The laxity of the social rules governing sexual partnerships, in part originated in men's receptivity to skid row's rare sexual opportunities.[82]

On one level, the relative acceptance of homosexuality on skid row echoed the more widespread behavior patterns of the nineteenth century, when sexual activity less strictly defined one's identity. Not unlike the broader situation in many postwar prison communities, such tolerance of same-sex relations, elaborately justified on the basis of situational necessity, nonetheless took place in a broader context of persistent racism. Although homosexuality remained categorized as a form of mental disorder by the American Psychiatric Association until 1973, social scientists studied same-sex relations in a variety of projects from academic research to sordid, popular paperback treatises. But the Columbia team and their colleagues in other cities did not find such an approach to skid row compelling, choosing instead simply to acknowledge the relatively open displays of homosexuality witnessed by researchers.[83]

The skid-row homeless maintained selective social customs and regulations from mainstream society. Their decisions in this regard served the interests of the majority of skid-row residents. Racial segregation reflected the ingrained attitudes of many among the era's middle-aged white population, which allowed impoverished white men to maintain a sense of cultural superiority. Similarly, the area's liberal attitudes toward sexual practices maximized the opportunities afforded homeless men for sexual release.

As a distinct geographic region, skid row was at once part of the city, yet set apart from its central functions. The area's marginal status paralleled that of its denizens, who remained residents of the city, yet obeyed unusual codes of behavior. The conflicting, often crude sentiments expressed by the homeless, preserved and presented in social science research, convey the perspectives of men struggling to impose and maintain social order in an atmosphere of seeming abandon. Their social practices sometimes closely reflected those of other city residents, and at other moments adapted them significantly. As shown by the careful research conducted in the 1960s, skid rows were not simply a physically separate zone; they also operated under a distinct code of behavior and ethics.

Although their work paid relatively little attention to questions of race and sexual activity, Bowery researchers hoped to rectify a major gap in the social scientific literature on another front. Acknowledging the paucity of knowledge about the lives and experiences of homeless women, they set out to collect the relevant data and compare it to their findings on homeless men. Their research revealed several stark differences between the two groups, alongside a number of similarities.

"The Bowery ain't no place for a lady"

In 1968, the Columbia University research team launched a two-year study of homeless women. The marked lack of social scientific research into the lives of homeless women stemmed in part from the differences between their recognizable life patterns and those of homeless men. On most of the nation's skid rows, women comprised a small minority. In Minneapolis, for instance, homeless men outnumbered their female counterparts twenty-three to one. Bogue's Chicago research, too, found women only 3 percent of the skid-row population. Rarely sleeping outdoors or congregating in skid-row districts, women had been largely ignored by previous social scientists.[84]

In order to avoid replicating the research pitfalls of their predecessors, the Columbia team crafted a program ensuring they would work with a sizable female population, including in their research not only those women lodged at the city's women's shelter, a population they termed "literally homeless," but also older women living elsewhere in the city in residential hotels and apartment buildings. The small rooms these women occupied sometimes provided longer-term lodgings than the overnight accommodations of skid row, yet the Columbia team felt their residents remained sufficiently isolated and alienated from mainstream society to warrant study under the project umbrella. They repeatedly compared the women's shelter population to that of Camp LaGuardia, while they saw the female hotel residents loosely paralleling their sample of working-class men.[85]

The team began the project with the premise that women were more often disaffiliated than men. This stemmed in part from their longevity, the theory held, as they outlived their husbands, partners, families, and friends, only to find themselves increasingly alone. Although the researchers acknowledged that some single women remained socially affiliated, they expected the loss of family ties to affect women more severely than men, given the era's continued emphasis on the centrality of marriage, children, and family to women's lives.[86]

In their pilot study of the women's shelter, the Columbia team encountered an extremely marginalized population. Of the ten random sample cases investigated, seven clients had been previously housed in psychiatric hospitals, while seven suffered from drinking problems. The extreme alienation and relative psychological abnormality of the women's shelter clients did not exclude the subjects from the project. By contrast, those traits made them more attractive to the researchers, who branded theirs "an extreme and most deviant form of disaffiliation," but found them an ever more desirable site for evaluating their hypotheses about "the etiology of homelessness, isolation, and disaffiliation." The research team set out to evaluate the relative affiliation of the women in their study based on social relationships, employment, and memberships in voluntary organizations.[87]

Whereas other cities' skid rows housed few women, the Bowery hosted the city's principal shelter for the era's single or unattached homeless women. Women with children were referred to the family shelter by the city, while those seeking assistance for only themselves were routed to the Emergency Assistance Unit in the Pioneer Hotel at Bowery and Broome Streets. In operation since 1959, the Unit provided round-the-clock services to unattached, homeless women needing lodgings.[88]

The services provided at the women's shelter, which occupied a portion of the Pioneer Hotel's rooms, emphasized shelter over programs assisting women out of homelessness. Vouchers enabled residents to eat in nearby restaurants, and access was granted to Alcoholics Anonymous, physicians, and psychiatrists. But the bulk of residents' time remained unstructured. They were not allowed to remain in their rooms during the day, so over half spent the bulk of their time in the facility's television room. As one woman remarked: "I sit in the TV room; I sit in the recreation room; I sit outside Broome Street; I sit in the park on Grand Street; I just sit."[89]

Although skid row was known for fostering little sense of community, its female residents proved especially alienated. Nearly two-thirds of the Camp LaGuardia residents reported having acquaintances in the Bowery area, but only one-fifth of the women's shelter residents maintained such relationships. Homeless women, overall, lived a more solitary existence, sometimes by choice. One woman expressed satisfaction with her social isolation, citing it as a personal philosophy: "I don't associate with people. That's my motto." The individualistic lives of many respondents lent credibility to researchers' hypotheses.[90]

The Columbia research team did not focus on issues pertaining to race or racism, all the more surprising in light of the 44 percent of women's shelter residents who were African American. The combined effects of structural racism and sexism left African American women doubly marginalized, facing obstacles ranging from employment and housing discrimination to cultural and social proscriptions. But such factors did not spur researchers to develop a critique of the systemic inequalities leading many women to homelessness. Instead, the research team framed their findings in terms reminiscent of the traditional dichotomies between the "worthy" and "unworthy" poor. Many clients at the women's shelter, they concluded, suffered less from unjust circumstances than their own personal problems. For many at the shelter, Caplow observed, "disaffiliation culminated a long series of wrong choices and personal failures, drunkenness and desertion, shoplifting and marital violence, abused children and neglected obligations." Locating many of the causative factors of homelessness in the actions and habits of the homeless women under study, the research team downplayed many relevant socioeconomic factors. In largely avoiding the topic of race and the effects of racism, they ensured minimizing a potentially significant factor.[91]

As Caplow observed, the family backgrounds of many women's shelter clients had been filled with strife. Many grew up in abusive or neglectful childhood homes, and many witnessed the departure of one parent through either desertion or divorce. In part due to these circumstances, many left home at a young age, later relying little on parental support. Yet the Columbia researchers emphasized not the economic impact of such "broken" homes, but the psychosocial ones, looking instead for patterns of subsequent disaffiliation.[92]

In their own marriages, too, most homeless women interviewed had not found stability. Over 75 percent of the women's shelter clients had been married, as compared to fewer than half the Camp LaGuardia men. Women also continued to pursue marital happiness, often via multiple marriages. To be sure, the economic realities of the era's elderly and middle-aged women, who often lacked skills for gainful employment, made the divorce or desertion of a husband a precipitating factor in many clients' homelessness. The limited and sometimes nonexistent resources available to such women left many with no alternatives to the public shelter.[93]

Widowhood proved especially devastating. The loss of a husband pressed many women into poverty, and some to such depths of inconsolable despair that everyday activities proved impossible. The experience of a Brooklyn native who participated in the Columbia study illustrates the economic and psychological devastation of such losses. Born in 1914, Carrie spent her childhood on the Lower East Side. After dropping out of high school, she worked in a garment factory. She married an older man, with whom she shared a happy and loving marriage; choosing to remain childless, the couple aborted two pregnancies. Ten years into the marriage, her husband died of cancer. After her parents died later that year, Carrie found herself homeless. She slept on the subway, in parks, and in public restrooms for the next twenty-five years, claiming not to mind her isolation: "I want to be left alone; I enjoy being alone; I'm individualistic." Widowhood left her not only unable to provide for herself, but also lacking the motivation to build a home.[94]

The Columbia team found few strong ties between homeless women and their children. Although they focused on the relative level of affiliation signified by such strained relationships, the economic impact also proved central to clients' lives. In an era when many working-class American families continued to provide financial support to aging relatives, the homeless women surveyed enjoyed few generous relationships with family members. Many had extremely limited contact with their children, including one who did not see her daughter for eight years, even though she lived less than two blocks away.[95]

Although the Columbia team foregrounded the significance of such problematic family relationships in women's journey to homelessness, they found no single causative factor at work, as was also the case in their study of male homelessness. Instead, they used multiple regression analysis to determine that aging was the strongest factor in producing disaffiliates, followed by income status, and then social interaction. As these factors played out in the experiences of the women under study, portraits emerged of complex lives filled with various challenges and difficult decisions. The researchers frequently encountered women struggling with the combined effects of mental illness, disorientation, desire for independence, alcoholism, belligerence, venereal disease, and drug use.[96]

The life history of one respondent offers an example of the complex, intertwined problems facing a single individual. A fifty-year-old Coney Island native residing at the women's shelter married at sixteen and had two daughters. On deserting her in 1963, her second husband took their ten-year-old daughter with him. The client reported working as a dancer and waitress over the years, but now displayed emotional and mental instability. Afraid of mysterious individuals she believed were attempting to kill her, she also objected to being "ordered around" at the women's shelter. In the past, she had spent time in a mental hospital; her physical health was also failing, as she complained of asthma, colitis, and gastric ulcers. She had received public assistance since 1965, but alcoholism and mental illness made managing funds difficult.[97]

Later researchers collected narratives from homeless women that reflected similarly complicated clusters of events. A woman who had worked at ABC television before suffering a breakdown later recalled,

I loved my job but the pressures were tremendous. I left thirteen
years ago in '67. I wasn't fired and I didn't say in so many words
that I was quitting. I just said I was so depressed. I can't pinpoint
it. But if I could I could cure myself. I think my mother dying, and
me being alone and the pressures of the job did it. I was thirty-
eight then and my mother and I lived together up until that point.
I was never married, then I was alone. I was like an old clock. I
just sort of ran down.[98]

The Columbia team concluded that women's homelessness differed from that
of men, resulting most often not from the loss of a job, but from the end of
either an official or common-law marriage. Rather than advocating for development of resources that might assist women in such a predicament, the
researchers limited their recommendations to the scope of their research para-
digm. The women they interviewed in residential hotels and apartments might
benefit from programs designed to foster increased social interactions. But for
the clients of the women's shelter, the researchers maintained little optimism.
"The bleakness of the program reflects the hopelessness of the underlying social technology," Caplow observed. "Something ought to be done about the
bleakness, for decency's sake, but the hopelessness is probably irremovable."[99]

Ironically, some homeless women surveyed maintained more hope for
their own future and offered suggestions for social services they felt would
improve Bowery conditions. When researchers probed homeless women's
attitudes toward skid row, most shelter residents did not fear the neighborhood, but many complained of the presence and behavior of homeless men.
Calling them "drunken bums," the women cited a need for increased programs to help the "sick." One advised, "Rehabilitate men and women on the
Bowery. Get them jobs, put them to work." She went on to urge increased
hospital admissions for both alcoholics and mental patients.[100]

The complex role of social scientists and journalists who visited the Bowery in search of information on homelessness involved navigating social hierarchies and inspiring trust. Although suspected of suffering from low self-
image, many homeless individuals maintained high levels of personal pride,
as articulated by "Pig Head Hattie," one of Harris's informants. Harris re-
counted a minor altercation with Hattie over an incident at the women's shelter. She defended her self-respect vigorously: "Do you think just because it
happened to so happen you met me on the Bowery, a girl ain't got her pride?
Me remind one of them lousy, crawling social workers anything? I got my

pride same's the next one or you, yourself, too. I got my pride." Hattie also offered a perceptive critique of the approaches adopted by area researchers a few weeks later: "You think you got us fooled. Go on, you ain't fooling nobody. Everybody's got your number. All you're doing around here is you're looking for types. I met a lady writer one time, she came from a newspaper though, said that right out."[101]

Many journalists who visited the Bowery did look for dramatic examples of despair and bizarre behavior. Social scientists, on the whole, focused on the more "average" cases they discovered. Although their efforts were considerably less crass than Hattie's estimation, researchers did seek to categorize the homeless into demographic groups and develop relatively simplistic understandings of their poverty and journey to the shelters. Women's homelessness, they discovered, reflected their role in society at large. The end of a romantic partnership or other family connection most often propelled them into poverty. The era's researchers pondered the women's "failures" at building stable relationships, wondering how such fates could be avoided. They focused little on the limited resources available to deserted women, especially those lacking marketable job skills, posing few practical improvements to their condition.

Homeless and impoverished women at mid-century thus faced a different set of experiences than did their male counterparts. Many shared the tendency toward alcoholism, substance use, and infrequent employment. Fewer congregated in shelters, though, remaining whenever possible in hotels and rented rooms. The Columbia team's innovative approach to tabulating the female homeless population, which allowed them to include among the homeless those individuals who were living in hotels and apartments, underscored the problematic nature of most definitions of homelessness. Especially in the case of women, focusing solely on the streets and shelters produced an incomplete picture of the population. Yet the distinction also emphasized the close connection between "homelessness" and the situation classified simply as "poverty." The inclusion of marginally housed individuals in any enumeration of the homeless makes clear the transitory nature of homelessness, but also the dangers of limiting an understanding of the issue to the concerns of those without shelter at a given moment.

New Social Services

Postwar urban, liberal policy makers often turned to social scientific data when developing urban policy, hoping for findings predicting positive outcomes. The most famous and successful such policy intervention was carried out by psychologists Kenneth and Mamie Clark, whose research into racial segregation had strongly influenced the Supreme Court in its *Brown v. Board of Education of Topeka, Kansas* decision. The Clarks' "Black doll experiment" tested young children's self-image and self-esteem in the context of racial segregation. When asked to color an outlined figure in a manner that resembled themselves, African American children routinely chose a lighter shade than their skin would warrant, and indicated that white dolls were more beautiful than black ones. Such findings were used to support the legal argument that segregation was damaging the self-esteem of African American children, leading to the integration of the nation's schools.[102]

Surely the most influential failed attempt to shape public policy through social science was that of Daniel Patrick Moynihan's report on "The Negro Family."[103] Like the Clarks, Moynihan grounded his work in the desire for social justice. Moynihan's report described the African American family as pathologically matriarchal. Weak men, aggressive women, and wayward children, Moynihan argued, were symptoms of a broken family structure that must be fixed before real social equality would be possible. Moynihan drew on the research to argue for programs designed to achieve racial equality. But his theories were quickly adopted by neoconservatives, who rejected aiding the African American population. By the 1984 publication of Charles Murray's *Losing Ground*, the rhetoric of pathology had become completely co-opted by neoconservative critics of public assistance. Scholars have observed in the trajectory of Moynihan's theories "the decline of liberalism."[104]

The 1960s witnessed urban officials using social science to address and end homelessness. As vagrancy and drunkenness charges were increasingly dismissed, they hoped to direct the homeless to appropriate facilities. Republican mayor John Lindsay, whose greatest legacy in the area of homeless policy was the pioneering "scatter-site" housing program, which secured apartments for homeless families in working-class neighborhoods, called for the establishment of a "drying-out" center for homeless alcoholics. Lindsay approached the innovative Vera Institute of Justice in May 1966, and planning began.[105]

Established as a nonprofit organization in 1961, the Vera Institute developed programs to improve the relationships between individuals and the justice system. With the aid of a Ford Foundation planning grant, the Vera Institute staff put into practice a type of program that Operation Bowery had envisioned. They secured a site at the muni, which was by then offering only day services to the homeless. They also enlisted the support of nearby St. Vincent's Hospital, which would admit men in crisis while also providing lab services to the program. After a pilot outreach study was completed, the Manhattan Bowery Project (MBP) was opened.[106]

Clients showered, then received a physical examination and sedation. After three days of intensive treatment, which sometimes included intravenous feeding, patients were moved to a recuperation ward, where they met with a caseworker to work on a referral plan. Many of the referrals were related to serious medical conditions, as nearly two-thirds of the patients suffered from pulmonary disease, 23 percent suffered from liver disease, nearly 40 percent were diagnosed with personality disorders, and one-third as schizophrenics.[107]

The program successfully recruited clients, with 73 percent of the men approached agreeing to receive assistance. After initial challenges communicating with African American homeless men, the MBP staff made a conscious effort to cross cultural divisions by increasing minority enrollment. After completing the five-day program, clients were referred to organizations including Camp LaGuardia, the Bowery Mission, Operation Bowery, the Rikers Island TB Unit, or the MBP's after-care clinic.[108]

In an effort to provide more comprehensive services, the MBP opened a "supported work" program that employed homeless alcoholics to clear vacant lots. This program was then expanded into Project Renewal, which employed homeless men to work part-time clearing lots for the City of New York. Program participants completed group therapy, individual counseling, and had access to educational and recreational opportunities. During four years of operation, Project Renewal reported over 20 percent of participants completing the program, with 75 percent of those men remaining sober. The MBP would build on this program to launch Supportive Therapeutic Environment Program (STEP) in 1973, lodging fourteen men in an SRO hotel while providing them with counseling and vocational and recreational activities.[109]

As a groundbreaking organization, the MBP early on faced some of the challenges that would occupy programs assisting the homeless throughout the coming decades, as residents of many communities refused to allow the homeless to live among them. After Project Renewal faced hostility in Brooklyn, program administrators exercised great care during future moves, working closely with neighborhood block associations and community groups. These strategies would become critical for residential facilities hoping to put down roots in often hostile working- and middle-class residential areas.[110]

During the 1960s, city officials had attempted to merge the findings of social investigators with the goals of social service providers in developing services for the homeless. Increasingly comprehensive programs included mental health services, medical care, job training and employment assistance, as well as traditional shelter facilities. Several of the new programs proved successful and enduring, fostering positive change in the lives of many homeless individuals. Because such programs were established away from the Bowery district, administrators developed strategies to convince area residents the homeless were not a population to be feared.

Yet by the late 1960s social turmoil and political protest had rendered the decade's early optimism distant and foreign. As President Lyndon Johnson's War on Poverty withered and paled beside the Vietnam conflict, poor Americans fell from the nation's agenda. The growing controversies around efforts to mobilize impoverished individuals, coupled with the mounting frustrations of many African Americans, left Johnson confused and bitter. He criticized Special Assistant Sargent Shriver for falling in with "kooks and sociologists." The federal urban programs sponsored by the Office of Economic Opportunity had brought money into the nation's cities and created new programs aiding many residents. Liberal Republican mayor Lindsay surprised many supporters when the number of residents receiving public assistance rose dramatically during his administration, exploding from 531,000 in 1965 to 1.25 million by 1972. The welfare crisis fueled the broader urban fiscal crisis of the 1970s. Across the country, cities struggled with "welfare crises" as benefit amounts increased.[111]

By the end of the 1960s, Oscar Lewis's culture of poverty thesis drew more condemnation than praise. Reviewing Lewis's work, Theodore Caplow described the publication of *The Children of Sanchez* as "an epical event," but called *La Vida* "a nasty book," that was "unreadable without its large component of pornography." Its author was "implacably hostile to his unfortunate subjects." Lewis fired back, accusing Caplow of misconstruing his intent, which was not to criticize impoverished individuals but the society that structured their reality. As he would time and again, Lewis defended his approach: "There is nothing in the concept which puts the onus of poverty on the character of the poor. Nor does the concept in any way play down the exploitation and neglect suffered by the poor." Not only were social scientific approaches to poverty under attack from politicians and community activists, the debate between the scholars involved had turned acrimonious.[112]

Although Caplow saw in Lewis's work flaws not inherent in his own, the two participated in similar efforts to locate the causes of poverty in the life histories of individual poor people. At their core, these social scientific approaches probed case histories for explanations of individual journeys to poverty. In so doing, they largely disregarded the broader structural factors causing poverty and homelessness. Economic trends, unemployment rates, racism, sexism, homophobia, deindustrialization, rising rents, and other possible causes of homelessness that would shape later sociological approaches to the subject, were eclipsed by the persistent focus on the individual. Studying the poor rather than poverty, the era's social scientists advanced only a partial understanding of homelessness. The skid-row homeless emerged from their studies as a diverse group of individuals who shared little other than long-term poverty, often heavy drinking habits, and a willingness to tolerate the conditions of shelter and hotel life.

As the 1960s ended, anomie faded from favor among poverty policy analysts. The work of Bahr, Caplow, and their peers on the nature of individual problems foreshadowed the key issues that would dominate the "new" homelessness of the 1970s and 1980s. One scholar termed the relationship between "assumed pathology" and skid-row life a "chicken-egg riddle." Untangling adaptive responses to the unfamiliar and difficult environment of skid row from the traits inherent to a homeless individual's character struck some as nearly impossible. In the coming decades, researchers would turn away from sociological disaffiliation, focusing instead on equally individual concerns such as substance abuse and mental illness in their efforts to understand and end homelessness.[113]

CHAPTER 6

THE END OF THE SKID-ROW ERA

I N his memoir of New York City homelessness, Lee Stringer described with biting irony the surprise of a professional coming across a cluster of homeless people sleeping in Grand Central Station. Summarizing the divide between even the era's iconic cocaine-snorting yuppie population and its crack-smoking homeless one, he observed, "I remember thinking, this guy's obviously no New Yorker. After four years' exposure to 'the homeless,' sights like this had ceased to startle the rank and file of Gotham. Like Ellison's *Invisible Man*, we had receded into that part of the landscape that refused to support the American Dream. And which few are wont to see. Nonpeople in a no-man's void." By the 1980s, those who used the city's streets as thoroughfares became increasingly adept at avoiding those for whom they served as a residence. The end of the skid-row era did not mean the end of homelessness, but the dispersal of the homeless population across the city. In New York, as in other cities, the homeless lived openly in both residential neighborhoods and business districts.[1]

Displaced from the city's residential, economic, and social systems, the homeless appeared on the streets in record numbers. Not since the Depression had "the flotsam of New York" so commanded the city's attention. Observers frequently drew comparisons between the situation of the 1930s and that of the late 1970s and early 1980s. Both eras witnessed thousands of poor individuals and families crowding into shelters and cowering in doorways seeking refuge from the elements.[2]

Yet the urban landscape of the 1970s proved in many respects even less hospitable than the bleakest days of the Great Depression. Whereas the

Roosevelt administration had responded to the economic crisis with the residential Federal Transient Program, the Carter and Reagan administrations avoided expansive programs adopting the homeless as charges of the federal government. In the bigger picture, even the Roosevelt administration's bold expansion of the nation's social welfare programs had not offered lasting protection to the homeless. Many of the working-class Americans who had benefited from the safety net, however, were now propelled into homelessness by the retraction of its provisions. The limits placed on programs, ranging from food stamps to disability benefits, chipped away at the fragile barrier between some impoverished individuals and the streets.

Policy developments at the state and city level also fueled the explosion of the homeless population. Across the nation, cities had demolished their skid rows by the 1970s, often in pursuit of renewed business districts. New York City also struggled to house the homeless in the wake of its previous efforts to eradicate their lodgings. The crush of homeless individuals, many with special needs, overwhelmed systems sponsoring fewer facilities than had been available in previous decades. As New York State and New York City wrangled over the financial and administrative responsibility for the mentally ill, thousands of people in need of care landed on the streets. Mayor Koch, who had admired Mayor LaGuardia in many regards, lacked a presidential counterpart such as Roosevelt to support his mayoral efforts. Instead, Koch battled the Reagan administration for support.[3]

The seemingly sudden appearance of the "new" homeless population in the late 1970s reflected changing mental health policies, shifting tax law, and the federal reduction of social programs. The era also witnessed a new discourse of rights as judicial orders established shelter facilities for the homeless. New advocacy coalitions made skillful use of the judicial system and media, drawing on their status as "outsiders" to achieve significant victories on behalf of the homeless in an era witnessing the growth of few other social programs. As its skid row gave way to the forces of gentrification, New York sought new ways to shelter its homeless population.

Mental Illness and SRO Hotels

Urban America's homelessness crisis resulted largely from short-sighted municipal and state policies. Politically charged efforts to alter the care of the mentally ill and to encourage urban real estate revitalization revealed the deep, official roots of the rise of the "new" homelessness. The political origins of such policies varied from socially liberal to fiscally conservative. Their cumulative effects, however, proved devastating for the nation's cities.

As early as the 1950s, mental health professionals had called for changes to the existing system of care for the mentally ill. Many accused the common, large-scale, warehouse-like institutions of failing to address patient needs. Through the use of new types of drug therapy and a system of community-based mental health care, many psychiatrists believed patients would receive better, more individualized treatment. The system would also allow greater individual freedom, enabling patients to retain more personal dignity and autonomy. State and federal politicians supported the program, in large part because it promised substantial financial savings to some public bodies. The states funded patient care for those housed in mental hospitals, but cities supported local facilities. City coffers also paid 25 percent of the Medicaid costs incurred by formerly institutionalized mental patients. New York State and California led the movement to release mental patients to local communities. By the late 1960s, the deinstitutionalization movement had wrought dramatic changes in New York. In 1965, the state housed 84,000 mental patients; by 1979, that figure had dropped to only 24,000.[4]

As formerly institutionalized patients returned to the city, the initially envisioned comprehensive system of after-care and outpatient services failed to materialize. State funds did not follow the patients, and the city proved unable and unwilling to develop adequate supplemental programs. As a result, many mentally ill individuals—lacking the cognitive and behavioral skills to maintain drug therapies, keep appointments, secure housing, or navigate the hostile bureaucracies of the public welfare system—struggled to manage their own care.

Analysts debated the precise number of former mental patients who joined the ranks of the city's homeless. One frequently cited estimate placed the number near 6,000. During the early 1980s, state officials publicly acknowledged that approximately one-fifth of the homeless in shelters were former mental patients, although they insisted that only approximately 2 percent of those individuals required further hospitalization, the rest presumably posing no public threat.[5]

The deinstitutionalization movement brought mentally ill homeless individuals into the public realm, but many families had long struggled to care for mentally ill relatives. Writing to Mayor Wagner pleading for help in 1962, a Bronx welfare recipient described her fifty-four-year-old alcoholic brother as "a mental case." Moved by his plea for help, she had invited him to join her and her grandchildren in a four-room railroad flat in 1961. But his drinking had led his condition to deteriorate in recent years; he walked with a cane, talked to himself, and believed he heard voices talking about him. Sleeping with the light on, hiding knives under his mattress, and growing increasingly irate while intoxicated, he posed a threat to the household. Frustrated and desperate, she confided to the mayor, "The answer to his problems is not just getting him a room some other place. I feel he needs medical help." The conflicting agendas of city and state governments over the care of the mentally ill had left many such families struggling for decades.[6]

Some warned against associating all homeless individuals with mental illness, fearing the categorization would disempower the homeless and further pathologize poverty. Many also stressed the fine line between cause and effect in this regard, as the intense strain of homelessness precipitated or caused mental problems for many individuals. As lawyer Robert Hayes remarked, "There is a difference between bizarre behavior brought on by fatigue and the paranoia of street living, and actual psychiatric disorder."[7]

Traditional homeless programs offering a bed and a meal were unsuited to caring for mentally ill individuals. Shelter residents complained of clients yelling all night, talking to themselves, and otherwise displaying abnormal behavior. As cities nationwide witnessed an increased number of mentally ill homeless, open public hostility sometimes erupted. In California, for instance, reports surfaced of a "troll buster" t-shirt mocking the mentally ill homeless population and calling for their removal.[8]

Single, unattached individuals released from mental hospitals often moved into SRO hotels, where they joined those living on a fixed income, whether from private pensions, personal savings, or government benefits, who were unable to afford the city's rising rents for even studio apartments. As early as 1974, large numbers of disabled, blind, and elderly individuals living in SROs had been rendered homeless by changing welfare policy. Local welfare budgets had allowed them SRO rooms, but transfer to the federal Supplemental Security Income program meant smaller payments, insufficient to meet even SRO rents.[9]

Many of the city's SRO hotels were clustered on the Upper West Side and in Midtown, where city officials considered them a nuisance. To rid itself of the problem, the city instituted a tax abatement known as the "J-51" program, yielding disastrous effects for SRO residents. Offering tax incentives to those who converted SRO properties to middle-income and luxury apartments, the program fueled the eviction of thousands of poor individuals. Some SRO owners forcibly evicted tenants, while others simply stopped making necessary repairs, shut off heat and hot water, and otherwise pressed tenants to leave.[10]

By the early 1980s, Mayor Koch stopped defending the city's tax abatement policies and approved a law offering tax incentives to those choosing instead to upgrade SRO hotels. But the late effort had little effect; some estimated that more than 10,000 rooms had closed between 1975 and 1979 alone. In 1975, studies estimated that 290 hotels rented rooms for less than $50 per week. By 1981, that number had dropped to approximately 120. In 1982, Koch took further steps to block tenant harassment. By then, however, the rising real estate values in Midtown and Upper West Side areas provided powerful incentives for continued conversion of the remaining hotels to luxury housing.[11]

Koch faced criticism not only from advocates for the homeless, but also from Governor Hugh Carey, with whom he bickered publicly over the situation of the city's homeless population. Koch pointed to the state's former policy of deinstitutionalization of the mentally ill, arguing that the state had dropped the problem on the city's doorstep. Carey fired back, insisting that Koch exaggerated the number of mentally ill homeless and that the J-51 tax abatements had precipitated the crisis. Political leaders continued to evade responsibility for the situation, more intent on deflecting the blame than in developing effective solutions.[12]

The state and the city had thus created much of the era's homelessness crisis. Although mental health providers had pursued deinstitutionalization in order to obtain preferable patient care, the program had become thoroughly politicized. Ultimately, it allowed state officials to abandon many mentally ill individuals, especially those too competent to require care in convalescent facilities. As the number of formerly hospitalized mentally ill homeless individuals increased, some moved into congregate shelters, alienating other residents. Others avoided such facilities, due to fear or a desire to live elsewhere. Simultaneously, the city's own tax abatement program had depleted the remaining stock of low-income housing. Although cramped, deteriorated, and often unhygienic, SRO hotels had offered individuals a modicum of privacy as well as access to a social network. The system of congregate shelters that arose in their place did not meet the need for privacy, a primary concern of many individuals.

By the late 1970s, the city's homeless population displayed significant diversity. Not only the mentally ill, but also people of color and women emerged as major subpopulations among them, bringing to light new needs and concerns. Most important, the homeless no longer clustered in the relative privacy of the Bowery. Instead, they conducted their lives in public.

The "New" Homeless

Throughout the mid-century, New York's skid-row homeless population had been dominated by middle-aged white men. The media and the public had grown accustomed to seeing such "skid-row bums" clustering on and near the Bowery, as similar populations did in other major cities. The urban homeless population that emerged in the 1970s bore little resemblance to that of mid-century, however, and included many women, youths, and African Americans. These "new" homeless, as they were termed by the media, reflected shifts in the socioeconomic realities of urban life that shocked many observers. These homeless individuals and families did not remain on the nation's skid rows. In New York, they appeared throughout Manhattan, even in high-priced neighborhoods and business districts, and eventually scattered to the outer boroughs.

The increasing presence of women among the homeless disturbed many onlookers. Homeless women were hardly a new phenomenon, and their existence (especially when the women in question were mothers) had inspired empathy among the general public historically. As had been the case for decades, widows appeared disproportionately among the homeless population, a husband's death often leaving a wife unprepared for economic survival. Adding to the growth of female homelessness, the rising divorce rate, coupled with the early financial effects of no-fault divorce, left increasing numbers of women in poverty. As widows and divorcees entered the economy as single individuals, many lacked the education and job skills necessary to find a secure position. Those who were older had often also failed to accrue enough employment history to qualify for Social Security benefits. Victims of domestic violence, substance abusers, and those suffering from mental illness also struggled to locate adequate and appropriate social services, sometimes finding themselves out of options and newly homeless.[13]

As the postwar, work-based welfare state expanded, it continued to exclude the labor performed by many women. Domestic workers, cooks, and child-care providers, among others, were frequently paid off the books, leaving them with no security net in their later years. One homeless woman recalled, "I always worked. I worked for a rich lady up on 77th Street. I was cooking for company and everything. You know, eight and nine tables. She had parties twice a week. She paid me but they didn't want to know about signatures or tax. Nothing. They tell you that they don't remember so they don't have the tax to write up and the paper work." Since the inception of the Social Security system, many domestic workers have remained outside its scope.[14]

Many of the women interviewed during these years reflected wistfully on past households, dreaming of futures in which they would once again maintain a stable residence. Some remained optimistic that they might also find productive relationships, as part of a broader, secure lifestyle. One homeless woman described her desires: "I want to get on welfare now so I can at least get on my feet, build a foundation. Then I can get a job. I'll be independent again, have my own apartment, pay my own bills, buy my own food, my clothes. But I don't need anyone to hurt me anymore. I need someone to love me and help me. I want a nice man to fall in love with me and I know I could fall in love with him eventually. He could work and I could work and we could build a life together." Socialized to speak more freely about their emotional needs, homeless women talked poignantly about the loneliness of life on the streets that few men articulated. Their journey to homelessness was also inextricably linked to their romantic history, in many cases; for widows, abandoned women, and victims of abuse, past periods of stability involved both regular shelter and a partner.[15]

Many homeless women feared for their physical safety, even inside shelters and hotels. One described her situation in stark terms:

> The last hotel I stayed in was a thievy hotel. You could get robbed as soon as you went out. It had no running water, no locks in the bathroom, people could even grab you from behind. There were murders there, thievery, killing, dope fiends. I was scared. I heard screaming there at night, a woman. I don't know why. That place was getting bad but you get so used to it. As soon as I go out at night I have fear because I don't know who's in back of me. I've been robbed so much.[16]

Such fears prompted many homeless women to spurn shelters in favor of life on the streets. The media and the general public alike were horrified and fascinated by the sight of homeless women toting mysterious sacks filled with their possessions, giving rise to the term, "bag ladies." In a society that had traditionally viewed women as the weaker, dependent sex, entitled to protection, grandmothers, mothers, sisters, aunts, and daughters now wandered the streets alone. Fearing attack in dimly lit and deserted areas, many homeless women loitered overnight in train stations and bus terminals, offering a constant and poignant reminder of the feminization of postwar poverty.[17]

Social scientists' public pronouncements on the psychology of homeless women echoed the discourse of the Depression era, as women were again described as especially degraded. One sociologist noted, "The women are much more ashamed than the men about living on the streets, and most find it demeaning to have to beg from strangers." Despite the interventions of the Women's Movement, women remained markedly unequal to their male counterparts in American society of the late 1970s. The rules governing social behavior continued to add psychological vulnerability to the physical dangers facing homeless women. Older women, especially, who had not anticipated lives without partners, struggled to accept the new realities of their experience.[18]

Private charities and public institutions alike targeted the emerging population of homeless women with new programs including a more accessible storefront center. But the causes of female homelessness stemmed from the continued broader economic inequality of the sexes in American society, as well as women's social inferiority in many domestic relationships. As a result, truly combating female homelessness would require far more than a few well-meaning and specific programs. Instead, it would mean revamping public policies and divorce laws, as well as educational and cultural traditions, some of which continued to be revered by many Americans.[19]

Alongside the increasing female population, the demographics of the male homeless population were changing rapidly. Younger men were joining the older men who had comprised the core of New York's skid-row population in the postwar years. While many younger men drank heavily, as did their older counterparts, some also used heavier drugs, like heroin and cocaine. Young, violent drug users often attacked and robbed older homeless men, creating a climate of fear on the streets and in the shelters.[20]

Since the 1950s, the number of homeless African American New Yorkers had been gradually rising. Similar to the plight of homeless women, homeless minorities often struggled against structural factors in their journey to the streets. Urban African Americans and Latinos in the postwar era often lacked access to education and employment, leaving them in disproportionate poverty and sometimes dependent on social services. When those programs faced funding cuts, some clients found themselves among the homeless.[21]

Academic and political debates raged over the relative poverty of urban

African Americans. Many argued that the community was no better off economically than it had been twenty years earlier, while some cited marginal improvements. By the early 1980s, some estimated that two-thirds of muni applicants were African American. Older men whose work histories left them outside the Social Security system, those who received inadequate benefits, and those struggling with alcoholism found themselves homeless. Younger men, poorly educated and often addicted to drugs, joined their older counterparts at the muni.[22]

The increasing numbers of African American youth also fueled the rise of homelessness. During the 1960s, the population of urban African American youths between sixteen and nineteen increased by almost 75 percent. These young people entered a newly competitive labor market, in which specialized skills assumed critical importance. Lacking access to formal education and job training, many young African Americans gravitated toward street life.[23]

As the homeless population increased, New York's shelter system was unable to keep up with the rising demand. By the mid-1970s, homeless people were congregating on city streets throughout Midtown, Times Square, and Central Park. As the new homeless population was not confined to a skid row, they shared the city with all New Yorkers, a prospect that made many city residents uncomfortable. As urban dwellers became accustomed to seeing homeless people on subway platforms, in the vestibules of apartment buildings, in the public libraries, and sleeping on the streets of fashionable neighborhoods, many learned to ignore them.[24]

By the 1980s, as the homeless were living even below ground in subway tunnels and steam pipes below prestigious hotels, journalists began to compare New York to Calcutta. While one might expect stark human suffering, destitution, and individuals begging for food in a distant, poverty-stricken nation, few could comprehend the justification for such scenes in one of the world's most financially successful cities. As the Democratic National Convention arrived at Madison Square Garden in 1980, city officials removed the homeless from the area, hoping to hide the growing population from journalists and visitors.[25]

The move was an overreaction on the part of New York's elite, because such trends were occurring in cities across the country and would probably have been less than shocking to Convention visitors. By the early 1980s, the Salvation Army was assisting over 40,000 homeless people nationwide, as public systems of assistance proved insufficient to meet the rising need. Some cities, including San Jose and San Diego, tried to relocate the homeless outside of desirable downtown areas, while others, including Houston and

Washington, D.C., were forced to open new facilities offering hundreds of new shelter beds. The term "Greyhound therapy" was coined to describe the trend of officials issuing mentally ill homeless individuals one-way bus tickets to Southern California, in a desperate effort to shift the problem population to another state.[26]

Programs for the homeless varied widely between states. Massachusetts offered one of the most generous, humane programs, as governor Michael Dukakis worked toward funding community shelters, a referral program, and low-income housing, and streamlined public assistance procedures for those without fixed residences. By contrast, a Phoenix Anti-Skid Row Ordinance adopted in 1981 pressured missions, blood banks, flophouses, and bars to close their doors.[27]

During the 1970s, the city of New York had been driven to the brink of financial collapse by a combination of external and internal factors. In the context of a declining national economy, officials were unable to meet the colossal expenses of operating a city proud of its tradition of providing vital public services. Following the highly publicized crisis, residents lost faith in the ability of city agencies to continue operating at past levels.[28]

The policies of "New Federalism" enacted by the Reagan administration reduced federal funding to state and local governments. For New York, the results were dramatic. By 1989, the city drew 36 percent of its general operating funds from federal and state sources, compared to 50 percent less than ten years earlier. Cuts to Supplemental Security Income and other federal programs left many individuals poor and some homeless. Even though the nation's overall economy was sound, the poor were suffering and applying to homeless shelters in record numbers.[29]

New York City's infamously high cost of living meant that even some individuals who received both veterans' benefits and Social Security payments could not afford a market-rate apartment. Instead, they lived on the Bowery in transient hotels that required no large deposits in advance or proof of creditworthiness. Many homeless individuals also struggled to locate and preserve the information required to receive the benefits to which they were entitled, lacking copies of birth certificates, Social Security cards, and other documentation after years without a stable residence.[30]

The "new" homeless population that had emerged in New York City and across the nation in the late 1970s reflected the era's persistent social inequalities. African Americans remained on the city's economic margins, and many remained in poverty. The changing job market, cuts to social programs, and the rise of powerful, popular drugs pushed many African Americans into homelessness, especially the young. Women, too, comprised an increasing proportion of the homeless population. Unskilled, undereducated, and ill-prepared for independent life, many widows and other single women were without resources. With family living patterns of earlier eras long eroded, such women often turned to public assistance and then to the streets. Observers found female homelessness especially shocking and objectionable, and many were stirred to take action. Most significantly, the homeless were no longer neatly concealed on the Bowery. Instead, they lined the passageways of the city's subway and commuter rail stations, and slept in the vestibules of residential buildings. Their presence moved many New Yorkers to criticize the city's seeming indifference to the suffering of its residents, and some to envision a new system for their shelter.

The New Advocates

As the crisis of homelessness mounted, new voices arose to criticize existing social services. Previous generations of social scientific investigators, from Jacob Riis to the Columbia Bureau of Social Research, had offered insightful criticisms of poverty policy. During the late 1970s, similar insights came from sociologists and activist lawyers, who publicized existing conditions while calling for radical changes to the shelter system. Unlike their predecessors, this generation of activists was strikingly successful. As political outsiders, they controlled few resources. Yet through careful strategizing and effective use of the courts, they achieved many of their goals.

A 1982 study by two Columbia University doctoral candidates, Ellen Baxter and Kim Hopper, skillfully documented the extent of the city's homeless problem. Focusing on the services available to the homeless mentally ill, they sought to gather information that they could use to argue for improved conditions and programs. Over the course of twenty months, they interviewed two hundred of the city's homeless. After meeting residents of shelters, missions, subway stations, and street corners, Baxter and Hopper determined that not all the city's homeless could be easily identified visually. Many went to great lengths to maintain standards of personal hygiene, grooming, and comportment, and were noticeable only through their presence in public places after business hours. The study drew media attention to the homeless living in the city's public spaces, including Grand Central Station. Newspaper articles featured photos of the young researchers, frequently describing occasions on which they had themselves been mistaken as members of their subject population.[31]

The most controversial aspect of their report proved to be their estimate of the size of the city's homeless population. Drawing on a variety of sources, and extrapolating from the number of individuals seeking shelter, they estimated 30,000 homeless men and 6,000 homeless women in the city. They added that at least 16,000 homeless adults were mentally disabled. By contrast, they noted that only 3,200 public shelter beds were available. These figures and the gap between them attracted significant media and political attention. They argued that the city deterred impoverished individuals from applying for assistance by limiting available beds. This reluctance to seek assistance explained, in their estimation, the gap between their figures and those of public agencies. Rejecting their widely publicized estimate, the Koch administration announced plans to conduct its own tally of the city's homeless.[32]

Baxter and Hopper's research spanned the city, but they paid significant attention to the Bowery area. They investigated traditional venues for the homeless, such as the Bowery Mission and the Salvation Army's Booth House, as well as more recent additions such as the Manhattan Bowery Project's outreach program. They especially emphasized the role of commercial lodging houses in the city's plan. At that time, once public facilities were full, the muni distributed up to 1,150 referral vouchers to commercial hotels—including the Union, the Kenton, the Palace, the Sunshine, the Delevan, and the Stevenson. Hopper visited the Palace Hotel, describing the decent accommodations in cubicle rooms for paying guests, but criticizing the state of the dormitory rooms occupied by individuals referred from the muni. Filthy and decrepit, outfitted with broken lockers and few mattresses and dominated by racially segregated bed assignments, the dormitory offered few advantages to sleeping outdoors save in inclement weather.[33]

By contrast, Baxter and Hopper commended smaller, nonprofit agencies' efforts to provide more individualized care. "Digger-type" shelters, run not by evangelical missions but by nonprofit communal groups, most of which were religious, instituted fewer rules and fostered a less formal atmosphere than traditional religious missions. Such organizations emphasized acceptance and the importance of treating residents as peers. Baxter and Hopper highlighted the achievements of several model, small facilities, including the thirteen-bed Dwelling Place run by Catholic Charities, the 27-bed women's Mary House and 35-bed men's Joseph House administered by the Catholic Workers, and the Star of the Sea Program.[34]

They especially praised the St. Francis Residence on East 24th Street, where a group of Franciscan friars and others interested in finding new solutions to the problems of the homeless had recently taken over operations of a welfare hotel. Their renovated facility housed one hundred men and women at rates of $35 to $50 per week, and offered meals and recreational and medical services. The organization stressed independent living and the dignity of the residents, many of them former mental patients. In other areas, they commended Boston's Pine Street Inn. Operating in the South End for over sixty years, the facility housed up to five hundred people. The staff provided comprehensive services, working to maintain especially high levels of courtesy and respect toward guests. Baxter and Hopper contrasted the substandard public accommodations and superior private shelters to enhance their argument that the poor quality of public facilities dissuaded needy individuals from seeking shelter. If decent opportunities were presented to the homeless, they argued repeatedly, many would accept assistance.[35]

In 1979, another "outsider" to the city's political scene launched an ambitious legal campaign on behalf of the city's homeless population. Robert Hayes, a young antitrust attorney, filed a lawsuit on behalf of three homeless men as a pro bono project. The suit named Governor Carey and Mayor Koch as responsible for the suffering of the homeless. *Callahan v. Carey* argued that the city shelter was understaffed and inadequate. It further charged that the lodging houses to which men were referred were unsanitary, and that even there, not all men found accommodations. Hayes insisted that squalid and demeaning conditions suppressed demand for city shelters. By offering only a "bed of nails," as the theory was known, the city dissuaded the poor from requesting and receiving assistance.[36]

Advocates for the homeless, who pressed for the right to shelter ordinances during the late 1970s and early 1980s, drew on a variety of legal strategies. Some based arguments on state constitutions or welfare laws, while others grounded their work in federal statutory rights and regulations. In *Callahan v. Carey*, Hayes cited the New York State Constitution's wording: "The aid, care and support of the needy are public concerns and shall be provided by the state and by such of its subdivisions, and in such a manner and by such means, as the legislature may from time to time determine." In 1977, the State Court of Appeals had ruled that that article of the State Constitution, drafted in response to the Great Depression, called for assistance for the needy.[37]

Victory for Hayes arrived quickly; in the first wave of the proceedings, State Supreme Court Justice Andrew R. Tyler ordered the city and state to create 750 additional beds for the homeless. He also barred city officials from closing the muni. Moving toward compliance with the order, the city quickly opened a new homeless men's shelter on Wards Island, located in the East River between Manhattan and Queens. The city and state paid nearly $250,000 to the Volunteers of America to operate the 180-bed facility. By late 1980, the Keener Building had become overcrowded, housing four hundred men. Because it was located too near the Manhattan Children's Psychiatric Center for comfort, an acrimonious relationship soon developed between the two organizations. The Psychiatric Center's staff complained of harassment by residents of the Keener shelter, some of whom allegedly exposed themselves. Some homeless men also resented the situation.[38]

In December 1980, one year after the original ruling, the Legal Aid Society brought a contempt of court motion against Mayor Koch and the City's Human Resources Commissioner Stanley Brezenoff, alleging that they had failed to meet the court's mandates. Efforts to comply with the court's decision met with formidable obstacles. Administrators sent more homeless men to Camp LaGuardia, a facility traditionally housing older men. The initiative was unsuccessful; almost 40 percent of those sent to the camp returned to the city the following day, finding the accommodations unsuited to their needs. As one young returnee remarked, "It's beautiful, if that's the place you want to retire at age 19." As a cold snap hit the region, the city housed residents displaced from their apartments by the frigid weather in an uptown armory and two Brooklyn centers. Pressed simultaneously to provide assistance to long-term homeless individuals and families, the city referred some to the temporary facilities. The two populations mixed uneasily; single women were housed in the basement, while the first floor housed single homeless men, instructed not to mingle with the other residents. The new, younger homeless did not assimilate into the city's existing facilities. At the same time, the city feared combining them with those without shelter for only a short time.[39]

By late August 1981, the Koch administration had agreed to a consent decree. Under the terms of the agreement, the city and state were to provide shelter upon request to any homeless man. Minimum standards were mapped out for facilities, mandating that they provide one shower for every ten men, a toilet for every six, weekly linen service, and sixty square feet of sleeping space. Recreation and dining areas were to be included, as well as a locker for each person's belongings. The decree also mandated additional security guards in the Bowery hotels and more intake centers for the homeless. The consent decree issued in *Callahan v. Carey* kept the court from addressing the core issues of the right to shelter, offering instead a temporary, patchwork resolution to the situation.[40]

The case served as a model for similar efforts at "impact litigation" for the homeless in other cities, to mixed results. In New Jersey, advocates obtained a restraining order against public welfare officials who refused assistance to the homeless due to lack of a permanent residence. Los Angeles County's early 1980s policy of issuing the homeless $8 checks and a referral to an area flop-house faced legal challenges when rooms could not be found for the price. Advocates who charged that a shelter system would be more cost effective won an injunction and a revamped voucher system. Although a New York-style "right to shelter" suit brought in West Virginia drew on the state's protective service laws, these developments did not trigger a nationwide movement toward guaranteed shelter for the homeless. The variation between states' constitutions meant that not many contained the specific grounds for any right to shelter legislation. Also, few states had the existing infrastructure of services in place that New York had, meaning that courts would not simply ask shelters to expand their services, but would be insist that shelters be established, a position few were willing to take.[41]

As New York officials searched for methods of meeting the demands of the decree, advocates urged them not to resort to the city's traditional strategy of shipping the homeless to remote destinations. Hayes argued that moving individuals beyond a "reasonable" distance from the city endangered their ability to reintegrate with the community. But Koch's efforts to open referral centers and shelters for the homeless in the city's residential neighborhoods triggered dramatic community protests. Upper West Side residents feared such facilities would draw an inordinate number of homeless individuals from across the city. Midtown facilities sponsored by churches also sparked protests. The secretary of a Midtown community board wrote to Koch: "A bag person couple were seen fornicating on the church steps one afternoon. Some of their male clients lie on our sidewalks exposing their genitalia. All of this, and there is more, is not only disgusting and dangerous to our adult population, but we have young children living here as well." More surprisingly, even the city's proposal to lodge the homeless in military barracks at Brooklyn's Floyd Bennett Field inspired complaints from community groups.[42]

Such neighborhood protests continued for years, turning the city's effort to meet the terms of the decree into a comedy of errors. Eventually, in a controversial, heavy-handed effort to avoid community protest over the opening of homeless shelters, the Koch administration stopped issuing advance notice of its plans. Elected officials and community boards received only twenty-four hours notice before each facility opened, so that they would be unable to mount demonstrations.[43]

As debates continued over location, advocates for the homeless grew increasingly disgusted with the city's inability and unwillingness to act. Reverend Donald Sakano of the Office of Neighborhood Preservation of Catholic Charities wrote to the *New York Times*: "As a civilized people we haven't the right to choose between life and death for the homeless. Yet we have witnessed months of discussion as to where just one shelter might be established. It is frightening to think of what will happen to homeless people again this winter."[44]

As winter 1981 approached, more men did, indeed, apply for shelter. City facilities and designated Bowery hotels were filled to capacity, so officials resorted to allowing some to sleep in city offices. By late October, a Supreme Court justice ordered the city to open an armory for use by the homeless. A site for a temporary shelter was finally procured, in the abandoned P.S. 63 in East New York. Four hundred beds and cots were placed in the former classrooms to accommodate the overflow homeless population. But such efforts remained inadequate to meet the rising need. By November, the city reported 30 percent more individuals seeking shelter than the previous year. In a dramatic gesture, State Assembly members held a news conference in front of the muni intake center, calling for immediate action on behalf of the homeless. As December began, the city announced a plan to use more of the armories as homeless shelters. Hayes continued to protest the city's actions as too limited in scope, calling the armories "nothing more than a municipal flophouse." Lacking sufficient plumbing and kitchen facilities, the armories fell short of the consent decree's standards. By the end of 1981, the city was housing homeless men in the Wards Island facility (and planning to add an additional 200 beds), the Flushing armory, Camp LaGuardia, the East New York shelter, and paying the lodging fees for over 1,000 men in Bowery hotels.[45]

Seeking a way out of the mounting crisis, Koch tried to forge partnerships with the city's churches and synagogues, calling on each to house ten homeless individuals. While the city would pay for beds and linens, the religious organizations would be responsible for food, shelter, and showers. Many religious leaders scoffed at the plan, branding it impractical and ill considered. But some responded to the call, immediately soliciting targeted donations from their congregations. Koch's appeal was replicated on a national scale in early 1982, when President Reagan, citing the influence of the Reverend Billy Graham, announced that poverty would be alleviated if each of the nation's congregations assumed responsibility for ten welfare families. The Episcopal bishop of New York called the proposals "naïve" and "dangerous," worrying they confused religious charity with public social justice. Rabbi Marc H. Tanenbaum of the American Jewish Committee similarly described the plight of the homeless as "morally obscene," and called on the city to take decisive action.[46]

But by late 1982, the Koch administration subsidized private agencies providing shelter to the homeless. By 1984, the Partnership for the Homeless coordinated a system of seventy-two small emergency shelters administered by churches and synagogues, a network they hoped would soon contain more than 1,000 beds. Public and private organizations had cooperated closely since the earliest days of the city's services to the homeless. From the Charity Organization Society's woodyard's connections to the muni, to the position of private organizations within the Temporary Emergency Relief Administration, through the postwar referrals of homeless men from the muni to the Salvation Army, public and private religious organizations had worked together to provide homeless services.[47]

Now, however, private organizations were asked to compensate for the explicit failures of public programs. The belief that public agencies hailed by activists of the 1920s and 1930s embodied the potential of standardized, rational care available only in the public realm no longer inspired optimism in observers. A fundamental faith in government ability to administer such programs had eroded, as the large, congregate public shelters and subsidized flophouses slid into disrepair.

The soaring numbers of homeless, now legally empowered to request and receive assistance, overwhelmed the city's crumbling, inadequate systems. The small, local, often religious facilities offered a model that appealed both to conservatives and liberals. Some maintained a modern version of President Coolidge's position that such expenditures belonged in the realm of private charity. More striking, though, were the pronouncements of liberals and advocates for the homeless who also called for public funding of privately administered, religious shelters. While government bureaucracies might manage to provide an assistance check after some wrangling, few trusted them with the care of the bodies and lives of the poor. Small-scale, humane programs, no longer tainted by the image of mandatory attendance at lengthy evangelistic sermons, attracted widespread support. Even as the crowded, filthy flophouse dormitories drew criticism, though, many homeless men continued to prefer the freedom such facilities offered. Many especially valued the anonymity conferred by the private rooms of SRO hotels.[48]

Outsiders to the political scene had orchestrated a movement to obtain higher quality and more abundant facilities for the city's homeless. By highlighting the unhealthy and depressing conditions of public facilities, they swayed popular and judicial support for the creation of new, significantly improved shelters. The city and state governments were left on the defensive, struggling to maintain popular media relations and to meet the minimum demands of the court. Yet for all such progress, neighborhood groups remained unwilling to accommodate new or expanded homeless facilities, out of fear that negative elements of skid row would taint their residential and business districts. By the late 1970s, no one wanted his or her neighborhood to serve as the city's skid row, even the residents of the Bowery.

The New Bowery

As rising numbers of homeless people appeared on the streets of New York, many observers viewed them as symptoms of the era's broader urban crisis. The nation's middle classes fled to the suburbs following the riots of the late 1960s, drawing desperately needed resources away from urban centers. Crime rates increased against a backdrop of abandoned buildings, as neighborhoods fell victim to disinvestment and neglect. The Lower East Side was no exception; images of drug users and criminals dominated public perceptions of the area.

The Bowery nonetheless led the way as a cultural revival took root in the Lower East Side. Its association with flophouses and homeless men had restricted its development for nearly a century. During the 1970s, these very associations would attract disaffected middle-class youths to the street and the surrounding neighborhood. Although they were enamored of the raw, grim filth of the Bowery, they would, ironically, be the first wave of the regentrification that would begin to sweep the neighborhood during the 1980s. The homeless remained a significant presence in the area, but now shared the street with an influx of new residents, ultimately weakening the traditional identification between the Bowery and homelessness. While in New York the tightening real estate market would be the driving force in shifting the Bowery away from its skid-row past, other cities had already demolished their skid rows through the more dramatic forces of urban renewal. These trends converged to bring about the end of the skid-row era nationwide.[49]

Some innovative programs for the homeless continued to operate on the Bowery during the 1970s. The Bowery Residents' Committee, for example, ad-

ministered a program in the building formerly housing Sammy's Bowery Fol-
lies. Founded by a social worker, the program allowed homeless men formal
input into its management. It maintained daytime lounge facilities for men
staying in area commercial lodging houses that forced their poorest guests to
remain outside the facility during the day. The program also provided alcohol
counseling, medical referrals, and job training programs to those looking to
change their lives. More traditional programs also continued; the city subsidized six Bowery flophouses, issuing lodging tickets as well as vouchers for
four used clothing stores.[50]

The Bowery neighborhood had finally entered the phase of revitalization
prematurely predicted by 1920s boosters and 1950s urban renewal advocates.
During the 1960s, nearby SoHo (South of Houston) had evolved from an industrial zone to a fashionable arts district. Gallery owners and artists, but also
urban planners, financiers, and politicians, had engineered the loft conver-
sions that came to characterize the neighborhood. Displaced by high rents
in that rapidly re-gentrifying district, some artists migrated to the Bowery,
initiating a cultural and commercial revival of the area. Amidst the remaining
flophouses and missions, art galleries began to open along the street, attracting artists and patrons no longer able to afford the SoHo gallery scene. The
First Street Gallery, the Bowery Gallery, and the Star Turtle Bowery show-
cased fine art for intrepid visitors willing to venture off the standard gallery
circuit.[51]

The 1970s also witnessed a revival of the northern Bowery's role as a site
of vibrant nightlife. Night clubs and restaurants made the Bowery a key element of the new "downtown scene" that attracted visitors and attention to the
area. Jazz was performed at the Ladies' Fort and the Tin Palace restaurant.
The La Mama off-Broadway theater had sparked a revival of downtown theater, which included Joe Papp's Public Theatre, the Astor Place Theatre, and
the Bouwerie Lane theatre, among others. The Great Gildersleeves rock club,
featuring heavy metal bands by 1980, drew a young crowd to the Bowery.[52]

The Bowery also provided space, atmosphere, and support for the burgeoning underground and punk rock music scene. Hilly Kristal's CBGB and
Omfug, on the Bowery near Bleecker Street, began featuring rock bands performing original music shortly after its 1973 opening. The club operated in
the ground-floor bar of the Palace, an infamous Bowery flophouse. The inexpensive rent allowed Kristal to pay the bands the entire cover charge, keeping
only the bar receipts. Its Bowery location added a ragged edginess to clubgo-
ers' experiences, as middle-class youth traversed undeniably gritty terrain to

Figure 20. The Ramones frequented CBGB, the rock club that brought a hip, young crowd to the Bowery. "Ramones—Outside CBGB," 1975. Copyright Bob Gruen.

hear up and coming musicians including Television, the Ramones, and Patti Smith. As Kristal observed, "Opening a club on the Bowery under a flophouse had its advantages and disadvantages—the rents were cheap, but the streets were strewn with the bodies of alcoholics who you had to step over to get in the door." The club became well known after hosting the acclaimed 1975 Summer of Rock Festival, which generated media attention and increased attendance. As Tommy Ramone recalled, "It got a lot of publicity and after that the place was always packed. This was in the Bowery, and nobody went to the Bowery, so it was a big deal."[53]

Many musicians affiliated with the club lived locally, providing the roots for a new artistic community. Three members of Talking Heads shared a loft a few blocks from the members of Blondie, and Arturo Vega, a Ramones insider, lived directly across from the club. The stark quality of the neighborhood and the bar itself complemented the raw and minimal sound of much of the emerging music. Kristal welcomed performers to visit the club on nights they were not performing, a practice Talking Heads front man David Byrne credited with fostering key relationships and encouraging a sense of artistic solidarity.[54]

As the area welcomed new entertainment and nightlife venues, speculators predicted rapid increases in residential real estate values. But by 1977, many remained sorely disappointed. Although investors had anticipated a pattern of conversion similar to that occurring in SoHo, the older, smaller, weaker Bowery buildings remained less suited to simple conversion. Some SRO owners did convert their properties to apartments. The Majestic Hotel was renovated into 40' x 75' lofts that rented for up to $500 per month. Overall, though, demand for area luxury and even middle-income housing lagged. Area businessmen complained that the remaining homeless population prevented the neighborhood from enjoying the spike in property values it would otherwise achieve. Floyd Feldman, an area lawyer active on the community board, observed, "Commercially, the Bowery has bounced up a bit. But you won't see a renaissance here because we've been chosen to be a dumping ground." Jack Klein, a real estate broker, commented succinctly: "The Bowery's gotten a lot better but it will never be a SoHo. There are too many bars, too many bums, and too many schlock joints." Even as their presence sparked renewed criticism, though, the number of homeless men seeking flophouse accommodations on the Bowery had dropped significantly. After declining for decades, the size of the area's homeless population stabilized. By 1978, only a dozen commercial hotels remained on the Bowery.[55]

Such improvements to the Bowery pleased many, but the city was unprepared to function without a skid row. Even as the area lost its identity as a skid row, city officials unable to house the homeless elsewhere, in compliance with the decree, tried once again to use the area as a homeless district. Since the decree, many homeless had been transported to the Bowery area for lodgings, triggering resentment on the part of area home and business owners. In 1981, a new 100-bed women's shelter on East Third Street prompted an angry reaction from Assemblyman Sheldon Silver, who felt his district held more than its share of the homeless already through the presence of the muni and commercial hotels. The following year, responding to Koch's call for nonprofit organizations willing to partner with the city to house the homeless, the Episcopal Mission Society proposed a homeless shelter on Mulberry Street. Protests from area residents led to the withdrawal of the plan. The executive director of the Society, Rev. James Gusweller, traced such criticism to the area's new population of young artists and professionals: "A shelter has to be somewhere, and I don't sympathize at all with the attitude of the NoHo people. They want their real estate to become more valuable—that's their big concern." Ironically, even the Bowery, the city's traditional skid row, was no longer considered by area residents an acceptable location for new homeless facilities by 1982.[56]

The homeless occupied a negotiated space on the Bowery by the early 1980s. Artists and musicians seeking inexpensive studio, gallery, and performance space led thousands of new visitors to the area. The Bowery nurtured emerging new movements of outsider music and art, expressing the perspective of many who felt alienated from the era's mainstream, corporate art culture. On the Bowery, the artists picked their way through the homeless, using some of their former establishments, and sharing space, for the most part amicably. Local lore included tales of the two cultures' famed moments of interaction, as when Chris Frantz of Talking Heads witnessed a homeless man defecating in the aisle of a local supermarket.[57]

The two groups coexisted relatively peacefully, yet the homeless began to be marginalized from the neighborhood. Since the urban renewal debates of the 1950s, city officials and real estate developers had longed to rid the Bowery of its skid-row population. Their efforts floundered, compromised by the stubborn presence of the homeless and the Welfare Department's continuing policy of subsidizing the institutions of skid row. Once again, the presence of the homeless served to dissuade many from buying property in the area, thwarting the plans of many eager speculators. But the shifting demographics of the homeless population, as well as the city's new housing strategies, ensured the continuing decline of the Bowery as a site for the homeless.

Debating Homelessness in the Reagan Era

The Legal Aid victories brought shelter to all who requested it, but offered little hope for the care of those too mentally ill to seek assistance or even know they required it. New York officials struggled for decades to develop effective policies to meet the needs of this population. Their efforts were complicated by the shifting national political climate. As the Reagan era dawned, federal officials and many of their constituents lost patience with the concerns of the homeless and began calling for greater personal responsibility and limited social welfare programs.

Viewing the homelessness crisis with increasing desperation, in 1981 Koch proposed to take the homeless into custody and detain them against their will for three days. While in the care of the city, they would be fed and bathed. On learning his plan was largely unconstitutional, the skeptical mayor remarked that if the Constitution didn't support him, it was "dumb." Nonetheless, the Department of Mental Health pursued a similar strategy of intervention in the cases of individuals who posed risk of harm to themselves or others, and who seemed unable to grasp the consequences of their actions. An October 1981 law authorized the city to take such individuals into protective custody for three days. Although the law was developed for use in the cases of elderly, housed individuals who refused assistance, the Koch administration hoped to invoke it when homeless people could not be convinced to enter shelters voluntarily.[58]

That winter, the Red Cross notified the city of an elderly woman living in a cardboard box on Tenth Avenue and Seventeenth Street who refused offers of assistance. Officials prepared to inaugurate the new law in her case. Before they could obtain a court order for forcible hospitalization, though, Rebecca Smith, a sixty-one-year-old diagnosed schizophrenic who had spent decades in and out of mental facilities, died of hypothermia. City officials resolved to act more quickly in the future during extreme weather conditions. The attention generated by the case had the positive effect of increasing popular knowledge of the city's homeless services programs, prompting city residents to report homeless people sighted sleeping outdoors.[59]

As the publicity over the Smith case slowed, Hayes and the Coalition for the Homeless brought a class-action suit on behalf of the mentally ill. Focusing on the state, the suit named Governor Carey and his staff as defendants, citing them with failing to meet the needs of the mentally ill homeless population. Hayes also brought a suit in February of that year that sought to expand the consent decree's provisions to include the female homeless population. Many homeless women reported their fear of being routed to a Bushwick, Brooklyn, facility that was widely regarded as extremely dangerous, as was its surrounding neighborhood. Noting that the Flushing armory lodged seventy women, but had only a single shower and three toilets, Hayes argued that the facility's deplorable conditions deterred homeless women from applying for assistance. These expansive suits helped to guarantee minimum standards and availability of accommodations for the city's homeless.[60]

Legal Aid suits had changed the terms of the debate over homelessness in New York City, and influenced the discourse around the subject in cities across the country. In creating the "right to shelter" system, advocates redefined the basic requirements of survival as a fundamental right. They operated against a broad backdrop of similar rights developments in other areas. The role of the courts, presidential executive orders, and federal legislation in expanding social policy from the mid-1960s to the mid-1970s has led some scholars to describe a "minority rights revolution." Such shifts spanned from civil rights issues to ones rooted in the environmental, consumer, and antiwar movements. Like the *Callahan v. Carey* consent decree and other victories for the homeless, however, such solutions remained temporary ones, spawned by perceived emergencies and not rooted in permanent legislation.[61]

The controversial approach to the problems of the homeless drew criticism from both ends of the political spectrum. Some argued that the advocates for the homeless glossed over significant differences between various homeless subpopulations, choosing as a matter of political expedience to present a unified, homogeneous group. Mental patients, substance users, and the unemployed might require distinct services, even if such divisions invited traditional categorizations of "worthy" and "unworthy" poor. Furthermore, by providing shelter as a matter of "rights" rather than as a social service, some argued, the government risked fueling "dependency." The broader public assistance system and minimum wage employment required "considerable responsibility," argued Thomas Main: "The shelters, on the other hand, give out something for nothing: Clients get plenty of services and have to give nothing in return."[62]

Some analysts also questioned the advocates' tactics in light of liberal policy development. By relying on the court system to institute policy change on home-less issues, J. Phillip Thompson argued, the advocates had neglected to develop broad popular support for the new programs and initiatives. The governmental agencies involved also did not seek significant input from community residents, especially impoverished ethnic minorities in the neighborhoods where shelters were planned, which engendering animosity toward the facilities. Various "elites" developed and instituted policies without acknowledging the concerns of the av-erage citizen. Due to these oversights, according to Thompson, "homeless policy was thus a failure."[63]

Such criticisms were not without merit. Occasional projects in other cities modeled the innovative results that could be achieved by soliciting and in-corporating community input into plans for the homeless. In downtown Los Angeles, for instance, an award-winning multipurpose park was constructed near skid row. After considering input from social workers, area residents, police officers, and the homeless themselves, the designers included basket-ball courts for area youth, a sandbox for young children, and benches, a rain shelter, restrooms, and chess tables for use by the homeless and others.[64]

Such interaction was rare, however, due to the political and economic pressures surrounding such projects. Further, the direction of urban home-less policy had been decided by "elites" since the turn of the century, at various moments dominated by charity reformers, religious evangelists, city, state, and federal officials, social scientists, and urban planners. The 1980s witnessed the temporary transfer of power to the new forces of law-yers and advocacy groups. As outsiders, they did not emerge from the en-trenched social service or political structures. Instead, the new advocacy groups aligned themselves squarely with the homeless and prioritized their concerns over those of any institutional bodies. Their lack of formal ties to political or religious organizations allowed them to make complex, occa-sionally contradictory demands, keeping the practical benefits to the home-less as their central focus.

The advocates agreed with the criticisms leveled against the city for ignoring community input, urging officials to adopt a dialogue-based ap-proach to shelter planning. They lacked the power to control such pro-cesses, though, and could do little more than advise. The judicial approach to agenda-setting accounted far less for the "failures" of the new homeless policies than the heavy-handed tactics employed by the Koch administra-tion in its implementation.

By late 1983, the Partnership for the Homeless predicted New York City's homeless population would soon double. Pressured by the courts, the city and state governments had been providing increasingly adequate services to the homeless. However, the zealous anti-poor actions of the federal government nonetheless outweighed such efforts, as the Reagan administration slashed social programs, low-income housing, and basic nutrition programs, including commodities distribution and food stamps, leaving the nation's poorest citizens more destitute, and thousands homeless.[65]

After Congress appropriated funds for homeless programs, the Reagan administration used the funding process to strip state and local governments of power. A 1983 allotment of $100 million for homeless programs gave federal officials the opportunity to weaken homeless programs while appearing compassionate. After announcing the need to bypass the "red tape" of the standard distribution channels, the administration dispersed the funds through the Federal Emergency Management Agency. Strict guidelines accompanied the funding, which was to be spent only on temporary expenses, such as commodities, food, cots, and leases. The funds could not be used to make needed investments in homeless programs by purchasing or renovating facilities. Some observers speculated that the guidelines were established to ensure that administrators did not spend all the funds, allowing the administration later to argue that such monies were not needed.[66]

The Reagan administration's hostility toward government-funded programs for the homeless was in keeping with popular frustration with public assistance programs in general. By the early 1980s, Reagan supporters were calling for lower taxes and reduced government spending. The era's popular culture caricatured "welfare queens" who allegedly lived lavishly from public support. Respected commentators and academics offered similar conclusions. Political scientist Charles Murray argued in the influential book *Losing Ground* that the social welfare programs expanded under the Great Society had been overly generous and encouraged poor Americans not to seek employment.[67]

In this context, Reagan made little effort to conceal his contempt for the homeless. In early 1984 on ABC's *Good Morning, America*, he noted that the homeless were not all to be pitied: "What we have found in this country, and we're more aware of it now, is one problem that we've had, even in the best of times, and that is the people who are sleeping on the grates, the homeless who are homeless, you might say, by choice." Reagan's adviser, Edwin Meese, remarked that many people visited soup kitchens not out of desperate need, but because doing so was "easier" than paying for food. While some tiny fraction of the homeless population might actively choose such a lifestyle from an array of options, their existence offered no excuse for federal inaction. Journalist Sydney Schanberg ridiculed Reagan's logic: "So if you can pretend the homeless choose to be poor and cold and hungry, you can then say you believe in freedom of choice and don't want to interfere with their personal desires."[68]

Not surprisingly, the Reagan administration continued to call for increased private sector programs for the homeless in lieu of public institutions. In his 1984 State of the Union address, nearly fifty years after FDR had returned the homeless to local and private care, Reagan similarly praised Covenant House, a nonsectarian, nonprofit New York City program for homeless youth established in 1968; he advanced it as a model for groups across the country concerned with the plight of the homeless. While Roosevelt had excluded the least sympathetic of the nation's poor in order to build a work-based public welfare system, Reagan actively sought to dismantle publicly funded poverty programs. Unemployable individuals, especially those without dependents, proved vulnerable targets for both ends of the political spectrum.[69]

As poverty mounted and visible homelessness increased, protest groups began to lobby for the rights of the homeless, hoping to use media attention to pressure the Reagan administration into addressing the issue. The Community for Creative Nonviolence served a Thanksgiving turkey dinner for the homeless near the White House. Not allowed to camp overnight, the group erected tents and a sign, "Welcome to Reaganville—Reaganomics at Work." Drawing on the image of the depression's Hoovervilles, the group framed the crisis of homelessness as one calling for a strong federal response. The National Coalition for the Homeless formed in May 1982, serving as an information resource for social service organizations working with the homeless in twenty cities.[70]

As the 1984 presidential election approached, homelessness emerged as a campaign issue. Candidate Walter Mondale assured voters that Reagan's callous attitude toward the homeless shared more with Coolidge than with Roosevelt. He insisted that Americans wanted to display more compassion toward their fellow citizens. In August, the Community for Creative Nonviolence again erected tents near the White House, this time to gain publicity for their campaign for funding the renovation of a 1,000-bed Washington, D.C., homeless shelter. Their previous "Reaganville" had resulted in an ironic Supreme Court ruling that such displays were allowed as long as the tents remained empty. Mitch Snyder, the group's leader, launched a hunger strike, attracting media attention. Fifty-one days into his strike, and two days before the election, Reagan's administration capitulated, just before a CBS *60*

Minutes story about the protest. Ever concerned with public relations, the administration's need to placate the protesters outweighed his commitment to limiting public assistance.[71]

Estimates of the size of the nation's homeless population ranged widely and reflected divergent political agendas. The Department of Housing and Urban Development estimated the country's homeless at only 250,000 to 350,000 individuals, but activist groups and service providers placed the number far higher. Snyder called HUD's estimate "utterly ridiculous" and estimated the figure at over two million. Others placed the figure as high as 2.5 million.[72]

The crack cocaine epidemic tainted popular opinion about the homeless. Stringer described the relationship between perceived substance use and charitable intent:

> In the mid eighties, when homelessness first emerged as an
> urgent national crisis, we were prepared to address it in the
> traditional way, with compassion and human interest, what I call
> the "sandwiches and sympathy" approach. However, once the
> crack connection became common knowledge—implying that
> homeless people might be complicit in their own destitution—a
> lot of people began to feel they had squandered their compassion
> on less-than-worthy subjects, and public sentiment soon began to
> turn.[73]

The trope of the worthy poor was never far from the American psyche.

Offering assistance to the homeless on request proved simpler than providing it to those who sought to be left alone. Once the preservation of human life through the provision of shelter was categorized as a duty of the local government, the limits of such responsibilities remained unclear. The Koch administration hoped to rid the city streets of the mentally ill homeless in part due to humanitarian concerns, especially given the negative publicity the population generated. Its streets increasingly tourist destinations, Manhattan developed by the 1980s in directions that left no room in doorways or on subway grates for the displaced mentally ill. The issue of forced hospitalization of mentally ill homeless individuals would plague the city for decades.

The expansion of city services to the homeless during these years reflected the tenacity and dedication of advocacy groups, who achieved results all the more remarkable for their occurrence during the Reagan era. After ignoring the plight of the nation's homeless, the administration eventually increased federal funding to homeless programs, even as their distribution methods limited the impact of such funding.

The Reagan administration sought to shift much of the responsibility for the nation's homeless to the private sector, where religious, nonprofit organizations might provide care according to their own moralistic guidelines. Such programs fit neatly into the administration's vision of a restructured role of the federal government in the public welfare system. Despite their internal struggles and debates, New York City and State stood against the Reagan administration's efforts to limit federal funding for urban problems, gradually expanding the public shelter system for homeless residents.

Pressured by the court to provide humane accommodations for the homeless, the efforts of the city and state yielded a qualified success. Between 1978 and 1985, New York City expenditures on the homeless skyrocketed from $8 million to over $100 million. Although administrators struggled to develop facilities, most of the city's homeless who requested shelter were housed. The accommodations they received were spartan, coarse, and inhospitable, whether in the armories or flophouses of Manhattan, the outer boroughs, or on Wards Island. Even though the homeless included among them several subpopulations, such as older men, young substance users, and women, each with different needs, the services they received were standardized and with little variation. The programs and services offered by the city met some of their basic needs, but did little to help them move toward social reintegration, or to preserve their individual dignity.[74]

Although the policy of deinstitutionalizing the mentally ill had ended, its long-term effects were devastating. By 1984, the American Psychiatric Association called the program "a major societal tragedy," due to the gross failings that accompanied its implementation. Similarly, by the time the Koch administration worked to end and counteract the city's J-51 tax abatement program, few SRO hotels remained to save. The delayed effects of past programs exacerbated the suffering of the homeless in 1980s New York.[75]

At the same time, new factors contributed to the rise of homelessness. As the Reagan administration continued to cut social programs, the number of homeless individuals and families in New York City increased. The limits placed on AFDC and other family assistance programs fueled the rise in family homelessness. In 1983 the city aided 6,000 individual homeless members of families; the following year, that number topped 10,000. Further, as the job market required specialized and technical skills, poor individuals who lacked access to such training and opportunities were increasingly excluded. As poverty rose across the nation, those individuals and families who fell through the cracks of the various "safety net" programs found themselves on the streets. Even efforts like the 1987 Stewart B. McKinney Homeless Assistance Act failed to receive presidential commitment, and were implemented in only a limited fashion.[76]

Homelessness became a category of analysis of increasingly limited use. While at mid-century, the homeless population of skid row had been relatively homogeneous, by the 1980s it exhibited a diversity it would maintain for decades. Substance users, older men, women, families, single mothers, youths, and the mentally ill each required specific services. On an individual level, each homeless person also reflected the complex series of events that had led him or her to the streets. While the city eventually managed to lodge many of its homeless, it often failed to address their various needs.

The evolution of American cities left the homeless fewer spaces to occupy during this second era of crisis. The skid rows that had long provided housing and services for the nation's homeless had been destroyed through the combined forces of benign neglect, active urban renewal, and surging gentrification. The homeless of the early 1980s were dispersed across the landscape of the nation's cities, often with no single district dedicated to their use.

Faced with the need to establish new shelters for the homeless, politicians struggled with the unpleasant and unpopular task of convincing city residents that mass shelters of homeless men, many of whom were former mental patients, would make good neighbors. Similar situations occurred in cities across the country, as neighborhood associations balked at the proposal of homeless shelters nearby. By the late 1980s, "NIMBY" was popularly understood as the abbreviation for "not in my backyard," the common reply to requests for not only homeless shelters, but also foster care facilities, drug rehabilitation centers, hazardous waste sites, and other unpopular public operations.[77]

The Koch and Reagan administrations and the advocates for the homeless agreed on a single point: each supported the expansion of private, religious-affiliated homeless shelters. Such programs fit the agenda of conservative politicians, who sought to limit the operations of the federal government, especially in the arena of public assistance. Homeless advocates approached the topic from another angle, seeking instead a solution to the problems of the homeless that involved more than warehouse-style dormitories, condescending staff members, and repressive security procedures. In small-scale, communal living programs, advocates saw the potential for homeless individuals to be treated with respect and aided toward pursuing their own goals, and urged officials to divert public funds to such private programs. Since Roosevelt had returned the care of unemployables to local and private organizations, a strand of liberal discourse had validated the characterization of the homeless as the concern not only of localities, but also of private charity.

Skid row was no longer the focal point of urban homelessness. In part, the Bowery's declining importance for the homeless stemmed from the neighborhood's changing role, as artists, musicians, and others began to move into the district and objected to their presence. Even had the neighborhood remained unchanged, though, the facilities skid row traditionally offered would not have met the needs of the "new" homeless population. Women were unsafe on the Bowery; some reported avoiding bathing and intentionally soiled themselves in a desperate attempt to dissuade rapists on the streets and in flophouses. Families obviously could not live in the cramped, squalid SRO hotels. The mentally ill, especially, required more intensive, specific services than the Bowery could offer. Even the single, unattached men who had traditionally flocked to skid rows deserved and demanded better accommodations than the shabby lodging houses of the Bowery. The Legal Aid lawsuits of the late 1970s and early 1980s would propel the homeless off the Bowery, to the outer boroughs, and into the center of a new series of debates.

CONCLUSION: WHITHER
THE HOMELESS

IN 1956, as the Hart Island rehabilitation facility was being closed, New York City Chief Magistrate John Murtagh, in front of whom vagrants appeared for sentencing, warned of the city's future. The modernizing Bowery, he cautioned, would no longer accommodate the homeless: "It is only because the Bowery is so large and so replete in lodging houses that the homeless have been relatively contained up to this time." He encouraged city officials to launch a new residential program for the homeless immediately, lest they infiltrate other neighborhoods and "knock Times Square silly." In the coming decades, as the skid-row district was redefined and the homeless scattered across the city, Murtagh's prediction would come to pass.[1]

After 1981, New York City's struggle with homelessness shifted profoundly. The "right to shelter" entitled the homeless to public assistance, but did not prevent successive mayoral administrations from implementing a complex array of new policies. Simultaneously, the gentrification of the Lower East Side brought dramatic changes to the streets of the Bowery, moving the homeless ever farther from the area. The skid-row era had finally come to an end.

Hoping to develop practical solutions to the problems of mentally ill homeless people, the Koch administration launched a controversial program to take them into protective custody. Diagnosing mental illness and convincing individuals to accept assistance was far from simple, as the first case proved. In October 1987, program staff picked up Joyce Brown, who lived in front of an air vent near the intersection of 65th Street and Second Avenue on Manhattan's East Side. Forty-year-old Brown had ceased contact with her middle-class New Jersey family the year before.[2]

Represented by the New York Civil Liberties Union (NYCLU), Brown contested her confinement. Although city psychiatrists described her as mentally ill, those called by the NYCLU found no signs of mental illness. Witnesses charged that Brown had destroyed money given by passersby. Brown argued she had only done so when the money was given to her against her will, noting, "I've heard people say: 'Take it. It will make me feel good.' But I say: 'I don't want it. I don't need it.' Is it my job to make them feel good by taking their money?"[3]

As the case played to national headlines, Brown's life history was tried in the press. Her family claimed that Brown, a secretary for ten years, had begun using cocaine and heroin in her early twenties, triggering mental deterioration and decline into unemployment, poverty, and antisocial attitudes. Acting justice Robert D. Lippmann of the State Supreme Court in Manhattan ordered Brown released from the Bellevue Hospital Center, arguing that city officials had not proven her mentally ill: "It cannot be reasoned that because Joyce Brown is homeless she is mentally ill. What must be proved is that because she is mentally ill she is incapable of providing herself with food, clothing and shelter."[4]

Lippmann urged a more rigorous analysis and more complex understanding of the connections between homelessness and mental illness. Lippmann, who had spent seventeen years as a Legal Aid attorney in the Bronx focusing on housing issues, went on to shift the blame to the city's shelter system: "She refuses to be housed in a shelter. That may reveal more about conditions in shelters than about Joyce Brown's mental state. It might, in fact, prove that she's quite sane." After several delays and appeals, Brown was released.[5]

The case inspired public debate over the relative importance of individual freedom and various community standards. Television executives suspended a local newscaster for questioning Brown in a hostile manner and asking Norman Siegel, her representative, "What about the rights of people like me who walk past the people who urinate? I'm a taxpayer. What about my rights?" A resident of the block where Brown lived outdoors for a year offered a more philosophical critique of the arguments made by the NYCLU: "It has been suggested that Ms. Brown is an eccentric living out an alternate lifestyle, and that her freedom should be returned to her. Second Avenue is not Walden Pond. She is not the personification of self-reliance that a judge and lawyer (who probably never saw her on the street) are making her out to be. She is utterly dependent on others for her daily ice cream and chicken cutlet, cigarettes, clothes, toilet paper and umbrellas." Thousands rallied behind Brown's cause, attending public demonstrations protesting her involuntary hospitalization.[6]

Although in inarguably crude terms, such polarized arguments captured the essence of the debate. Siegel painted a frightening picture of "vans roaming the streets of New York looking for people to take to Bellevue Hospital." Meanwhile, Koch critiqued an emerging "lofty new attitude, wrapped in the rhetoric of civil liberties," accusing Siegel and his supporters of attempting to "justify their heartlessness by calling it a defense of freedom."[7]

The Brown case prompted public discussion of the ability of mentally ill homeless individuals to make decisions regarding their lives and care. Faced with an inadequate, dangerous, and alienating shelter system, many homeless opted for the city streets. In so doing, they came into direct conflict with other city residents, some of whom advocated more intensive policing of public spaces to ensure proper hygiene and safety. Some law and order urban conservatives found themselves allied with homeless advocates hoping that mandatory care would improve patients' lives.

Conflicting ideas about use of public space also sparked a battle in Tompkins Square Park in 1988. The Lower East Side park was attracting an increasing number of homeless people, prompting officials to enact a 1 a.m. curfew. The prolonged riot that ensued yielded over 120 charges of police brutality. By the following year, homeless encampments in the park angered area business owners and city officials. In July, two hundred police officers destroyed a shantytown housing approximately one hundred individuals. City officials allowed the homeless to continue sleeping in the park, but barred their use of structures and encampments.[8]

The gentrification of the Lower East Side fueled city efforts to minimize its visible homeless population. One homeless carpenter quipped, "You got people paying $2,000 a month in rent, and they don't want this eyesore." The rising tensions between new and long-time area residents attracted media attention. In 1989, journalists savored a violent incident involving the Christadora building, which had been converted to condominiums. Area radicals reportedly smashed the entrance glass, chanting, "Die, yuppie scum," echoing similar events in cities like San Francisco. Squatter evictions and smaller riots continued on the Lower East Side through the late 1980s.[9]

Public and private agencies worked together to sponsor the Tompkins Square Park Help Center, offering referrals to homeless individuals as the park was cleared in late 1989. But Robert Hayes of the Coalition for the Homeless noted that such referral programs would remain of little use until alternative housing programs had been implemented. City officials continued to raze shelters built in the park, ultimately closing it for year-long renovations and thereby effectively evicting the homeless.[10]

After officials chased the homeless from Tompkins Square, shantytowns were established in other areas of the East Village, several of which were destroyed by city bulldozers in October 1991. Mary Brosnahan of the Coalition for the Homeless described the situation involving city removal of the homeless from large, visible encampments as a "three-card monte game." The Transit Authority simultaneously mounted an aggressive campaign to evict homeless individuals who violated subway policies against panhandling, fare evasion, and public sleeping.[11]

As the city cracked down on homelessness at Tompkins Square and Columbus Circle, Nancy Wackstein, Mayor David Dinkins's director of the Office of Homelessness and SRO Housing Services, described the areas as "situations that the Mayor felt were out of control." In an ironic reversal of the era's struggles over community gardens and other public spaces, she continued, "The Mayor feels there's not one segment of the public that can privatize a public area." By 1991, many other cities were following New York's policy of shutting the homeless out of public spaces. Atlanta, Santa Barbara, Chicago, Phoenix, Cincinnati, Miami, and Los Angeles were among cities pursuing ordinances to "turn down the comfort level in public places." San Diego officials cleared a homeless encampment out of Balboa Park. Father Joe Carroll of the St. Vincent de Paul Center explained his opposition to establishing a publicly funded, open-air homeless settlement in the park, citing New York's Tompkins Square experiences: "Once you let them believe they have a right to it, the city in effect loses control of the property. San Diego says it is not going to let that happen. They've seen what happened in New York."[12]

In 1972, the *Papachristou v. City of Jacksonville* Supreme Court decision had branded vagrancy ordinances overly vague and no longer useful. In the following years, most municipal ordinances and campaigns targeted the homeless as impediments to commercial activity. A decade later, policy experts James Q. Wilson and George L. Kelling advanced their controversial "broken windows" theory about policing urban spaces. They argued that a single broken window, if left unrepaired, conveyed the impression that an area was out of control, inspiring youths and others to break additional windows.

Wilson and Kelling urged police forces to maintain a highly visible presence in urban environments to foster a sense of community order. They described "the ill-smelling drunk," "the importuning beggar," and "the unchecked pan-handler" as key signs of "urban decay." They insisted that ensuring a neigh-borhood's orderly appearance justified the arbitrary arrest of the homeless: "Arresting a single drunk or a single vagrant who has harmed no identifiable person seems unjust, and in a sense it is. But failing to do anything about a score of drunks or a hundred vagrants may destroy an entire community."[13]

Inspired by this theory, New York City mayor Rudolph Giuliani waged a series of "quality of life" campaigns across the city. He and Police Chief Bratton employed strategies ranging from harassment charges to traffic laws to clear the homeless from public spaces, triggering accusations of cater-ing to business interests and wealthy residents. In 1999, Giuliani observed: "Streets do not exist in civilized societies for the purpose of people sleeping there. Bedrooms are for sleeping and a society moves as a progressive so-ciety as it convinces more and more people that they shouldn't be sleeping on its streets." Many activists and service providers found such behavioral approaches to homelessness overly simplistic and naïve. On a practical level, where were the homeless to go? As the Giuliani administration pursued ag-gressive removal tactics, many homeless evacuated areas like Grand Central Terminal, Madison Avenue near 42nd Street, and the southern half of Central Park. Instead, they built shantytowns in several areas: Chelsea Piers, Hunts Point in the Bronx, along FDR Drive, below the Brooklyn-Queens Express-way, and in Flushing Meadows Park and Forest Hills in Queens.[14]

The Giuliani administration also scaled back city homeless services. Ironically, during his 1989 mayoral campaign, Giuliani had proposed allo-cating more SRO apartments and transitional housing for shelter residents. By 1993, the administration alienated homeless advocacy groups with a bold proposal to challenge the 1981 consent decree, citing other cities, including Boston and Philadelphia, which reduced services to the homeless. Extend-ing the Dinkins administration's strict eligibility requirements for shelter services, the Giuliani administration opposed using the shelter system as an entry to low-income housing. By 1995, following the lead of governor Mario Cuomo, officials tightened entrance requirements for homeless facilities.[15]

The following year, the Giuliani administration attempted to extend its "Work Experience Program," commonly referred to as "workfare," to include families housed in homeless shelters. Parents of children age three to thirteen would be required to perform assigned maintenance and clerical tasks, while their children attended day care. Shelter administrators refused to enforce the policies, which required them to expel noncompliant parents and report their children to child welfare authorities. Advocates for the homeless found the policy cruel, unfair, and at best misguided. In response, first deputy mayor Peter J. Powers drew on rhetoric reminiscent of that of welfare administrators from the Charity Organization Society to President Roosevelt: "We think it's positive to ask people to work for their benefits. It's a way of building up self-esteem, and people in the shelter system should also be asked to contribute something back." After prolonged legal struggle, state courts found some of Giuliani's plans to violate the 1981 consent decree.[16]

As the administration cracked down on homelessness, a series of highly publicized attacks revived frenzied debate over the care of mentally ill homeless people. In January 1999, twenty-nine-year-old schizophrenic Andrew Goldstein pushed Kendra Webdale, a thirty-two-year-old receptionist, in front of an oncoming N train in a Chelsea subway station. Webdale's death garnered headlines for weeks, fascinating and terrifying city residents. Goldstein had repeatedly requested admission to heavily supervised treatment facilities, but was referred instead to inexpensive, single-room residences and group dormitory facilities, where he stopped taking his medications and missed mental health appointments. Three months later, forty-three-year-old Julio Perez, a homeless man lodged in a Washington Heights shelter program for the mentally ill, pushed forty-six-year-old Edgar Rivera in front of an oncoming subway train, severing both legs.[17]

In November, an assailant brazenly struck Nicole Barrett, a twenty-seven-year-old office worker from Athens, Texas, over the head with a paving stone near 42nd Street and Madison Avenue in the middle of the day. The media speculated that the perpetrator would once again prove to be a mentally ill homeless person. Three days later, Mayor Giuliani and police commissioner Howard Safir announced a plan to approach homeless individuals, offer them services, and arrest those who refused, at the discretion of police officers. The police investigated the homeless on the city streets as well as those lodged in shelters.[18]

Giuliani described the suspect as a panhandler who lived in the Port Authority bus station, concluding, "He fits every description of homelessness." Advocates for the homeless argued that such inaccurate stereotyping of the homeless as violent criminals misled the public. Brosnahan noted that public dialogue furthered confusion: "Maybe the problem is we have only one word, 'homeless,' that is supposed to suffice for the woman fleeing domestic violence, the man with a five-year crack addiction, someone who just got burned out of their home." Ironically, the man arrested and charged with the brick assault was not homeless. The mainstream press took little note of this fact, leaving city residents to continue to fear their homeless neighbors.[19]

Brosnahan's point proved sound; the homeless population of New York City at the turn of the twenty-first century remained extremely diverse. In 2001, scholars estimated that the city's family shelter system housed over 16,000 individuals. The number of homeless families had increased 500 percent since 1980. The average homeless parent was an African American or Hispanic female receiving public assistance. Half were high school graduates, but 8 percent had been homeless as children, and 13 percent had spent time in the foster care system.[20]

Fear of homelessness plagued many impoverished families. Darlene, a woman who became homeless after ten years of military service, explained the difficulties facing many Americans:

> So, you're lookin' at the fact that you need to make at least five or six dollars an hour. The new minimum wage, what's it gonna be? $4.25? That's still not enough. You'll have to get two minimum wage jobs and work 60 hours a week. And you'll maybe have to do that for two months before you've saved enough to move in. Now, where are you gonna stay while you're doing that? How will you stay clean? And if, say, you're in the predicament where you have two children, not even all that will begin to close the gap.

The homeless during the postwar years had been primarily white men; by the 1980s and 1990s, they included many women and children, many of whom were minorities.[21]

When mayor Michael R. Bloomberg took office in 2002, he distanced his administration from several of the quality-of-life issues that had tarnished the final months of the Giuliani administration, including several policies on homelessness. Often characterized as a "social liberal," Bloomberg called for improved conditions in shelters, additional beds, and the movement of many homeless families into Section 8, low-income housing. Yet he also continued to press for a version of Giuliani's plan to force homeless families out of shelters if they failed to accept housing placements.[22]

Conservative groups celebrated the 2003 court decision authorizing city shelters to evict residents who failed to comply with facility regulations.

Heather MacDonald, the outspoken representative of the Manhattan Institute, assured *New York Post* readers, "Enforcing expectations of reasonable behavior is not just essential to shelter management, it is a vital prerequisite to bringing vagrants back into society. Until street colonists learn to obey the most minimal rules for decent conduct, they cannot expect to hold a job or an apartment." Such calls for the disciplining of wayward vagrants harkened back to nineteenth-century rhetoric.[23]

Homeless and domiciled residents had shared America's cities through skid rows for nearly a century. The presence of the homeless on the Bowery and the nation's other skid rows reflected a long-term compromise by city officials, charity administrators, area residents, business owners, and the homeless. By segregating the homeless into a separate district, city officials ensured that the norms and laws governing city life were not violated. Homeless people often lived directly on the streets, eating, sleeping, and urinating in public places. Such behavior was banned elsewhere in America's cities, shielding working- and middle-class neighborhoods from such sights. This division of space also protected those outside skid-row neighborhoods from fear of being accosted by the homeless. Brawling vagrants were a common sight on skid row; it was not considered newsworthy because middle-class individuals were not under attack.

Yet skid rows had also served as tools of social control, regulating the behavior of the homeless through both direct and indirect means. The homeless had to follow directions in order to receive organized assistance, listen to sermons, and navigate arcane administrative systems in exchange for food and lodging. Nearly all facilities banned the consumption of alcohol, further limiting the behavior of relief recipients. Those who slept in bars and SRO hotels followed the rules dictated by the owner or operator, while those who preferred more freedom often slept in the open air. In the bigger picture, the boundaries of skid rows themselves created another regulatory system. As long as the poor were not allowed to leave the area for any significant length of time, they remained tied to the poverty zone of the Bowery, fueling the conflation of the poor and the place where they lived. The homeless were often understood only in narrow ways, becoming a people apart who lived differently and followed different rules. They were often seen as an undifferentiated mass whose actions were assumed to have caused their situation. They were "skid-row bums" who belonged on the Bowery.

Even though they were grim, filthy, and often dangerous places, skid rows were not leveled out of humanitarian concerns for the nation's home-

Figure 21. In 2011, amid the upscale markets and lofts of the contemporary Bowery, the Bowery Mission, a fixture in the area since 1879, continued to feed and minister to the area's homeless. Courtesy Andrew Russeth, 16 Miles of String (16miles.com).

less. After urban renewal projects eliminated some skid row areas, the forces of gentrification led to the redevelopment of others, including the Bowery. For nearly a century, many American cities had used skid rows to manage homelessness; maintaining them was a type of informal urban welfare policy. Rooted in the spatial segregation approach to poverty common during the late nineteenth century, officials had maintained skid rows long after near-by tenement-dwelling populations had thinned. Skid rows had reflected the continuation of a nineteenth-century solution to an urban problem through-out most of the twentieth century.

By the mid-1980s, observers no longer described the Bowery as primarily a skid row. Estimates placed 3,000 beds on the Bowery for the use of the homeless, 900 of them city flophouse beds. Since the mid-1970s, though, the Chinatown portion of the Bowery had expanded, bringing new waves of in-dividuals seeking inexpensive area lodgings. New owners renovated the Ful-ton Hotel, which had long catered to transients, rechristening it the Fu-Shin Hotel. Chinese men made up the majority of those lodged in its small rooms. The Salvation Army and the Bowery Mission continued to offer services to the area's homeless, even as the city changed around them.[24]

By the turn of the twenty-first century, only six traditional flophouses re-mained on the Bowery: the World, Grand, Sunshine, White House, Prince, and Providence. Rooms rented for approximately $10 per night, although those that had been renovated rented to tourists for up to $30 or $40. By 2005, the White House was a youth hostel and the Pioneer Hotel catered to budget visitors as the Sohotel. Roughly 1,500 rooms on the Bowery remained acces-sible to homeless men, while illegal boarding houses in the outer boroughs arose to meet the demand for housing. Outer borough operators routinely forced guests to sleep in shifts, amid inadequate sanitary facilities and fire haz-ards. Undocumented workers proved especially vulnerable to such schemes, as operators routinely overcharged them for substandard accommodations. Even those receiving workfare, food stamps, and other government assistance often found themselves unable to afford the rents in such flophouses.[25]

After decades of delay and gradual change, dramatic waves of gentrifica-tion eventually brought some real estate values on the Bowery to luxury lev-els. The Avalon Chrystie Place at Houston Street and the Bowery houses the upscale supermarket Whole Foods, while at 195 Bowery, luxury apartments include a sixteenth-floor penthouse worth over $4 million. Observers have been startled by the rapid gentrification, as flophouses suddenly gave way to luxury lofts.

Once skid rows no longer contained the homeless and their habits, waves of conflict ensued between the homeless and officials in cities across the country. Where were the homeless to sleep? What sanitation facilities would be available for their use? At stake was the power to control the city streets and determine appropriate public behavior. Arresting the homeless for performing basic life functions in public amounted to the criminalization of abject poverty, a concept that struck many officials and urban residents as not only inappropriate but also unethical. Homeless advocates rated New York City number fourteen of the "Top 20 Meanest Cities" in terms of anti-homeless regulations. Yet cities across the nation also enacted ordinances blocking the actions and presence of the homeless. As of 2005, nearly 30 percent of the nation's cities prohibited "camping" in specific areas, 27 percent barred individuals from sitting or lying down in some public areas, almost 40 percent banned loitering in some areas, and 43 percent barred begging in some places. These ordinances represent the efforts of frustrated city officials to use behavioral deterrents to attempt to solve a social and economic problem.[26]

Since the beginning of the recession in 2007, concerns over homelessness have increased. According to the Annual Homeless Assessment Report, nearly 1.6 million Americans used emergency shelters or transitional housing programs in 2009. A single-night survey found over 643,000 homeless, approximately one-third of them unsheltered, meaning they slept outdoors, in abandoned buildings, or in automobiles. Individuals in homeless facilities made up 37 percent of survey subjects; one-sixth of homeless individuals lived in Southern California, Las Vegas, New Orleans, or New York. Homeless families and youth made up an alarmingly large proportion of the homeless population. Between 2007 and 2009, the number of sheltered homeless families increased by 13 percent; nearly 240,000 family members were homeless. Some reports estimated as many as 110,000 youth were among the unsheltered homeless, with youth leaving the foster care system especially vulnerable. Approximately 107,000 military veterans were homeless, many suffering the lingering effects of post-traumatic stress disorder, traumatic brain injury, or sexual abuse.[27]

Although today's public servants address the needs of a population that no longer always resembles that of skid row, lessons remain in the history of urban homelessness. The moderate effectiveness of skid-row policies in addressing the needs of the homeless stemmed in part from their collaborative nature. As skid rows evolved, they reflected public-private partnerships at work. The initial charity structure forged by private organizations had later been bolstered and expanded by an infusion of local, state, and briefly, federal support. On skid row, governmental agencies were not in conflict with private religious charities. Instead, they had shared the overlapping goals of sheltering, feeding, and clothing the homeless. By issuing vouchers for private establishments, and other means, governmental agencies actively supported skid rows. This arrangement allowed cities to house the homeless through flexible strategies, without committing to large-scale building or funding schemes.

Skid-row policies were often weakened by the lack of federal support. The local nature of homeless assistance programs remained constant throughout the twentieth century, interrupted only by the intervention of the Federal Transient Program. Although a degree of local authority in implementing public assistance programs can help to ensure that the needs of the local population are addressed, relying solely on local authorities often led to wildly varying levels of assistance, institutionalization of local prejudice, and discrimination against the transient homeless. Federal neglect of the homeless occurred also as the government and private employers left many homeless Americans outside the social insurance and private pension programs central to the burgeoning welfare state. Abandoned by federal authorities, the homeless turned to skid rows in search of assistance.

Large-scale efforts to understand and end homelessness were carried out on the Bowery and other skid rows at mid-century. These interventions, first in the hands of the alcoholism movement, and later the work of social scientists studying social affiliation, focused public as well as academic attention on the problem of homelessness. Both efforts struggled to yield meaningful results, too deeply buried in single-issue research to reach broader conclusions about the causes and effects of homelessness. Viewing the skid-row population in the 1970s and 1980s often as monolithic led to the misconception that the homeless were all mentally ill or substance abusers. Although the deinstitutionalization of many mentally ill individuals and drug addiction had furthered urban homelessness, so had an array of other factors, including urban development policy, the real estate market, and cuts to public assistance programs.

In 1986, President Reagan approved the Stewart B. McKinney Homeless Assistance Act. The act and its subsequent reauthorizations allocated federal support to homeless assistance programs. By 2009, congressional funding of such programs topped $1.67 billion. McKinney Act programs have included educating homeless youth and assistance to mentally ill homeless.[28]

In 2010, the U.S. Interagency Council on Homelessness issued "Opening

Doors: Federal Strategic Plan to End Homelessness." The plan builds on exist-ing programs, embracing ambitious goals, including ending chronic home-lessness and the homelessness of veterans in five years, that of families and children in ten years, and beginning to "end all homelessness." There are en-couraging signs that its authors have learned from history. The plan stresses the importance of collaborative programs, and mentions the need for work-ing with nonprofit agencies assisting the homeless. It also clarifies the impor-tance of fostering cooperation between local, state, and federal authorities, a goal sorely lacking through most of the twentieth century. The plan also emphasizes the crucial element of flexibility in programming. Although it acknowledges the problems that plague many homeless people, such as sub-stance abuse and mental illness, it reminds readers of the individual paths that lead people to homelessness and calls for careful evaluation of each client to aid them in an appropriate manner.

Unlike the approaches toward homeless policy throughout most of the twentieth century, the plan also highlights the structural causes of homeless-ness by identifying lack of affordable housing, inadequate income supports for the near homeless, and a broken health care system as causes. It outlines strategies to improve the care available to veterans and victims of domestic violence, in particular, to keep them from falling into homelessness, while also emphasizing the importance of keeping families together as they receive assistance. The authors caution against relying on programs targeting home-lessness in isolation, calling instead for the support of mainstream programs that also address the needs of the homeless.

In these ways, the current proposal draws on the lessons of history and may be poised to intervene meaningfully in the current crisis. The plan em-phasizes the long-term cost effectiveness of early structural intervention into homelessness, citing fewer emergency room visits, less reliance on hospital care for advanced conditions, fewer police staff hours and jail space spent. In the current recession, it remains to be seen if the nation is willing to follow the example of the New Deal years, summoning the political will necessary to set aside individualistic judgments long enough to invest in social service programs of this scale.

NOTES

Introduction

1. Robert Wagner, quoted in "Bowery Clean-Up Planned," *NYT*, 31 October 1961; Howard M. Bahr, *Homelessness and Disaffiliation* (New York: Bureau of Applied Research, Columbia University, 1968), 261.

2. Jacob Riis, *How the Other Half Lives* (1890; New York: Dover, 1971).

3. "Many Captives," *NYT*, 17 February 1886; "Patrick McGurk's Resort Raided," *NYT*, 21 March 1893; "Many Doors Smashed in Bowery Raid," *NYT*, 23 November 1901; "Jerome Backs Raids of Bowery Resorts," *NYT*, 25 January 1902; "Police Make Raid on Bowery Dives," *NYT*, 16 February 1902; "Filth and Foul Odors, Another Visit to the Lowest Class of Lodging-Houses," *NYT*, 25 January 1882.

4. Kenneth L. Kusmer, *Down and Out, and On the Road: The Homeless in American History* (New York: Oxford University Press, 2002), 147–67.

5. See Christopher Mele, *Selling the Lower East Side: Culture, Real Estate, and Resistance in New York City* (Minneapolis: University of Minnesota Press, 2000); Samuel Zipp, *Manhattan Projects: The Rise and Fall of Urban Renewal in Cold War New York* (New York: Oxford University Press, 2010); Tyler Anbinder, *Five Points: The 19th-Century New York City Neighborhood That Invented Tap Dance, Stole Elections, and Become the World's Most Notorious Slum* (New York: Plume, 2002); Wendell Pritchett, *Brownsville, Brooklyn: Blacks, Jews, and the Changing Face of the Ghetto* (Chicago: University of Chicago Press, 2003); Martha Biondi, *To Stand and Fight: The Struggle for Civil Rights in Postwar New York City* (Cambridge, Mass.: Harvard University Press, 2003); Thomas Kessner, *Fiorello H. La Guardia and the Making of Modern New York* (New York: McGraw Hill, 1989); Vincent J. Cannato, *The Ungovernable City: John Lindsay and His Struggle to Save New York* (New York: Basic Books, 2001); Jonathan Soffer, *Ed Koch and the Rebuilding of New York City* (New York: Columbia University Press, 2010).

6. Michael B. Katz, *The Undeserving Poor: From the War on Poverty to the War on Welfare* (New York: Pantheon, 1990); Katz, *In the Shadow of the Poorhouse: A Social History of Welfare in America* (New York: Basic Books, 1986).

7. Kim Hopper, *Reckoning with Homelessness* (Ithaca, N.Y.: Cornell University Press, 2003), 93–100; Joel Blau, *The Visible Poor* (New York: Oxford University Press, 1992).

8. Don Mitchell, *The Right to the City: Social Justice and the Fight for Public Space* (New York: Guilford Press, 2003), 1–12.

9. Alex Vitale, *City of Disorder: How the Quality of Life Campaign Transformed New York Politics* (New York: New York University Press, 2009); Leonard C. Feldman, *Citizens Without Shelter: Homelessness, Democracy, and Political Exclusion* (Ithaca, N.Y.: Cornell University Press, 2004).

10. Doris Wykowsky, in Ann Marie Rousseau, *Shopping Bag Ladies: Homeless Women Speak About Their Lives* (New York: Pilgrim Press, 1981), 107.

11. Moses, quoted in Gwendolyn A. Dordick, *Something Left to Lose: Personal Relations and Survival Among New York's Homeless* (Philadelphia: Temple University Press, 1997), 13.

12. John Benton, "Rest for Weary Willie," *Saturday Evening Post* 208, 10, 5 September 1936, 5, 6, 79, 81, 82; Howard M. Bahr and Kathleen C. Houts, "Can You Trust a Homeless Man? A Comparison of Official Records and Interview Responses by Bowery Men," *Public Opinion Quarterly* 35, 3 (Fall 1971): 374–82.

13. Sara Harris, *Skid Row U.S.A.* (New York: Tower, 1961); Samuel E. Wallace, *Skid Row as a Way of Life* (New York: Harper & Row, 1968); Rousseau, *Shopping Bag Ladies*; Joseph Hart, *Down and Out: The Life and Death of Minneapolis' Skid Row* (Minneapolis: University of Minnesota Press, 2002); Steven Vanderstaay, *Street Lives: An Oral History of Homeless Americans* (Philadelphia: New Society, 1992); Dordick, *Something Left to Lose*.

14. John, quoted in Vanderstaay, *Street Lives*, 78–79.

15. Kusmer, *Down and Out*, 4–6; Todd DePastino, *Citizen Hobo: How a Century of Homelessness Shaped America* (Chicago: University of Chicago Press, 2003), xxiv–xxv.

16. Doris Wykowsky, quoted in Rousseau, *Shopping Bag Ladies*, 107.

17. See Elaine S. Abelson, "'Women Who Have No Men to Work for Them': Gender and Homelessness in the Great Depression, 1930–1934," *Feminist Studies* 29, 1 (Spring 2003): 104–26; Marsha A. Martin, "Homeless Women: An Historical Perspective," in *On Being Homeless: Historical Perspectives*, ed. Rick Beard (New York: Museum of the City of New York, 1987), 33–41; Lynn Weiner, "Sisters of the Road: Women Transients and Tramps," in *Walking to Work: Tramps in America, 1790–1935*, ed. Eric Monkkonen (Lincoln: University of Nebraska Press, 1984), 171–88.

18. DePastino, *Citizen Hobo*; Don Mitchell, *The Right to the City: Social Justice and the Fight for Public Space* (New York: Guilford, 2003).

19. Kenneth T. Jackson, "The Bowery: From Residential Street to Skid Row," in Beard, ed., *On Being Homeless*, 74–75.

20. Kim Hopper, "The Public Response to Homelessness in New York City—the Last Hundred Years," in Beard, ed., *On Being Homeless*, 89–101; "163, 176 in Almshouses," *NYT*, 11 July 1906; David J. Rothman, "The First Shelters: The Contemporary Relevance of the Almshouse," in Beard, ed., *On Being Homeless*, 12.

21. David T. Courtwright, *Violent Land: Single Men and Social Disorder from the Frontier to the Inner City* (Cambridge, Mass.: Harvard University Press, 1996), 170–97.

22. See also Tim Cresswell, "Tramps, Knowledge and Mobility," in *The Tramp in America* (London: Reaktion, 2001), 9–22; DePastino, *Citizen Hobo*, xviii–xix; Kusmer, "The Underclass in Historical Perspective: Tramps and Vagrants in Early America, 1870–1930," in Beard, ed., *On Being Homeless*, 20–31; Frank Tobias Higbie, *Indispensable Outcasts: Hobo Workers and Community in the American Midwest, 1880–1930* (Urbana: University of Illinois Press, 2003).

23. Nels Anderson, *The Homeless in New York City: A Study of Their Needs and of the Community's Resources for Assisting Them* (New York: Welfare Council of New York City Research Bureau, February 1934), 28; CSS Papers, Box 132, Columbia University Archives; Kusmer, *Down and Out*, 73–98. See *Leslie's Weekly* 21, 4 October 1865, 39, *NYT*, 13 February 1874, both cited in Anderson, *The Homeless in New York City*, 29.

24. Kusmer, *Down and Out*, 6, 55–56; Charity Organization Society, press release, June 1943, CSS Papers, Box 191, Folder: Woodyard and Laundry, Columbia University; To Members of the Executive Committee, memorandum, 16 December 1933, CSS Papers, Box 191, Folder: Woodyard and Laundry; Charles E. Merrill, Jr., Chairman, Committee on Industrial Building of Woodyard, to Mortimer H. Singer, Esq., 2 December 1912, CSS Papers, Box 189, Folder: Woodyard—1909–24.

25. Nels Anderson, *The Homeless in New York City: A Study of Their Needs and of the Community's Resources for Assisting Them* (NY: Welfare Council of New York City Research Bureau, February 1934), 459; "Woodyard's Long Record," *Evening Post*, 5 August 1908, CSS Papers, Box 189, Folder: Woodyard—1909–24; C.O.S., press release; Johnson de Forest, Wayfarers' Lodge, to Stanley P. Davies, 8 April 1937, CSS Papers, Box 190, Folder: Woodyard—1930–38; Hopper, "The Public Response to Homelessness," 91–94; Standing Committee on Vagrancy to the Conference of Charities, 13 May 1896, CSS Papers, Box 182, Folder: Vagrancy; "Days Work Performed in the Wood Yard, 1910–11, 1911–12," chart, CSS Papers, Box 189, Folder: Woodyard—1909–24.

26. Office of the Chief of Police, Police Department of the City of New York, to Precinct Captains, Special Order No. 2610, 11 February 1896, CSS Papers, Box 182, Folder: Vagrancy

27. S. S. Bogert, Chairman, Office of the 3rd District Committee, to the Secretary of Committee on Wayfarers' Lodge, 20 July 1894; Charles E. Merrill, Jr., Chairman, Committee on Industrial Building of Woodyard, to City Editor of the *NYT*, 8 January 1909, CSS Papers, Box 189, Folder: Woodyard—1909–24.

28. Lawson Purdy, Secretary, C.O.S., to Our Members and Contributors, November 1921, CSS Papers, Box 189, Folder: Woodyard—1909–24; Charles W. Ogden, Chairman, Fundraising Appeal for the Woodyard of the C.O.S., January 1933, CSS Papers, Box 190, Folder: Woodyard—1930–38; Johnson De Forest to Lawson Purdy, Secretary, C.O.S., 22 December 1927, CSS Papers, Box 191, Folder: Woodyard and Laundry.

29. Kusmer, *Down and Out,* 79–80; "A Farm Colony for Paupers," *NYT*, 2 April 1896;

"Mrs. Lowell on Vagrancy," *NYT*, 17 February 1897; "To Start a Farm Colony," *NYT*, 22 February 1897.

30. W. Frank Persons, "The Charity Organization Society's Woodyard & the Municipal Lodging House," 30 October 1916, CSS Papers, Box 189, Folder: Woodyard—1909–24; Farm Colony Committee, Section on the Homeless, Welfare Council of New York City, June 10, 1932, A Work Relief Project for the Homeless, CSS Papers, Box 185, Folder: Welfare Council—Coordinating Committee on Unemployment 1934–35; "The City Overrun with Homeless Men," NYT, 28 December 1907; "Bread Lines Long at Charity's Doors," NYT, 29 December 1907; "The Growing Problem of the American Tramp," NYT, 14 June 1908; "Facing the Problem of the Unemployed," NYT, 25 October 1908.

31. For media coverage of the proposed farm colony, see "To Start a Farm Colony," NYT, 22 February 1897; "Farm Colony for Vagrants," NYT, 8 January 1898; "City Farm Crop Wins Prizes," NYT, 20 November 1910; "Colony Farm Proposed as a Solution of the Tramp Problem," NYT, 21 May 1911; "Vagrancy Growing All over the State," NYT, 24 May 1911; "Protest Against Poor Farm," NYT, 25 September 1912; "Farm Colony for Women," NYT, 10 December 1914; "Shows Need of Hobo-Farm," NYT, 4 February 1917.

32. Kusmer, *Down and Out,* 79–80.

33. Frank Charles Laubach, "Why There are Vagrants: A Study Based Upon an Examination of One Hundred Men," PhD diss., Columbia University, 1916, 5, 7, 10, 12, 113–14, 118, 119.

34. "Nation to Help Aid the Jobless," *NYT*, 8 March 1915; "New York to Have Repair Shop for Humanity," *NYT*, 23 April 1916.

35. Luc Sante, *Low Life: Lures and Snares of Old New York* (New York: Vintage, 1992), 11–16; Christine Stansell, *City of Women: Sex and Class in New York, 1789–1960* (Urbana: University of Illinois Press, 1987); I. L. Nascher, *The Wretches of Povertyville: A Sociological Study of the Bowery*, sketches and illustrations by George Toner (Chicago: Jos. J. Lanzit, 1909); Kathy Peiss, *Cheap Amusements: Working Women and Leisure in Turn-of-the-Century New York* (Philadelphia: Temple University Press, 1986), 139–62.

36. Alvin F. Harlow, *Old Bowery Days: The Chronicles of a Famous Street* (New York: D. Appleton, 1931), 403–5; Nascher, *The Wretches,* 168–83.

37. Sante, *Low Life,* 104–40; Harlow, *Old Bowery Days,* 417–24; Nascher, *The Wretches,* 20–22; Jacob Riis, *How the Other Half Lives* (New York: Scribner's, 1890), 11, 4–8.

38. Kusmer, *Down and Out,* 47–67; "The Mission House Fire," *NYT*, 15 March 1898; Riis, *How the Other Half Lives,* 11, 4–8.

39. Nascher, *The Wretches,* 10, 9, 13–16, 18–19; "Latter Day Diversions of the Bowery," in Harlow, *Old Bowery Days,* 454–86.

40. Jackson, in *On Being Homeless,* ed. Beard, 73, 69, 74; Nascher, *The Wretches,* 33, 49–50, 80–81.

41. Nascher, *The Wretches,* 70–97, 93.

42. Anbinder, *Five Points,* 241–68.

43. Nels Anderson, "Some Observations on the Bowery," sent 24 July 1928 from William Hodson, Executive Director, Welfare Council of New York City, to Miss Anna Kempshall, Charity Organization Society, 7–8, CSS Papers, Box 131, Folder: Homeless—1927–33; Logan L. Thomas, *Report on the Greater New York Gospel Mission* (New York: Welfare Council of New York City, Research Bureau, September 1931), 5.

44. "Bowery Mission's New Home," *NYT*, 19 September 1908; "Bowery Breadline Is Back," *NYT*, 27 November 1908; "Mission Accuses Lodging House Men," *NYT*, 10 February 1908; "Bowery Mission to Expand," *NYT*, 6 November 1920.

45. Mr. William Warner Hopkins, Chairman of the Board, quoted in Annual Report of the Association in 1881, cited in "The Bowery Branch of the Y.M.C.A. of New York City: A Short History Compiled April 15, 1927," CSS Papers, Box 131, Folder: Homeless—Clippings—Articles; Ernest Poole, "Something Is Wrong," *NYT*, 18 February 1930; Anderson, *Homelessness in New York City*, 89–92.

46. Anderson, *Homeless in New York City*, 74, 76; Lieutenant William C. Davis, "Nomads: The Salvation Army Method of Dealing with the Homeless Man Problem," *War Cry*, 21 January 1933, 4, 13.

Chapter 1. The Challenge of the Depression

1. Nels Anderson, "Some Observations on the Bowery," sent July 24, 1928 by William Hodson, Executive Director, Welfare Council of New York City, to Miss Anna Kempshall, Charity Organization Society, 8–9, CSS Papers, Box 131, Folder: Homeless—1927–1933; "Snowfall a Boon to the Jobless," *NYT*, 10 March 1928; "Mr. Zero to Give Out Food," *NYT*, 17 June 1931; "Thanksgiving Feast Stewing at the Tub," *NYT*, 27 November 1929; "Mr. Zero Holds Open House," *NYT*, 21 April 1930; Franklin Folsom, *America Before Welfare* (New York: New York University Press, 1991), 226–27.

2. "Dramatizing the Bowery Boy," *NYT*, 3 January 1925; "City's Thanksgiving a Feast of Bounty," *NYT*, 30 November 1928; "Jobless Set Pace in Fashion Parade," *NYT*, 28 March 1932.

3. "The Bowery Branch of the YMCA of New York City, A Short History compiled April 15, 1927," CSS Papers, Box 131, Folder: Homeless—Clippings—Articles; Cleveland A. Dunn, former chairman of the Bowery Committee of Management, "Policy of the Bowery Branch," CSS Papers, Box 131, Folder: Homeless—Clippings—Articles; Elmer Galloway, "Homeless Men Make Up Unique Bowery Problem," *NYT*, 26 January 1930; Nels Anderson, *The Homeless in New York City: A Study of Their Needs and of the Community's Resources for Assisting Them* (New York: Welfare Council of New York City Research Bureau, February 1934), 127, Table 21.

4. Andrew S. Dolkart, *New York City Landmarks Preservation Commission Guide to New York City Landmarks* (New York: Wiley, 2003), 25.

5. *New York Charities Directory* (New York: New York Charity Organization Society, 1920), 164, 58.

6. Catherine Brody, "New York's One Hotel for Old Women Only," *New York Herald Tribune*, 26 October 1924.

7. *New York Charities Directory*, 71, 72, 16, 77, 157.

8. Ibid., 22, 216.

9. Ibid., 46.

10. Ibid., 289, 265, 318; Judith Weisenfeld, "The Harlem YWCA and the Secular City, 1904–1945," *Journal of Women's History* 6, 3 (Fall 1994): 62–78.

11. *New York Charities Directory*, 206.

12. Beth S. Wenger, *New York Jews and the Great Depression: Uncertain Promise* (New Haven, Conn.: Yale University Press, 1996), 136; Marc Dollinger, *Quest for Inclusion: Jews and Liberalism in Modern America* (Princeton, N.J.: Princeton University Press, 2000), 19, 11, 14; Anderson, *Homeless in New York City*, 85–88; Mark Wischnitzer, *Visas to Freedom: The History of HIAS* (New York: World, 1956), 37–48, 28–30, 52, 67–69, 34–35.

13. Anderson, "Some Observations," 7–8; Marian J. Morton, "The Transformation of Catholic Orphanages: Cleveland, 1851–1996," *Catholic Historical Review* 88, 1 (January 2002): 65–89; Dorothy M. Brown and Elizabeth McKeown, Introduction to *The Poor Belong to Us: Catholic Charities and American Welfare* (Cambridge, Mass.: Harvard University Press, 1997), 1–12, 3, 4, 6; June Hopkins, *Harry Hopkins: Sudden Hero, Brash Reformer* (New York: St. Martin's, 1999), 71–90.

14. Studs Terkel, *Hard Times: An Oral History of the Great Depression* (New York: Pantheon, 1970), 30.

15. Anderson, "Some Observations," 4; "Call Breadlines Longest Since 1916," *NYT*, 13 February 1928; "Homeless Men Crowd City Lodging House," *Better Times* 10, 17 (29 April 1929): 11, Box 131, Folder: Homeless—Clippings—Articles; Anderson, *Homelessn in New York City*, 92; "600 New Jobs a Day Promised for Idle," *NYT*, 24 November 1930; "City Votes $30,000 for Lodging Annex," *NYT*, 14 February 1931.

16. Anderson, *Homeless in New York City*, 162, 308, 155–56, 146, 160, 171–72, 164–66, 161, 170.

17. Ibid., 112, 108–9, 89; Press Release from Welfare Council of New York City, 3 November 1930, CSS Papers, Box 131, Folder: Homeless—1927–33.

18. Press Release from Welfare Council, 3 November 1930; Anderson, *Homeless in New York City*, 308–9.

19. Lieutenant William C. Davis, "Nomads: The Salvation Army Method of Dealing with the Homeless Man Problem," *War Cry*, 21 January 1933, 4, 13; Anderson, *Homelessness in New York City*, 79, 76, 77. "City to Consider Relief for Idle," *NYT*, 13 March 1930. "The Bowery Eats," *War Cry*, 20 September 1930, 4; "Laundry Is Supplied for Destitute Men," *NYT*, 16 March 1932; "Cheer Lodge Raises Morale of Jobless," *NYT*, 17 July 1932.

20. Anderson, *Homeless in New York City*, 77; Esther H. Elias, "Gold Dust Lodge," *War Cry*, 31 December 1932, 3, 15; Jean Johnson, "Pure Gold at Gold Dust Lodge," *War Cry*, 4 November 1933, 3.

21. "That's Where I'd Go," Bowery YMCA brochure, CSS Papers, Box 131, Folder Homeless—Clippings—Articles.

22. Ibid.; "Reports More Jobless," *NYT*, 15 January 1928; "Bowery Y.M.C.A. is Short on Budget," *NYT*, 19 February 1930; Anderson, *Homeless in New York City*, 162; John H. Henry, "Bowery Mission Needs Help," *NYT*, 20 February 1930; "Bowery's Y.M.C.A. Seeks $67,000 Fund; Haven for Educated Men in Distress," *NYT*, 12 February 1933; "Bowery Branch of the YMCA"; "Y.M.C.A. to Erect Buildings in 1930," *NYT*, 19 January 1930; "New Harlem Y.M.C.A. to be Started Today," *NYT*, 10 November 1931.

23. Anderson, *Homelessness in New York City*, 141–46; Wenger, *New York Jews*, 15–24.

24. Wenger, *New York Jews*, 40, 138–45.

25. Logan L. Thomas, *Report on the Greater New York Gospel Mission* (New York: Welfare Council of New York City Research Bureau, 1931), 7–10, 42.

26. Anderson, *Homeless in New York City*, 72.

27. Thomas, *Report*, 13–16, 33–35, 64, 73. Kenneth L. Kusmer, *Down and Out, and On the Road: The Homeless in American History* (New York: Oxford University Press, 2002), 84–89.

28. Elaine S. Ableson, "'Women Who Have No Men to Work for Them': Gender and Homelessness in the Great Depression," *Feminist Studies* 29, 1 (Spring 2003): 104–27; Agnus V. O'Shea, "Development of the Care of Transient Women," *The Transient* 1 (November 1934); Anderson, *Homeless in New York City*, 125, Table 7.

29. Anderson, *Homeless in New York City*, 92, 130.

30. Ibid., 130–32.

31. Ibid., 124–25, 128, Table 7; Emily Hahn, "Women Without Work," *New Republic*, 31 May 1933, 63–65.

32. "Women's Canteen and Rest Room," *War Cry*, 31 January 1931; "Rallying to Aid the Army's Emergency Relief Activities," *War Cry*, 21 November 1931, 13; "Solving the Women's Problem," *War Cry*, 3 September 1932, 5; "A Nation-Wide Chain of Free Food Depots," *War Cry*, 24 October 1931, 3; "The E. F. Hutton Free Food Depot," *War Cry*, 3 January 1931, 9.

33. "Jobless Women Shy at Free Lunch Room, But Dainty Service and Flowers Tempt Them," *NYT*, 5 December 1930.

34. Anderson, *Homeless in New York City*, 132–33, Table 12; Virginia Pope, "Future of Women Workers: Lessons of the Depression," *NYT*, 13 March 1932; Anderson, Table 7.

35. Anderson, *Homelessness in New York City*, 384–85; Isabel E. Weaver, "Why Women Work," *NYT*, 5 August 1933.

36. Cheryl Lynn Greenberg, *"Or Does It Explode?" Black Harlem in the Great Depression* (New York: Oxford University Press, 1991), 44. Anderson, *Homeless in New York City*, 137.

37. Report of Seven Harlem Cases brought to office by Mr. Winters and Mr. Mayer, 13 November 1931, Case #2874, CSS Papers, Box 158, Folder: Relief—Harlem—Mt. Morris District—1931–32; "Additional Cases of Families in Need of Immediate Relief Cited by Harlem Committee on Unemployment," *New York Age*, 21 March 1931, CSS Papers, Box 158, Folder: Relief—Harlem—Mt. Morris District—1931–32.

38. Anderson, *Homeless in New York City*, 179, 140.

39. Ibid., 77; "Concerning the Homeless Man," *War Cry*, 24 October 1931, 10; Charity Organization Society Report on Relief in Harlem and Mt. Morris District, CSS Papers, Box 158, Folder: Relief—Harlem—Mt. Morris District—1931–32; Esther H. Elias, "Where Harlem's Hungry Hordes are Fed, Scenes at the Salvation Army Colored Men's Hotel and Food Depot," *War Cry*, 11 March 1933, 3; Commissioner Alexander M. Damon, "The Salvation Army Review of Welfare Activities in Greater New York for the Year Ending September 30, 1936," Salvation Army Archives; "Dispo" for Eastern Territory Men's Social Service Department, Hotel for Colored Men, New York City, Salvation Army Archives.

40. Welfare Council of New York City, "Central Registration Bureau for Women, Outstanding Facts Brought Out by Statistics for October, November, and December 1932," Box 184, CSS Papers, Folder: Welfare Council Central Registration Bureau, 1933–34; Welfare Council of New York City, "Report of the Work of the Central Registration Bureau for Women from March 1st to September 30, 1932," Box 184, CSS Papers, Folder: Welfare Council—Central Registration Bureau, 1933–34; Anderson, *Homeless in New York City*, 135.

41. "The Harlem Cooperating Committee on Relief and Unemployment, Campaign Facts Brochure," CSS Papers, Box 158, Folder: Relief—Harlem—Mt. Morris District—1931–32; "'Work, Not Charity,' Asked by Jobless," *NYT*, 5 February 1931.

42. Mrs. Addiss to Miss Kempshall, memorandum, 28 June 1932, CSS Papers, Box 158, Folder: Relief—Harlem—Mt. Morris District—1931–32.

43. Anderson, *Homeless in New York City*, 161.

44. American Association for Organizing Family Social Work, Minutes on the Meeting of the Committee on the Homeless, 18 April 1929, CSS Papers, Box 131, Folder: Homeless 1927–33; Anderson, *Homeless in New York City*, 218–19.

45. Anderson, *Homeless in New York City*, 134–41.

46. "Free Bed Seekers Under Official Fine," *NYT*, 5 January 1928; "4 Bowery Lodgings Closed by Harris," *NYT*, 1 April 1928; "Health Orders Met in Bowery Lodgings," *NYT*, 4 April 1928; "Health Rule Defied by Rescue Mission," *NYT*, 6 April 1928; "Harris Yields Point on All-Night Mission," *NYT*, 7 April 1928; "'Bowery Bishop' Heeds Dr. Harris," *NYT*, 8 April 1928; "Harris Asks Bureau to Allot Free Beds," *NYT*, 10 April 1928.

47. "Bored Bums Can't Dig Up Even Work," *Daily News*, 13 April 1928, 8.

48. Martin Sommers, "Truth About Bowery Homeless and Jobless," *Daily News*, 9 April 1928, 3–4; "Imp in Bottle Enslaves Bowery," *Daily News*, 10 April 1928, 3–4; "No Cash-No Job Rule Breeds Bowery Bums," *Daily News*, 11 April 1928, 2, 4; "The News Reporter and His Pal Are Hired But Have Good Excuse to Quit," *Daily News*, 12 April 1928, 2, 6; "Bored Bums Can't Dig Up Even Work."

49. Charles Burlingham, Chairman, New York Association for Improving the Condition of the Poor, to Arthur Woods, Commissioner of Police, 1 December 1914, Box 159, Folder: Saloons—Investigation of 1915–16; Press Release from the Welfare Council of New York City, 3 November 1930, CSS Papers, Box 131, Folder: Homeless—1927–33; "2,347 Begin Count of City's People," *NYT*, 3 April 1930.

50. "Smith Group warns of Begging Menace," *NYT*, 7 December 1930; "Asks Public to Curb Begging in Streets," *NYT*, 4 January 1932.

51. "Relief Groups Clash on Free Meal Tickets; Council Attacks Plan to Curb Begging," *NYT*, 12 September 1932; "Relief Fund Acts to Curb Begging," *NYT*, 12 November 1932.

52. "Of 574 Breadlines, Only 25 Want Jobs," *NYT*, 22 March 1916; "Flock of Crippled Beggars Go To Jail," *NYT*, 27 May 1921; "Plan Drive Against Wealthy Beggars," *NYT*, 5 September 1922; "Well-To-Do Beggars," *NYT*, 23 May 1929; "Beggars Get Millions in Generous New York," *NYT*, 15 August 1926; "Moneyed Beggar Exiled from City," *NYT*, 19 December 1928; "Beggars Said to Get $125,000 Daily in City; Subways Called Best 'Shake-Down Spots,'" *NYT*, 24 July 1929; Interview with Stuart A. Rice, 8 July 1927, stapled to Minutes, Sub-Committee on the Homeless, 11 July 1927, with information from Rice's articles, "The Municipal Lodging House–A Hybrid Institution," *American Labor Legislation Review*, March 1922, and "The Failure of the Municipal Lodging House," *National Municipal Review*, November 1922, CSS Papers, Box 132, Folder: Homelessness— Subcommittee—Welfare Council—1927–29.

53. Anderson, *Homeless in New York City*, 404, 406–7.

54. Ibid., 405–6.

55. Marilyn Cohen, *Reginald Marsh's New York: Paintings, Drawings, Prints, and Photographs* (New York: Whitney Museum of Art with Dover, 1983); "Breadlines Inspire Art Show Canvases," *NYT*, 25 February 1931.

56. "Calls it Unwise Charity," *Tribune*, 13 April 1901; "Bread for all at 'Sun' Depot," *New York Sun*, 9 March 1914; Kusmer, *Down and Out*, 81–82; Bailey B. Burritt, Acting General, New York AICP, to Editor of the *Sun*, 14 March 1914, CSS Papers, Box 97, Folder: Breadline 1914–15; COS Protests; "No Pauperization in Free Bread Charity," *New York Sun*, 14 March 1914; "Women Dodge Bread Line, But Get Loaves," *New York Morning Sun*, 18 March 1914.

57. Burritt to Editor of the *Sun*; "No Pauperization in Free Bread Charity."

58. "Breadline Meals to be Regulated," *NYT*, 12 February 1931; Lilian Brandt, *An Impressionistic View of the Winter of 1930–31 in New York City* (New York: Welfare Council of New York City, February 1932), 41.

59. Robert S. McElvaine, *The Great Depression: America, 1929–1941* (New York: Times Books, 1984), 78–79; "Sees Relief Abused in Bread Lines Here," *NYT*, 16 December 1930; "Church Scores Bread Line," *NYT*, 25 October, 1931; Kusmer, *Down and Out*, 84–89; "A Nation-Wide Chain of Free Food Depots," *War Cry*, 24 October 1931, 3.

60. "Breadline Meals to be Regulated," *NYT*, 12 February 1931; "30th Anniversary, 1925 to 1955," Welfare and Health Council of New York City, brochure, and "The Welfare Council of New York City, Some Questions Answered," brochure, 1928, CSS Papers, Box 184, Folder: Welfare Council: Beginnings; "Opens Food Depot Founded by Hutton," *NYT*, 19 December 1930; "Feeds 2,000 Jobless on His 51st Birthday," *NYT*, 18 April 1929; See "Irving T. Bush Weds Miss Marian Spore in Reno One Hour After His Wife Gets Divorce Decree," *NYT*, 10 June 1930; "New Lady Bountiful Aiding the Bowery," *NYT*, 21

February 1930; "Lady Bountiful Continues Her Aid," *NYT*, 25 February 1930; Marion Spore, "My Work on the Bowery," *North American Review*, August 1930, 245–49, 247.

61. Cora Kasius, "COS Program in Relation to Community Developments During the Depression Years 1929–1936," May 1938, Box 115, CSS Papers, Folder: Depression Years—COS Program, 1929–36, 8.

62. Kasius, "COS Program," 7; City of New York Emergency Work Commission, "Standards for Rating the Eligibility of Applicants for Work Relief," 11 March 1932, Box 149, Folder: New York City—Commission Work Bureau 1931–32; City of New York Emergency Work Commission Report, December 28, 1931 to May 31, 1932, Box 150, Folder: New York Emergency Work Commission Report—December 1931–May 1932; William W. Bremer, *Depression Winters: New York Social Workers and the New Deal* (Philadelphia: Temple University Press, 1984), 32; "$1,400,000 Raised in Drive to Provide Jobs for Idle; Harkness Gives $500,000," *NYT*, 19 November 1930; "Church Scores Bread Line," *NYT*, 25 October, 1931; Kusmer, *Down and Out*, 84–89; "120 Cities Abandon Breadline Relief," *NYT*, 26 January 1931.

63. "Over 12,000 Brooklyn Unemployed In Mighty Relief Demonstration," *Daily Worker*, 9 January 1931; "3 Red 'Hunger' Riots Stir Only the Police," *NYT*, 9 January 1931; "600 Rioters Here Battle 100 Police at Relief Bureau," *NYT*, 27 May 1934; "Police Attack Jobless in N.Y. Demonstration," *Daily Worker*, 28 May 1934; "Wide Appeal Made to Aid Unemployed," *NYT*, 20 March 1930; "Welfare Leaders See Growing Need to Aid the Jobless," *NYT*, 11 February 1928; "Urges Federal Aid for the Jobless," *NYT*, 17 February 1928; "Turn Away 1000 at Bowery Mission," *Daily Worker*, 17 February 1928.

64. "3,000 Jobless 'Demand Shelter' Give Real Feed!" *Daily Worker*, 5 January 1931; "Reds Lead Jobless in Lodging Demand," *NYT*, 4 January 1931.

65. R. L. Duffus, "New York Coordinates Relief for Unemployed," *NYT*, 8 November 1931; "Final Plea by Smith for Aid to Jobless," *NYT*, 19 December 1932; Anderson, *Homeless in New York City*, 226–27.

66. Ernest Poole, "Personal Reports of What Goes On in the Bowery and the East Side," *NYT*, 4 April 1932; "Hoover Endorses Gibson Fund Appeal," *NYT*, 26 October 1932; "Expenditures on Outdoor Relief," Research Bureau, Welfare Council of New York City; William Hodson Papers, New York Public Library Special Collections, Box 5, Folder: Miscellaneous Personal—Prior to 1934; McElvaine, *The Great Depression*, 78–79, 88.

67. James R. McGovern, *And a Time for Hope: Americans in the Great Depression* (Westport, Conn.: Praeger, 2000), 3–5.

68. David M. Katzman, "Ann Arbor: Depression City," in *Hitting Home: The Great Depression in Town and Country*, ed. Bernard Sternsher (Chicago: Quadrangle, 1970), 47–59; reprinted from *Michigan History* 50 (December 1966): 306–17.

69. Bonnie Fox Schwartz, "Unemployment Relief in Philadelphia, 1930–1932: A Study of the Depression's Impact on Voluntarism," in *Hitting Home*, 60–84; reprinted from *Pennsylvania Magazine of History and Biography* 92 (January 1969): 86–108.

70. Josephine Chapin Brown, "The President's Organization on Unemployment Re-

lief; State Governments Rise to the Emergency," in *Public Relief, 1929–1939* (1940; New York: Octagon, 1971), 85–102.

71. Bremer, *Depression Winters*, 65, 70; "Cities Prefer Own to Federal Relief," *NYT*, 6 September 1931.

72. J. Brooks Atkinson, "The Now and Here: Tragedy of the Jobless in a Floundering Play that Visualizes the Great Emergency of These Times," *NYT*, 20 December 1931.

73. Terkel, *Hard Times*, 30–31.

74. Bernard Sternsher, "Victims of the Great Depression: Self-Blame/Non-Self-Blame, Radicalism, and Pre-1929 Experiences," *Social Science History* 1, 2 (Winter 1977): 137–77.

75. Anderson, *Homelessness in New York City*, 386, 392, 215–17.

76. "Says Agencies to Track Jobless," *NYT*, 7 April 1930; Britt cited in Anderson, *Homelessness in New York City*, 293; Anderson, *Homeless in New York City*, 391.

77. Anderson, *Homeless in New York City*, 347–70.

78. Ibid., 388, 222–26.

79. Ibid., 383.

80. Ibid.,380, 383, 381.

81. Ibid., 386, 389.

82. "Pleas of Idle Grow as City Expands Aid," *NYT*, 30 October 1930; "24 Homeless Men Arrested," *NYT*, 12 March 1935.

83. Robert Neuwirth, "Squatters in New York," in Neuwirth, *Shadow Cities: A Billion Squatters, a New Urban World* (New York: Routledge, 2005), chap. 6, 205–37.

84. Alan Bloom, "Women and Children: The Forgotten Homeless of the Nineteenth Century," Organization of American Historians Annual Meeting, Thursday, 20 April 2006; Daniel R. Kerr, *Derelict Paradise: Homelessness and Urban Development in Cleveland, Ohio* (Amherst: University of Massachusetts Press, 2011), 39–70.

85. Anderson, *The Homeless in New York City*, 64, 59, 60; Boris Israel, "Shantytown, U.S.A.," *New Republic*, 24 May 1933, 39–41; "Men of 'Jungles' Win Vote Right by Court Order," *New York World-Telegram*, 13 October 1932.

86. "Park Squatters Defy Critics of Huts' Neatness," *New York Herald Tribune*, 23 September 1932.

87. "Call Breadlines Longest Since 1916," *NYT*, 13 February 1928; "The Army of the Unemployed Has Drawn Strange Recruits," *NYT*, 16 November 1930; "2 Breadlines Feed 2,000 Daily Here," *NYT*, 19 March 1930.

88. Helen R. Wright, "The Families of the Unemployed in Chicago," *Social Science Review* 8, 1 (March 1934): 17–30.

89. Edwin H. Sutherland and Harvey J. Locke, *Twenty Thousand Homeless Men: A Study of Unemployed Men in the Chicago Shelters* (Chicago: Lippincott, 1936; reprinted New York: Arno Press and New York Times, 1971), 88.

90. Ibid., 75.

91. Wenger, *New York Jews*, 150; Dollinger, *Quest for Inclusion*, 28–29, 33.

92. Sternsher, "Victims of the Great Depression," 165.

93. Matthew Josephson, "'Relief': The Last Gasp on Private Charity," *New Republic*, 10 May 1933, 354–56.

Chapter 2. A New Deal for the Homeless

1. Franklin D. Roosevelt, "The Forgotten Man," radio address, Albany, N.Y., 7 April 1932, in *The Public Papers and Addresses of Franklin D. Roosevelt, 1928–32* (New York: Random House, 1938), 1:624.

2. Joan Crouse, *The Homeless Transient in the Great Depression, New York State, 1929–1941* (Albany, N.Y.: SUNY Press, 1986), 42; Ernest Poole, "The Work of Relief: Personal Reports of What Goes on in the Bowery and the East Side," *NYT*, 4 April 1932; "1,130,000 Lodgings by City This Year," *NYT*, 28 October 1932; Ellery F. Reed, *FTP: An Evaluative Survey, May to July, 1934* (New York: Committee on Care of Transients and Homeless), 21–22.

3. Joseph R. Mason, "The Political Economy of Reconstruction Finance Corporation Assistance During the Great Depression," *Explorations in Economic History* 40 (2003): 101–21; Daniel C. Vogt, "Hoover's RFC in Action: Mississippi, Bank loans, and Work Relief, 1932–1933," *Journal of Mississippi History* 47, 1 (1985): 35–53; William Bremer, *Depression Winters: New York Social Workers and the New Deal* (Philadelphia: Temple University, 1984), 88–100; Edith Abbott, "The Fallacy of Local Relief," *New Republic*, 9 November 1932, 348–50.

4. Swift quoted in Josephine C. Brown, *Public Relief 1929–1939* (New York: Henry Holt, 1940), 116.

5. Brown, *Public Relief*, 153.

6. Joanne Goodwin, "'Employable Mothers' and 'Suitable Work'": A Re-Evaluation of Welfare and Wage-Earning in the Twentieth-Century United States," *Journal of Social History* (Winter 1995): 253–74; Ernest Poole, "The Work of Relief: Personal Reports of What Goes on in the Bowery and the East Side," *NYT*, 4 April 1932.

7. Bremer, *Depression Winters*, 114–25; Franklin D. Roosevelt, "The Forgotten Man," in David W. Houck, *Rhetoric as Currency: Hoover, Roosevelt, and the Great Depression*, Presidential Rhetoric Series 4 (College Station: Texas A&M University Press, 2001).

8. State of New York Department of Social Welfare, "Compilation of Settlement Laws of All States in the United States" (Albany, N.Y.: State Office Building, January 1931); National Association of Travelers Aid Societies, "A Community Plan for Service to Transients" (Washington, D.C.: U.S. GPO, 1931), 3, 4, 17; Reed, *FTP*, 13, 17.

9. Crouse, *Homeless Transient*, 134–35; Ellen C. Potter, *After Five Years: The Unsolved Problem of the Transient Unemployed 1932–1937* (New York: Committee on Care of Transient and Homeless, May 1937), 4; "H.R. 4606," *Statutes at Large* 48 (12 May 1933): 55–58; Potter, *After Five Years*, 4–5; "Recent Observations on the Transient Program," *Public Welfare News* 4, 1 (January 1936): 1–9; 3.

10. Boyden Sparkes, "The New Deal for Transients," *Saturday Evening Post*, 9 October

1935, 94; James T. Patterson, "The New Deal and the States," *American Historical Review* 73, 1 (October 1967): 70–84.

11. Sparkes, "The New Deal," 23; Reed, *FTP*, 28, 31; Potter, *After Five Years*, 2.

12. "Recent Observations on the Transient Program," 1–9, 3; "Intake," *The Transient*, September 1934, 2; Potter, *After Five Years*, 6.

13. Reed, *FTP*, 91, 90; Lorena Hickok to Harry Hopkins, 25 June 1934, in Lorena Hickok, *One Third of a Nation: Lorena Hickok Reports on the Great Depression*, ed. Richard Lowitt and Maurine Beasley (Urbana: University of Illinois Press, 1981), 298; Peter Fearon, "Relief for Wanderers: The Transient Service in Kansas, 1933–35," *Great Plains Quarterly* 26, 4 (Fall 2006): 250; Jeffrey S. Cole, "'Hopeful People on the Move': The Urban South and the Transient Problem During the Great Depression," in *The New Deal and Beyond: Social Welfare in the South Since 1930*, ed. Elna C. Green (Athens: University of Georgia Press, 2003), 53–56.

14. Sparkes, "The New Deal," 92; C. M. Bookman, "The Federal Transient Program," *The Survey*, April 1935, 104–5.

15. John Benton, "Rest for Weary Willie," *Saturday Evening Post* 209, 10 (5 September 1936): 5, 6, 79, 81, 82; "Recent Observations on the Transient Program," 1–9, 3. See also John Webb, "The Transient Unemployed," reviewed in *The Transient* (May 1936): 12–15.

16. Walter C. Reckless, "Why Women Become Hoboes," *American Mercury*, February 1934, 175–80; Agnes O'Shea, "Development of the Care of Transient Women," *The Transient* 1, 5 (November 1934): 6; Meridel Le Sueur, "Women Are Hungry," *American Mercury*, March 1934, 316–26.

17. Lieutenant William C. Davis, "Nomads: The Salvation Army Method of Dealing with the Homeless Man Problem," *War Cry*, January 21, 1933, 4, 13; 4; Todd DePastino, *Citizen Hobo: How a Century of Homelessness Shaped America* (Chicago: University of Chicago Press, 2003), xvii–xxv; Stephanie J. Shaw, "Using the WPA Ex-Slave Narratives to Study the Impact of the Great Depression," *Journal of Southern History* 69, 3 (August 2003); Davis, "Nomads," 4; O'Shea, 1, 3, 6–7; "Analysis of Census Figures," *The Transient* 1, 5 (November 1934): 3.

18. Anne Loftis, "Steinbeck and the Federal Migrant Camps," *San Jose Studies* 16, 1 (Winter 1990): 76–90. On the evolution of Steinbeck's thoughts on the depression, see Morris Dickstein, "Steinbeck and the Great Depression," *South Atlantic Quarterly* 103, 1 (Winter 2004): 111–31.

19. Hickok to Hopkins, 27 June 1934, in *One Third of a Nation*, 300, 301; Errol Lincoln Uys, *Riding the Rails: Teenagers on the Move During the Great Depression* (New York: TV Books, 1999), 43; "7,400,000 Children Listed on Relief," *NYT*, 5 January 1935.

20. George Chauncey, *Gay New York: Gender, Urban Culture, and the Making of the Gay Male World 1890–1940* (New York: Basic Books, 1994), 65–97.

21. Hickok to Hopkins, 6 May 1934, in *One Third of a Nation*, 244.

22. Matthew Josephson, "The Other Nation," *New Republic*, 17 May 1933, 14–16.

23. "City Lodgings Crowded," *NYT*, 16 December 1933.

24. "Hartford House," *The Transient* (January 1935): 4, 5, 8; "Hartford House May Go," *NYT*, 20 September 1935; "Health Club Buys 54th St. Building," *NYT*, 22 May 1937. See also Homer Borst, Director, Transient Division, to Morris Lewis, Director of Transient Activities, February 9, 1934, National Archives, Records of the Transient Division, RG 69, Box 40, Folder: New York.

25. Farm Colony Committee, Section on the Homeless, Welfare Council of New York City, "A Work Relief Project for the Homeless," 10 June 1932, CSS Papers, Columbia University, Box 185, Folder: "Welfare Council—Coordinating Committee on Unemployment 1934–35."

26. "Park Experiment is a Big Success," *NYT*, 12 March 1933; Research Bureau, Welfare Council of New York City, "Temporary Shelter of Homeless Persons in New York City, Confidential Report," March 1933, CSS Papers, Box 131, Folder: Homeless 1927–33.

27. Welfare Council of New York City, "Summary of Minutes, Meeting of the Executive Committee of the Coordinating Committee on Unemployment," 16 May 1934, CSS Papers, Box 185, Folder: Welfare Council—Coordinating Committee on Unemployment, 1934–35; "Summary of Minutes, Meeting of the Executive Committee of the Coordinating Committee," 10 October 1934. In May 1935, camp residents approved the facility name change to Camp LaGuardia, to shed the association with the Greycourt prison formerly occupying the site, and honor the achievements of the current mayor. "City Camp Marks First Anniversary," *NYT*, 12 May 1935; Joan M. Crouse, "The Remembered Men: Transient Camps in New York State, 1933–1935," *New York History* 71, 1 (January 1990): 68–94, 75, 74, 76.

28. "The Need of Case Work Service for Applicants to the CRB for Women," 6 December 1934, approved by Executive Committee of the Coordinating Committee on Unemployment, 20 February 1935, CSS Papers, Box 184, Folder: Welfare Council-Central Registration Bureau, 1933–34, 2; Elaine S. Abelson, "'Women Who Have No Men to Work for Them': Gender and Homelessness in the Great Depression, 1930–1934," *Feminist Studies* 29, 1 (Spring 2003): 104–26; "Camp TERA, Confidential Report," 4 August 1933, CSS Papers, Box 98, Folder: "Camp TERA"; Gretta Palmer, "Uncle Sam Offering Jobless a Vacation," *New York Telegram*, 2 June 1933, Clipping, CSS Papers, Box 98, Folder: "Camp TERA."

29. Central Registration Bureau for Women to Executives of Agencies Interested in Unattached and Homeless Women, memorandum, 10 October 1933, CSS Papers, Box 98, Folder: "Camp TERA"; Miss A. A. Buffington, The Welfare Council, to Executives of Family Agencies, memorandum, 5 December 1933, CSS Papers, Box 98, Folder: "Camp TERA."

30. "School for Young Transients," *The Survey*, August 1935, 241. See also Homer Borst, Director, Transient Division, New York TERA, to Col. Geo. D. Babcock, TERA, 16 April 1935, National Archives, Records of the Transient Division, RG 69, Box 40, Folder: New York.

31. David Scheyer, "Flop-House," *The Nation*, 2 August 1934, 216–18.

32. "Average Daily Census of Homeless Persons Sheltered in New York City, 1932–1935," table in "Temporary Shelter," Research Bureau, Welfare Council of New York City,

Columbia University Special Collections, CSS, Box 186, Folder: "Temporary Shelter of Homeless"; see also chart, "Resident and Transient Women, New York City, 1932–35," Research Bureau, Welfare Council.

33. "2,200,000 in State on Relief in March," *NYT*, 27 May 1935; "Text of Addresses by Mayor LaGuardia and the New Relief Director," *NYT*, 8 April 1935.

34. Ellen C. Potter, M.D., "Mustering Out the Migrants," *The Survey*, December 1933, 411–12.

35. "Subway Beggars Barred on B.M.T. Trains; Sad Tales and Serenades Held Nuisances," *NYT*, 8 June 1933; "Magistrates Back Drive on Panhandling, No Need for Anyone to Beg, It Is Held," *NYT*, 19 December 1933.

36. "'Panhandler' Drive Marked by Leniency," *NYT*, 4 January 1934; "Reform of Beggars Sought in Court," *NYT*, 4 March 1933; "Medical Aid Urged in War on Beggars," *NYT*, 22 January 1934; "Mendicancy in New York City," *The Transient* (March 1935): 6–7; "743 Jailed in City in Drive on Begging," *NYT*, 2 August 1934; "City Beggars Fewer," *NYT*, 1 April 1935; "Few Beggars Rate Normal in Tests," *NYT*, 25 April 1935.

37. "Shoppers Warned of Street Beggars," *NYT*, 18 December 1935; "Street Begging Here Called Unjustified; Public Asked to Cease Contributing Alms," *NYT*, 23 April 1934; Walter Wile, Chairman Mendicancy Committee, Welfare Council, "Eradicating Mendicancy," Letter to the Editor, *NYT*, 3 May 1934; "Alms Cards Issued as Curb on Begging," *NYT*, 6 June 1934.

38. "Hobo Debates on Radio," *NYT*, 13 May 1934.

39. Reed, *FTP*, 26; Welfare Council of New York City, "Summary of Minutes, Meeting of the Executive Committee of the Coordinating Committee on Unemployment," 28 February 1934, CSS Papers, Box 185, Folder: Welfare Council—Coordinating Committee on Unemployment, 1934–35.

40. Fred Schatz, quoted in Uys, *Riding the Rails*, 179.

41. H. I. Brock, "'The Bowery, The Bowery': Then and Now," *NYT*, 27 January 1929; "Arcade Taxpayer for the Bowery," *NYT*, 4 November 1934; "Bread Lines Disappearing from the Bowery as Destitute Get Work and Pay Their Way," *NYT*, 14 January 1934.

42. Potter, "After Five Years," 6–7; "What Next for Transients?" *The Transient* (September 1934): 2.

43. Words as Sign-Posts to Attitudes and Prejudices," *The Transient* (May 1935): 3, 6–7.

44. Reed, *FTP*, 26–27; Hickok, in *One Third of a Nation*, 245.

45. Potter, "Mustering Out the Migrants," 411.

46. Kim Phillips-Fein, *Invisible Hands: The Making of the Conservative Movement from the New Deal to Reagan* (New York: Norton, 2009); Kenneth S. Davis, *FDR: The New Deal Years 1933–1937, A History* (New York: Random House, 1986), 436–563.

47. Roosevelt, "Annual Message to the Congress," 4 January 1935, *Public Papers and Addresses*, 4: 19–20; David M. Kennedy, "What the New Deal Did," *Political Science Quarterly* 124, 2 (2009): 251–68.

48. Linda Gordon, *Pitied But Not Entitled: Single Mothers and the History of Welfare, 1890–1935* (New York: Free Press, 1994), 1–13; Edward D. Berkowitz, *America's Welfare*

State: From Roosevelt to Reagan (Baltimore: Johns Hopkins University Press, 1991), 1–10; Jeff Singleton, *The American Dole: Unemployment Relief and the Welfare State in the Great Depression* (Westport: Greenwood, 2000), 302–3, 213.

49. Anderson, *The Homeless in New York City*, 383; "The Unattached in the New Program," *The Transient* (May 1935): 5; "Shelter Is 4 Years Old," *NYT*, 2 December 1935.

50. Russell H. Kurtz, "No More Federal Relief?" *The Survey* 71, 2 (February 1935): 35–37; Kurtz, "How the Wheels Are Turning," *The Survey*, August 1935, 227.

51. William J. Ellis, "Inter-State Co-operation Viewed by the Public Administrator," *The Transient*, (March 1936): 5; George Hallawachs, "New York City's Transient Problems," *The Transient* (March 1936): 9.

52. *Elks Park Digest*. 2, 10, March 1, 1936; National Archives, FERA Transient Division, Transient Camp newsletters, Box 2, Folder: New York; Cholly, "Help Help," and "Josiah Simpkins," *Contact* 2, 34, October 18, 1935. National Archives, FERA Transient Division, Transient Camp newsletters, Box 1, Folder: District of Columbia.

53. It seems likely that at least some of these editorials were written by staff members of the Transient Program. *The Highlander* quoted in "With the Transient Press," *Elks Park Digest* 2, 2, September 5, 1935, published by Elks Park Camp, Port Jervis, N.Y., National Archives, Records of the Transient Division, RG 69, Box 2, Folder: New York; "The Editorial," *Contact*, 2, 35, October 25, 1935, National Archives, FERA Transient Division, Transient Camp newsletters, Box 1, Folder: District of Columbia.

54. "What Next for Transients?" *The Transient* (September 1934): 2; Potter, *After Five Years*, 10; Gordon, *Pitied But Not Entitled*, 1–13.

55. Edwin Amenta, *Bold Relief: Institutional Politics and the Origins of Modern American Social Policy* (Princeton, N.J.: Princeton University Press, 1998), 7; Edward D. Berkowitz, "Social Security or Insecurity?" *Reviews in American History* 24, 1 (1996): 126–31.

56. Potter, *After Five Years*, 8; Benton, "Rest for Weary Willie," 81; Singleton, *The American Dole*, 145–46; Letter from Othel Baxter, Newark, N.J., to Stanley Davies, Charity Organization Society, October 10, 1935; National Archives, Records of the Transient Division, RG 69, Box 55, Folder: Closing of Programs—Approvals.

57. Potter, *After Five Years*, 5; Joanna C. Colcord and Russell H. Kurtz, "Relief Policies and Practices, 1932–1935," *The Survey*, December 1935, 374–76; "15,000 at Offices to Apply for Jobs," *NYT*, November 28, 1933; Russell H. Kurtz, "Relief from Relief," *The Survey* 69, 12, December 1933, 403–5.

58. Colcord and Kurtz, "Relief Policies and Practices"; "2,200,000 in State on Relief in March," *NYT*, 27 May 1935.

59. Matthew Josephson, "'Relief': The Last Gasp on Private Charity," *New Republic*, 10 May 1933, 355–56.

60. Kenneth J. Heineman, *A Catholic New Deal: Religion and Reform in Depression Pittsburgh* (University Park: Pennsylvania State University Press, 1999), 70–71.

61. Heineman, 11–33.

62. Nancy L. Roberts, *Dorothy Day and the Catholic Worker* (Albany: State University of New York Press, 1984), 17–33.

63. Harry Murray, *Do Not Neglect Hospitality: The Catholic Worker and the Homeless* (Philadelphia: Temple University Press, 1990), 81.

64. Murray, 61. Herman Hergenhan, *Catholic Worker*, May, June 1934.

65. Murray, *Do Not Neglect Hospitality*, 56.

66. Murray, 79; Day, quoted in Murray, 72.

67. Murray, 74; Day, cited in Murray, 70.

68. Murray, 66.

69. "Transient Order Arouses Protest," *The Survey*, October 1935, 310–11.

70. "The Case of the Transients," *The Survey*, October 1935, 303–4; Stanley P. Davies, General Director, Charity Organization Society, to Harry Hopkins, Public Works Administration, DC, telegram, September 18, 1935, CSS Papers, Box 180, Folder: "Transients"; "End of Federal Aid for Transients Scored; Charity Leader Sees City Facing a Crisis," *NYT*, 7 October 1935; Davies to Senator Royal S. Copeland, 22 October 1935, CSS Papers, Box 180, Folder: "Transients"; "Transient Relief Is Demanded Here," *NYT*, 24 October 1935. Protests over the closure of the FTP fill several folders in the Transient Division Records. Protest letters and telegrams appeared from across the country, including the following: David Donovan, Chairman, Transient Relief Committee, Baltimore, to Mrs. Franklin D. Roosevelt, 16 January 1936, Box 55, Folder: Clients Answered; Cyrus Greene, Executive Secretary, Tampa Urban League, to Harry Hopkins, September 4, 1935; Earl M. Kouns, Executive Secretary, Official Colorado State Relief Committee, to Hon. Edward P. Costigan, 27 September 1935; Katherine Cate, Chairman, County Council of Social Agencies, Santa Barbara, California, to Senator William McAdoo, September 26, 1935, all in Box 55, Folder: Protests Answered Congressional with Enclosures.

71. Salvation Army, "Review of Welfare Activities in Greater New York for the Year Ending September 30th, '36," presented by Commissioner Alexander M. Damon, Salvation Army Archives; George Hallwachs, Director, Joint Application Bureau, "New York City's Transient Problems," *The Transient*, March 1936, 9; Walter T. Diack, General Secretary, YMCA of the City of New York, to Elmer Galloway, 22 November 1935, Box 9, Folder: "Study of Problems Arising as a Result of Discontinuation of Relief for Transients, Bowery Branch, 1935–36," Kautz Family YMCA Archives, Minneapolis.

72. "Moses Charges WPA Sent Him 1,000 'Bums'; Will Reject Them as Useless in Park Jobs," *NYT*, 10 September 1935; "Moses Calls WPA 'Stupid, Arrogant'; Johnson Hits Back," *NYT*, September 11, 1935; C. M. Bookman, "FERA: Yesterday–Today–Tomorrow," *The Survey*, June 1934, 194–98; James T. Patterson, *America's Struggle Against Poverty, 1900–1985* (Cambridge, Mass.: Harvard University Press, 1986), 56–57.

73. "Recent Observations on the Transient Program," 1–9; 3; Potter, *After Five Years*, 8; Crouse, "Remembered Men," 91.

74. "Mr. Zero Parades Band of Derelicts," *NYT*, 13 April 1936.

75. See Christopher Howard, *The Hidden Welfare State: Tax Expenditures and Social Policy in the United States* (Princeton, N.J.: Princeton University Press, 1997); Jacob S. Hacker, *The Divided Welfare State: The Battle over Public and Private Social Benefits in*

the United States (New York: Cambridge University Press, 2002); Jennifer Klein, *For All These Rights: Business, Labor, and the Shaping of America's Public-Private Welfare State* (Princeton, N.J.: Princeton University Press, 2003).

Chapter 3. Skid Row in an Era of Plenty

1. Michael Harrington, *The Other America: Poverty in the United States* (New York: Macmillan, 1962; Penguin, 1968), 88, 94.

2. James T. Patterson, *America's Struggle Against Poverty, 1900–1985* (Cambridge, Mass.: Harvard University Press, 1986), 13; Alex S. Vitale, *City of Disorder: How the Quality of Life Campaign Transformed New York Politics* (New York: New York University Press, 2008).

3. Alan Brinkley, "Reflections on the Past and Future of Urban Liberalism," in *Rethinking the Urban Agenda: Reinvigorating the Liberal Tradition in New York City and Urban America*, ed. John Mollenkopf and Ken Emerson (New York: Century Foundation Press, 2001), 13–22; Michael B. Katz, *The Undeserving Poor: From the War on Poverty to the War on Welfare* (New York: Pantheon, 1990); Alice O'Connor, *Poverty Knowledge: Social Science, Social Policy, and the Poor in Twentieth-Century U.S. History* (Princeton, N.J.: Princeton University Press, 2001), 3–22.

4. Elmer Galloway to Mr. Cooley, 2 March 1942; and brochure, "Is Anything Blitzproof?"2 February 1942; both in Box 10, Folder: Mail Appeal—Stuart/Blitzproof, Bowery Branch, Kautz Family YMCA Archives, Minneapolis; "Mayor Orders Clean-Up of Bowery; Draft Act Will Be Principal Weapon," *NYT*, 18 November 1942; "Life Visits the Bowery," *Life*, 21 December 1942, 116–18; "Surprise Attack Made on Bowery," *NYT*, 19 November 1942; "'Bowery Bums' Are Making Good under Manpower Salvage Program," *NYT*, 25 March 1943; *Homeless Men in New York City: Report of the Project Committee on Homeless Men of the Welfare Council of New York City* (New York: Welfare Council of New York City, 1949), 23; Department of Welfare, "Supplementary Analysis of Report on Administration Issued by Public Administration Service," 14 December 1950, Box 4, Folder 77, Mayor O'Dwyer Papers, Department Files, New York City Municipal Archives; "The Post-War Decade in Welfare," *The Welfarer*, March 1955, 3–12, Box 159, Folder: 1816, Mayor Wagner Papers, NYCMA; "Persons Supported by Public Assistance, January 1932-May 1950," reproduced from *The Welfarer*, July 1950, 12, Box 64, Folder: 628, O'Dwyer Papers.

5. For characteristics of the general population of New York City, see U.S. Census, "General Characteristics of the Population, for Standard Metropolitan Areas, Urbanized Areas, and Urban Places of 10,000 or More: 1950," vol. 2 of *Characteristics of the Population, New York*, part 32 of *Census of Population: 1950* (Washington, D.C.: U.S. GPO, 1952), 32–108.

6. For educational background of first-time applicants to muni, March-May 1948, see "Homeless Men in New York City," 28, 33.

7. Robert Straus and Raymond G. McCarthy, "Nonaddictive Pathological Drinking Patterns of Homeless Men," *Quarterly Journal of Studies on Alcohol* 12, 4 (1951): 601–11,

604–5; Francis E. Feeney, Dorothee F. Mindlin, Verna H. Minear, and Eleanor E. Short, "The Challenge of the Skid Row Alcoholic; A Social, Psychologial and Psychiatric Comparison of Chronically Jailed Alcoholics and Cooperative Alcoholic Clinic Patients," *Quarterly Journal of Studies on Alcohol* 16, 4 (1955): 645–67; David J. Pittman and C. Wayne Gordon, "Criminal Careers of the Chronic Police Case Inebriate," *Quarterly Journal of Studies on Alcohol* 19, 2 (1958): 255–68.

8. Edward E. Rhatigan, Commissioner of Welfare, to Mayor O'Dwyer, memorandum, 8 October 1946, Box 19, Folder: 157, O'Dwyer Papers, Department Files; "17 Perish as Fire Sweeps 42nd Street Lodging House," *NYT*, 25 December 1943; "Bowery Hotel Suit Fails," *NYT*, 23 April 1946.

9. Edward E. Rhatigan, Commissioner of Welfare, William M. Ellard, Director of Real Estate, and Abraham D. Beame, Asst. Director of the Budget, to Mayor O'Dwyer, interdepartmental memorandum, 2 December 1946, Box 19, Folder: 157; Rhatigan to Bennett, memorandum, 30 January 1947, Box 34, Folder: 287; Rhatigan to O'Dwyer, 20 May 1947, Box 34, Folder: 288; Rhatigan to O'Dwyer, 28 August 1947, Box 34, Folder: 288, all in O'Dwyer Papers, Department Files.

10. Wilfred B. Kirk, Charman of the Bowery Improvement Committee of the East Side Chamber of Commerce, to O'Dwyer, 29 October 1947, Box 12, Folder: 115, O'Dwyer Papers, Subject Files; "Bureau of Institutional Administration, the Men's Shelter," *The Welfarer*, November 1958, 6–7, Box 159, Folder: 1819, Wagner Papers, Department Files; "Camp LaGuardia," *The Welfarer*, December 1955, 6–8, Box 159, Folder: 1816, Wagner Papers, Department Files.

11. Community Service Society to Welfare Commissioner, report, 22 July 1949, Box 56, Folder: 528, O'Dwyer Papers, Department Files.

12. "Committee on Homeless Men," *The Welfarer*, August 1949, 1, 3, Box 56, Folder: 530, O'Dwyer Papers, Department Files; "400 Men Sleep on Floors and Benches in Shortage of Beds at Municipal Shelter," *NYT*, 18 November 1949; "Mayor O'Dwyer Appoints Committee on Homeless Men," Department of Welfare Press Release, 22 July 1949, Box 56, Folder: 528, O'Dwyer Papers, Department Files; "Scarlet Fever Here," *NYT*, 27 March 1948; "Lower Court Facilities Scored; Some Said to be like 'Dungeons,'" *NYT*, 6 July 1950.

13. "Increase in Wartime Jobs Merges Women's Shelter, Lodging House," *NYT*, 9 June 1943. Benjamin J. Ralin, Representative of the 24th District, to O'Dwyer, 13 January 1947, Box 156, Folder 1677, O'Dwyer Papers, Subject Files.

14. J. S. Eisenger, Secretary, University Settlement Society, to O'Dwyer, 13 January 1947, H. Daniel Carpenter, Hudson Guild, to O'Dwyer, 14 January 1947, Charles Axelrod to O'Dwyer, 13 January 1947, Harry Levine to O'Dwyer, 14 January 1947, all in Box 156, Folder: 1677, O'Dwyer Papers, Subject Files.

15. Rhatigan to Mayor O'Dwyer, memorandum, 14 January 1947, Box 156, Folder: 1677, O'Dwyer Papers, Subject Files.

16. "Family's Ritzy Relief Cost $500 in Month," *New York World-Telegram*, 9 May 1947; "Relief Family of 7 Gets $640 a Month; Mayor Is Aroused," *NYT*, 20 May 1947; "In

the Matter of the Inquiry by the Department of Social Welfare of the State of New York into the Management and Operations of the New York City Welfare Department," vol. 1, 29 October 1947, 13–30, Box 44, New York State Archives, Albany, Social Services Commissioner Files, Record Series Number 16034–90.

17. "Urges Council Probe Lavish Relief by City," *New York Journal American*, 20 May 1947; "More Rhatigan Relief-de-Luxe!" *New York World-Telegram*, 20 May 1947; "Relief Family Kept in Hotel," *New York Sun*, 9 May 1947; "New York's Relief Policy Wins World Reputation for Generosity," *New York Sun*, 20 May 1947; "State to Make Full Relief Inquiry Here; City Pays Housekeepers for Aid Recipients," *New York Sun*, 23 May 1947; "Rhatigan Silent on Charges of Wasteful Relief Practices," *New York Sun*, 27 May 1947.

18. "Relief in Hotels Sanctioned by State Unit, Rhatigan Says," *NYT*, 28 May 1947.

19. "Gross Negligence in Relief Policies Charged in Report," *NYT*, 13 November 1947.

20. "The Financing of Public Welfare Costs 2," Box 25, Folder 328, Impellitteri Papers, Department Files; "The Post-War Decade in Welfare," *The Welfarer* 7, 3, 3–12, Box 159, Folder: 1816, Wagner Papers, Department Files; "$1,000,000 Welfare Cost Shifted by State to City," *NYT*, 27 December 1950; Hilliard to O'Dwyer, 2 June 1950, Box 64, Folder: 627, O'Dwyer Papers, Department Files.

21. Michael Reisch and Janice Andrews, *The Road Not Taken: A History of Radical Social Work in the United States* (Philadelphia: Brunner-Routledge, 2001), 87–114; "Housing Shortage Costs City $640 Month for Relief Family," *Daily Worker*, 20 May 1947; "Clique of Disgruntled Demos, GOPers Out to Wreck City Welfare Program," *Daily Worker*, 23 May 1947; "New Tragedies Hit Victims of 'Ritzy Relief' Slanders," *Daily Worker*, 28 May 1947.

22. Joshua B. Freeman, *Working-Class New York: Life and Labor Since World War II* (New York: New Press, 2000), 84–87; "Tighter Controls on Relief Spending Installed by City," *NYT*, 18 October 1947; Ellen Schrecker, *Many Are the Crimes: McCarthyism in America* (Princeton, N.J.: Princeton University Press, 1998), 383–85; "Rhatigan Asserts Reds Were Factor in Relief Activities," *NYT*, 3 December 1947; "Rhatigan Defends His Relief Policy," *NYT*, 27 October 1947; Daniel J. Walkowitz, *Working with Class: Social Workers and the Politics of Middle-Class Identity* (Chapel Hill: University of North Carolina Press, 1999), 185–96.

23. "Press is Assailed on Relief Stories," *NYT*, 28 May 1947; "Advisory Council to be Named to Aid City's Relief Head," *NYT*, 3 November 1947.

24. James T. Patterson, *America's Struggle Against Poverty 1900–1985* (Cambridge, Mass.: Harvard University Press, 1986), 90; Theda Skocpol, "The Limits of the New Deal System and the Roots of Contemporary Welfare Dilemmas," in *The Politics of Social Policy in the United States*, ed. Margaret Weir, Ann Shola Orloff, and Theda Skocpol (Princeton, N.J.: Princeton University Press, 1988), 293–312.

25. Frances Fox Piven and Richard A. Cloward, *Regulating the Poor: The Functions of Public Welfare* (New York: Pantheon, 1971), 123–46; Caleb Foote, "Vagrancy-Type Law and Its Administration," *University of Pennsylvania Law Review* 104 (1956): 603–50; "Work Relief Plan Begins Tomorrow," *NYT*, 4 July 1950; John A. Mullaney to Welfare Commissioner

McCarthy, memorandum, Box 155, Folder: 1781, Wagner Papers, Department Files; Arnold J. Vander Meulen, *Skid Row Life Line: The Story of the Haven of Rest Rescue Mission, Grand Rapids, Michigan* (Grand Rapids, Mich.: Zondervan, 1956), 11–14.

26. Martha Biondi, *To Stand and Fight: The Struggle for Civil Rights in Postwar New York City* (Cambridge, Mass.: Harvard University Press, 2003), 3; Dorothy K. Newman, Nancy J. Amidei, Barbara L. Carter, Dawn Day, William J. Kruvant, and Jack S. Russell, *Protest, Politics and Prosperity: Black Americans and White Institutions, 1940–75* (New York: Pantheon, 1978), 260; Kim Hopper, *Reckoning with Homelessness* (Ithaca, N.Y.: Cornell University Press, 2003), 147–71, 231, 135, 254; David Isay with Stacy Abramson, "The Sunshine Hotel," *The Sunshine Hotel & Charlie's Story* (New York: Sound Portraits Productions, 1999); Cheryl Lynn Greenberg, *"Or Does It Explode?" Black Harlem in the Great Depression* (New York: Oxford University Press, 1997), 46, 155; "The Salvation Army: Review of Welfare Activities in Greater New York for the Year Ending September 30, 1936," pamphlet, New York Collection, Salvation Army Archives; *Homeless Men in New York City*, 25, 27, 35–37, 43.

27. "City Lodging House Offers No Luxury," *NYT*, 23 May 1947. See also "The Welfare Problem," *NYT*, 29 May 1947; "Statistics from October 1960," *The Welfarer*, December 1960, 2, Box 156, Folder: 1789, Wagner Papers, Department Files.

28. "Statement of Edward E. Rhatigan, 27 October, 1947," interviewed by Victor J. Herwitz, typescript, 3, Box 44, Social Services Commissioner Files, Record Series Number 16034–90, New York State Archives, Albany; "A Temporary Home: The Family Shelter," *The Welfarer*, April 1954, 6–7, Box 158, Folder: 1815, Wagner Papers, Department Files; Felicia Kornbluh, *The Battle for Welfare Rights: Politics and Poverty in Modern America* (Philadelphia: University of Pennsylvania Press, 2007), 1–13.

29. Jerome Beatty, "The Most Hated Man in Town," *American Magazine*, Clipping, Box 64, Folder 628, O'Dwyer Papers, Department Files; "New Man for Welfare," *NYT*, 13 March 1948; "Raymond M. Hilliard Dies at 58; Reformed City Welfare Agency," *NYT*, 5 July 1966; Mark H. Maier, *City Unions: Managing Discontent in New York City* (New Brunswick, N.J.: Rutgers University Press, 1987), 57–59; "City Relief Regime Accused by State of Misapplying Aid," *NYT*, 27 January 1952.

30. Christopher Howard, *The Hidden Welfare State: Tax Expenditures and Social Policy in the United States* (Princeton, N.J.: Princeton University Press, 1997); Jacob S. Hacker, *The Divided Welfare State: The Battle over Public and Private Social Benefits in the United States* (New York: Cambridge University Press, 2002), 16.

31. "On the Bowery," *Time*, 15 April 1957, 122.

32. Booth cited in Adjutant Don Pitt, "Alcoholism: The Army's Role," in *The Salvation Army and the Alcoholic*, brochure (New York: National Research Bureau, Salvation Army, 1948), 5; Diane Winston, *Red Hot and Righteous: The Urban Religion of the Salvation Army* (Cambridge, Mass.: Harvard University Press, 1999), 23, 249; Captain Ralph I. Miller, "The Best-known Salvationist in the Country," *War Cry*, 7 March 1953, 7. See also "Philosophy of Present-Day Treatment of Alcoholics," remarks by Lt.-Colonel Gilbert S. Decker, 8 May 1953, at Eastern Shore Section Meeting, Maryland Conference

of Social Work, Salisbury, Md., Alcoholism Vertical File, Salvation Army National Archives and Research Center, Alexandria, Va.

33. "Promotion to Glory," Funeral Programs for Brigadiers Luella B. Larder and Olive McKeown, Biographical Vertical Files, Salvation Army Archives; "Resolution on Bowery Alcoholic Problem," 26 January 1946, RG 4.5, Box 207, Folder: 14, Salvation Army Archives; Adjutant Olive McKeown, "Report on Present Program and Proposals: The Salvation Army Bowery Corps," 1 July 1947, RG 4.5, Box 207, Folder: 14, Salvation Army Archives.

34. "Lay Cornerstone for Bowery," *War Cry*, 20 October 1951, 9; "His Victorious Life Meant So Much to So Many," *War Cry*, 26 September 1953, 10.

35. "The Salvation Army Bowery Corps and Alcoholic Rehabilitation Center," pamphlet, 1953, ARC-East, NYC File, Salvation Army Archives; "Doors Are Closed to Bowery Haven," *NYT*, 16 July 1951; "Alcoholics to 'Dry' in $500,000 Center," *NYT*, 21 May 1952.

36. Captain Luella B. Larder, "New York Bowery Corps. Narrative Report. September 1946," RG 4.5, Box 207, Folder: 14, Salvation Army Archives; "International Leader Dedicates New Bowery Corps Building," *War Cry*, 14 June 1952, 8, 9.

37. "Brief by Director, Rehabilitation Center for Alcoholics, the Salvation Army Bowery Corps, New York City, 1958–59," 1, 3, RG 4.5, Box 207, Folder: 7, Salvation Army Archives; Decker, 5; Captain Luella B. Larder, "The Development and Training of the Converted Alcoholic for Soldiership," 6, RG 4.5, Box 207, Folder: 14, Salvation Army Archives.

38. "George Bolton, Bowery Pastor," *NYT*, 31 July 1959; Thorp McClusky, "Lighthouse on Skid Row," *Christian Herald*, December 1949, 36–39, 82–83.

39. John W. Crowley and William L. White, *Drunkard's Refuge: The Lessons of the New York State Inebriate Asylum* (Amherst: University of Massachusetts Press, 2004), 4–11; Sarah W. Tracy, *Alcoholism in America: From Reconstruction to Prohibition* (Baltimore: Johns Hopkins University Press, 2005), 1–24; Gerald R. Garrett, "Alcohol Problems and Homelessness: History and Research," *Contemporary Drug Problems* (Fall 1989): 305–7; Nels Anderson, *The Hobo: The Sociology of the Homeless Man* (1923; Chicago: University of Chicago Press, 1961), 96–98; Jim Baumohl, "Alcohol, Homelessness, and Public Policy," *Contemporary Drug Problems* (Fall 1989): 284.

40. John Frendreis and Raymond Tatalovich, "'A Hundred Miles of Dry': Religion and the Persistence of Prohibition in the U.S. States," *State Politics & Policy Quarterly* 10, 3 (Fall 2010): 302–19.

41. Herbert Finagrette, *Heavy Drinking: The Myth of Alcoholism as a Disease* (Berkeley: University of California Press, 1988), 18; Joseph R. Gusfield, "Deviance in the Welfare State: The Alcoholism Profession and the Entitlements of Stigma," in Gusfield, *Contested Meanings: The Construction of Alcohol Problems* (Madison: University of Wisconsin Press, 1986), 185–204; Lori Rotskoff, *Love on the Rocks: Men, Women, and Alcohol in Post-World War II America* (Chapel Hill: University of North Carolina Press, 2002), 66–69, 105–48; "Alcoholics to Get Aid as Ill Persons," *NYT*, 3 October 1944.

42. Finagrette, *Heavy Drinking*, 13–30.

43. E. M. Jellinek, "Phases of Alcohol Addiction," in *Society, Culture, and Drinking Patterns*, ed. David J. Pittman and Charles R. Snyder (New York: Wiley, 1962), 356–68.

44. E. M. Jellinek, "The Alcohol Problem: Formulations and Attitudes," *Quarterly Journal of Studies on Alcohol* 4, 3 (1943–44): 446–61; Penny Booth Page, "E. M. Jellinek and the Evolution of Alcohol Studies: A Critical Essay," *Addiction* 92, 12 (1997): 1619–24, 1622; Dwight Anderson, "Alcohol and Public Opinion," *QJSA* 3, 3 (1942–43): 392.

45. Jellinek, "Phases of Alcohol Addiction"; Robert Straus, "Alcohol and the Homeless Man," *QJSA* 7, 3 (1942–43): 366–67.

46. Robert Straus, "Excessive Drinking and Its Relationship to Marriage," *Marriage and Family Living* 12, 3 (August 1950): 79–81, 94; Donald J. Bogue, *Skid Row in American Cities* (Chicago: University of Chicago Community and Family Study Center, 1963), 272–76.

47. William W. Wattenberg and John B. Moir, "Factors Linked to Success in Counseling Homeless Alcoholics," *QJSA* 15, 4 (1954): 587–94; Bogue, *Skid Row in American Cities*, 274–78; W. Jack Peterson and Milton A. Maxwell, "The Skid Road 'Wino,'" *Social Problems* 5, 4 (Spring 1958): 308–16; Joan K. Jackson and Ralph Connor, "The Skid Road Alcoholic," *QJSA* 14, 3 (1953): 468–86; Earl Rubington, "The Changing Skid Row Scene," *QJSA* 32, 1 (1971): 125; Robert Straus and Raymond G. McCarthy, "Nonaddictive Pathological Drinking Patterns of Homeless Men," *QJSA* 12, 4 (1951): 602–7; Straus, "Excessive Drinking," 94.

48. Bogue, *Skid Row in American Cities*, 127–28; Martin A. Block, M.D., "A Program for the Homeless Alcoholic," *QJSA* 23, 4 (1962): 644.

49. Robert Straus, "Alcohol and the Homeless Man," *QJSA* 7, 3 (1946–47): 361; David J. Myerson, "An Approach to the "Skid Row" Problem in Boston," *New England Journal of Medicine* (15 October 1953): 646–49; Myerson, "The 'Skid Row' Problem; Further Observations on a Group of Alcoholic Patients, with Emphasis on Interpersonal Relations and the Therapeutic Approach," *New England Journal of Medicine* (21 June 1956): 1168–73.

50. Robert Straus, "Medical Practice and the Alcoholic," *Annals of the American Academy of Political and Social Science* 315, *Understanding Alcoholism* (January 1958): 117–24; George E. Vaillant, *The Natural History of Alcoholism Revisited* (Cambridge, Mass.: Harvard University Press, 1995), 376–82.

51. Gusfield, *Contested Meanings:*, 36–37; Page, "E. M. Jellinek and the Evolution of Alcohol Studies," 1634; Vaillant, *The Natural History of Alcoholism Revisited*; Gusfield, "Benevolent Repression," 399–424.

52. "E. J. McGoldrick, City Aide, Dead," *NYT*, 22 November 1967; "Secret City Bureau Cures Alcoholics," *NYT*, 10 May 1944; Department of Welfare, Bureau of Alcoholic Therapy, "Bridge House," Box 18, Folder: 154, O'Dwyer Papers, Department Files; Edward J. McGoldrick, Jr., "New York City's Bureau of Alcoholic Therapy," *Public Welfare*, September 1946, Clipping, Box 19, Folder: 157, O'Dwyer Papers, Department Files; "Bridge House Report 1959," *The Welfarer*, May 1960, 2, 6, Box 156, Folder: 1788, Wagner

Papers, Department Files; "1960 Annual Report, Bridge House," Box 156, Folder: 1788, Wagner Papers, Department Files.

53. Straus, "Alcohol and the Homeless Man," 371; Bogue, *Skid Row in American Cities*, 272–304.

54. Jellinek, "The Alcohol Problem."

55. Elmer L. Andersen, "Report of the Minnesota Interim Commission on Alcoholism," *QJSA* 14, 2, 340–49.

56. Ibid.

57. Francis E. Feeney, Dorothee F. Mindlin, Verna H. Minear, and Eleanor E. Short, "The Challenge of the Skid Row Alcoholic: A Social, Psychological and Psychiatric Comparison of Chronically Jailed Alcoholics and Cooperative Alcoholic Clinic Patients," *QJSA* 16, 4 (year): 645–67; Anthony Zappala and Frank S. Ketcham, "Toward Sensible Rehabilitation of the Alcoholic: The District of Columbia Program," *Public Health Reports (1896–1970)* 69, 12 (Dec. 1954): 1187–96.

58. David Myerson, "An Approach to the Skid Row Problem in Boston," *The New England Journal of Medicine* 249,16 (15 October 1953): 646–649; David J. Myerson and Joseph Mayer, "Origins, Treatment and Destiny of Skid-Row Alcoholic Men," *New England Journal of Medicine* 275, 8 (August 25, 1966): 419–25; William W. Wattenberg and John B. Moir, "Factors Linked to Success in Counseling Homeless Alcoholics," *QJSA*, 15, 4 (1954): 587–94.

59. Ernest M. Gruenberg and Raymond G. McCarthy, "Reports on Government-Sponsored Programs," *QJSA* 14, 4 (1953): 674–84; Besse Hirschberg, "Alcoholism in the Case Load of the New York City Welfare Department: A Statistical Analysis," *QJSA* 15, 3 (1954): 402–12.

60. Department of Welfare, "Facilities on Hart Island Transferred to the Department of Welfare," press release, 23 February 1950, Box 64, Folder: 626, O'Dwyer Papers, Department Files; "Hart Island Used as a Prison by Navy," *NYT*, 12 June 1944.

61. "The Hart Island Program for Alcoholics in New York City," *QJSA* 14, 1 (1953): 140–46; Hilliard to Thomas J. Patterson, 14 November 1949, Box 56, Folder: 529, O'Dwyer Papers, Department Files; "Report on Alcoholism," *The Welfarer*, March 1954, 5, Box 158, Folder: 1815, Wagner Papers, Department Files; "Bowery Derelicts 'Come to Life' Under the City's New Recovery Plan," *NYT*, 1 January 1951.

62. "Neighbors Oppose Hart Island Plan," *NYT*, 4 February 1950; "Assail Hart Island Plan," *NYT*, 22 February 1950; Haley & Fusfeld, Attorneys at Law, Bronx, to Board of Estimate, Department of Correction, Commissioner Hilliard, and Commission for Homeless Men of the City of New York, petition, 7 February 1950, Box 64, Folder: 622, O'Dwyer Papers, Department Files; Elizabeth J. Carbon, Asst. Secretary of Cooper Union, to Mayor O'Dwyer, 5 April 1950, Box 64, Folder 626, O'Dwyer Papers, Department Files; Barnett August, Asst. Secretary of East Side Chamber of Commerce, to Deputy Mayor Ried, telegram, 2 February 1950, Box 64, Folder: 628, O'Dwyer Papers, Department Files; "Hart Island Plan Approved by City," *NYT*, 24 February 1950.

63. "Report on Alcoholism"; Deputy Mayor Henry Epstein to Welfare Commissioner McCarthy, 30 December 1954, Box 155, Folder: 1780, Wagner Papers, Department Files; Department of Welfare, "Magistrates' Court Department of Welfare Program for Homeless Men at Hart Island," press release, 18 December 1950, Box 64, Folder: 627, O'Dwyer Papers, Department Files; "Bowery Derelicts 'Come to Life.'" See also Joel Blau, *The Visible Poor: Homelessness in the United States* (New York: Oxford University Press, 1993).

64. "Aid to Alcoholics in City Criticized," *NYT*, 22 January 1954; "'Others' Is Creed of Shelter Head," *NYT*, 5 September 1955.

65. "Hart Island Correction," *The Welfarer*, September 1954, 9, 7, Box 158, Folder 1815, Wagner Papers, Department Files; "City Aid to Alcoholics Hailed; Harts Island project is Inspected," *NYT*, 16 November 1955.

66. "Mrs. Simon Scores City on Alcoholics," *NYT*, 24 October 1957; "Alcoholism Aid Urged," *NYT*, 23 Jan. 1957.

67. Department of Welfare, press release, 27 August 1954, Box 158, Folder: 1815, Wagner Papers, Department Files.

68. Block, "A Program for the Homeless Alcoholic."

69. I. Jay Brightman, "The Future of Alcohol Programs," *Public Health Reports (1896–1970)* 75, 9 (September 1960): 775–77.

70. Kenneth L. Kusmer, *Down and Out, on the Road: The Homeless in American History* (New York: Oxford University Press, 2002), 225; Charles Hoch and Robert A. Slayton, *New Homeless and Old: Community and the Skid Row Hotel* (Philadelphia: Temple University Press, 1989), 104–6, 108–9.

Chapter 4. Urban Renewal and the Challenge of Homelessness

1. City Planning Commission Minutes for 1957, 71, 72. "Plan Board Backs New City Housing," *NYT*, 30 June 1956; "Proposal to Rename Bowery Heard Again," *NYT*, 21 November 1947; "New Group Will Aim to Improve Bowery," *NYT*, 30 April 1953; "Bowery Clean-Up Mapped by Group," *NYT*, 21 May 1953; *Manhattan Yellow Pages* (1940, 1960); "Preacher Proposes Ellis Island Refuge for Bowery Drifters to Greenwich Village," *NYT*, 11 February 1957.

2. "1 Dead, Score Hurt in Bowery Blaze," *NYT*, 28 July 1937; "Man Killed in Fire in Bowery Hotel," *NYT*, 13 July 1938; "City Housing Order Denied by Court," *NYT*, 29 November 1939; "Lodging House Ruling Blocks Safety Drive," *NYT*, 30 November 1939; "Lodging Houses to be Inspected," *NYT*, 18 November 1955.

3. Gail Radford, *Modern Housing for America: Policy Struggles in the New Deal Era* (Chicago: University of Chicago Press, 1996), 29–57, 181–90; Richard M. Flanagan, "The Housing Act of 1954: The Sea Change in National Urban Policy," *Urban Affairs Review* 33, 2 (November 1997): 268–69.

4. Otto Davis, "Economics and Urban Renewal: Market Intervention," in *Financing the Metropolis: Public Policy in Urban Economies*, ed. John P. Credine, *Urban Affairs Annual Review* 4 (1970): 75–76; Flanagan, "The Housing Act of 1954," 271; Ashley A. Foard and

Hilbert Fefferman, "Federal Urban Renewal Legislation," in *Urban Renewal: The Record and the Controversy*, ed. James Q. Wilson (Cambridge, Mass.: MIT Press, 1966), 93–95.

5. Foard and Fefferman, "Federal Urban Renewal Legislation," 97–98; Clarence J. Davies, Jr., *Neighborhood Groups and Urban Renewal* (New York: Columbia University Press, 1966), 8.

6. Flanagan has called the Housing Act of 1954 a "sea change in national urban policy," "The Housing Act of 1954," 267, 276.

7. Jon C. Teaford, *The Rough Road to Renaissance: Urban Revitalization in America, 1940–1985* (Baltimore: Johns Hopkins University Press, 1990), 123–25, 135; Christopher Mele, *Selling the Lower East Side: Culture, Real Estate, and Resistance in New York City* (Minneapolis: University of Minnesota Press, 2000), 127; Arnold Hirsch, *Making the Second Ghetto: Race and Housing in Chicago, 1940–1960* (Chicago: University of Chicago Press, 1983); Thomas J. Sugrue, *The Origins of the Urban Crisis: Race and Inequality in Postwar Detroit* (Princeton, N.J.: Princeton University Press, 1996).

8. Dolores Hayden, *Building Suburbia: Green Fields and Urban Growth, 1820–2000* (New York: Pantheon, 2003), 154–80.

9. Davis, "Economics and Urban Renewal," 78; Radford, *Modern Housing*, 189–90.

10. Howard M. Bahr, "The Gradual Disappearance of Skid Row," *Social Problems* 5, 1 (1967): 41–45, 43; Barrett A. Lee, "The Disappearance of Skid Row: Some Ecological Evidence," *Urban Affairs Quarterly* 16, 1 (September 1980): 81–107, 90.

11. Stephen Metraux, "Waiting for the Wrecking Ball: Skid Row in Postindustrial Philadelphia," *Journal of Urban History* 25, 5 (July 1999): 691–716.

12. Joseph Hart, *Down and Out: The Life and Death of Minneapolis's Skid Row* (Minneapolis: University of Minnesota Press, 2002), 39, 40–42, 51.

13. Ibid., 48, 51–52.

14. Tenants Relocation Bureau, *The Homeless Man on Skid Row* (Chicago: the Bureau, 1961), 57–61; Charles Hoch and Robert A. Slayton, *New Homeless and Old: Community and the Skid Row Hotel* (Philadelphia: Temple University Press, 1989), 117–19, 121; Teaford, *The Rough Road*, 148–49; Ronald Vanderkooi, "The Main Stem: Skid Row Revisited," *Society* 10, 6 (1973): 64–71.

15. John Stainton, *Urban Renewal and Planning in Boston* (Boston: Citizens Housing and Planning Association and Boston Redevelopment Authority, 1972).

16. Jennifer R. Wolch, Michael Dear, and Andrea Akita, "Explaining Homelessness," *Journal of the American Planning Association* 54 (Autumn 1988): 443–53.

17. Samuel Zipp, *Manhattan Projects: The Rise and Fall of Urban Renewal in Cold War New York* (New York: Oxford University Press, 2010).

18. Charles G. Bennett, "Moses, 70 on December 18, Won't Quit," *NYT*, 3 December 1958.

19. Kenneth T. Jackson, "Robert Moses and the Planned Environment: A Re-Evaluation," Keynote Address, Conference on Robert Moses and the Planned Environment, Hofstra University, June 10–11, 1988, in *Robert Moses: Single Minded Genius*, ed. Joann P. Krieg (New York: Long Island Studies Institute, Hofstra University), 21; Hilary Ballon, "Robert Moses and Urban Renewal: The Title I Program," in *Robert Moses and the Mod-*

ern City: The Transformation of New York, ed. Hilary Ballon and Kenneth T. Jackson (New York: Norton, 2007), 94–115.

20. Joseph Anthony Panuch, *Building a Better New York for Those Who Live and Work in Growing New York City: Final Report to Mayor Robert F. Wagner* (New York: Mayor's Independent Survey on Housing and Urban Renewal,1960), 51, 52.

21. Ibid., 54.

22. "Moses Protests Article in Times," *NYT*, 1 July 1959; Housing and Home Finance Agency, Urban Renewal Administration, Urban Renewal Project Directory, September 30, 1959, cited in Panuch, *Building a Better New York*, 54.

23. Zipp, *Manhattan Projects*, 197–242; Mele, *Selling the Lower East Side*, 121, 1301–31; "Reorganize FHA, Moses Demands," *NYT*, 1 December 1954; Robert Moses, "Remarks by Robert Moses at Seward Park," 11 October 1958, 1, Box 7, Bound Volume 1958, Robert Moses Papers, City Planning Commission Collection, New York City Municipal Archives; Mark Gelfand, *A Nation of Cities: The Federal Government and Urban America, 1933–1965* (New York: Oxford University Press, 1975), 212–13; Joshua B. Freeman, *Working-Class New York: Life and Labor Since World War II* (New York: New Press, 2000), 114; Charles G. Bennett, "Moses, 70 on December 18, Won't Quit," *NYT*, 3 December 1958; Jackson, "Robert Moses and the Planned Environment," 21–33; Joel Schwartz, *The New York Approach: Robert Moses, Urban Liberals, and the Redevelopment of the Inner City* (Columbus: Ohio State University Press, 1993); Leonard Wallock, "The Myth of the Master Builder," *Journal of Urban History* 17 (Aug. 1991): 339–62; Robert Caro, *The Power Broker: Robert Moses and the Fall of New York* (New York: Knopf, 1974).

24. The Reminiscences of Abraham Kazan, The Oral History Research Office, Columbia University, 1970, 519; New York City Planning Commission, "Master Plan of Sections Containing Areas Suitable for Development and Redevelopment," December 1954, 13; Minutes of the City Planning Commission of the City of New York for 1957, 71; "The Reminiscences of Abraham Kazan," Oral History Research Office, Columbia University, 1970, 33, interview by Lloyd Kaplan at Otisville, New York, begun 30 September 1967, 55, 73–74, 128, 148, 150, 144, 164, 153, 316–18, 519; Joshua B. Freeman, *Working-Class New York: Life and Labor Since World War II* (New York: New Press, 2000), 118; United Housing Foundation, "United Housing Foundation: Purpose, Program, Principles, Progress, Plans," pamphlet, 1966, vertical file, Tamiment Library and Robert F. Wagner Labor Archives, New York University; "United Housing Foundation: Years of Accomplishment," pamphlet, 1970, Tamiment Library.

25. Francis Sugrue, "City's Big Headache: 10,000 on the Bowery," *New York Herald Tribune*, 16 March 1959; David Isay with Stacy Abramson, "The Sunshine Hotel," *The Sunshine Hotel and Charlie's Story*, radio documentary (New York: Sound Portraits Productions, 1999); *Manhattan Yellow Pages*, 1954.

26. Title I Slum Clearance Progress, 30 September 1958, 28–29, Commissioner Felt Subject Files, Box 30, Folder: 5, City Planning Commission Papers, New York City Municipal Archive; *Alternate Plan*, 69, 31–37.

27. Major D. W. Moulton, Conference Minutes, 14 November 1958, RG 4.5, Box 208, Folder: 1, Salvation Army Archives.

28. "Third Avenue Blossoms as El Disappears," *NYT*, 6 February 1956; Tony Schuman, "Labor and Housing in New York City: Architect Herman Jessor and the Cooperative Housing Movement," http://home.comcast.net/~coopcity/design.html, accessed 15 August 2009; Freeman, 116; "Plan of Sections Containing Areas Suitable for Development and Redevelopment," Item CP-11256, CPC Minutes 1957, 72; Reminiscences of Abraham Kazan, 520–22; Robert Moses to Abe Stark, President of Council, City Hall, 27 February 1958, Box 117, Folder "Housing," Moses Papers, New York Public Library, Special Collections. See also Moses to Justice Felix Frankfurter, U.S. Supreme Court, 12 March 1958, same folder.

29. City Planning Commission Minutes for 1957, 71, 72; "Plan Board Backs New City Housing," *NYT*, 30 June 1956. For the condition of housing units along the Bowery, in Manhattan, and in New York, see 1960 Census City Block Statistics.

30. Thelma Burdick to Moses, 26 March 1959, RG 4.5, Box 208, Folder: 2, Salvation Army Archives; "Bowery's 'Skid Row' Going for Housing and Factories," *New York Herald Tribune*, 15 March 1959; McKeown to Pepper, 28 April 1959, RG 4.5, Box 208, Folder: 1, Salvation Army Archives; "Bowery Area Changes: A Review as of August 18, 1959, Based upon Minutes of Community Meetings and Newspaper Articles of 1959," RG 4.5, Box 208, Folder: 2, Salvation Army Archives; "Bowery's 'Skid Row' Going for Housing and Factories," *New York Herald Tribune*, March 15, 1959.

31. Teaford, *The Rough Road*, 153–62; see "Mayor Hears Please on 'Village' Traffic," *NYT*, 19 April 1958; "Project Foe Hits 'Village' Group," *NYT*, 14 March 1961; "City Gives Up Plan for West Village," *NYT*, 1 February 1962.

32. Jennifer Hock, "Jane Jacobs and the West Village: The Neighborhood against Urban Renewal," *Journal of the Society of Architectural Historians* 66, 1 (March 2007): 16–19.

33. Cooper Square Development Committee and Businessmen's Association, *An Alternate Plan for Cooper Square*, 1959, 1; Thelma J. Burdick and Staughton C. Lynd, Co-Chairmen, Committee on Community Development, flyer, RG 4.5. Box 208, Folder: 2, Salvation Army Archives.

34. Radford, *Modern Housing*, 188–89.

35. *Alternate Plan*, 8, 11, 15, 29–30, 54.

36. Author's interview with Walter Thabit, New York, 17 December 2003; *Alternate Plan*, 69.

37. *Alternate Plan*, 25.

38. Burdick to Moses, 26 March 1959, RG 4.5, Box 208, Folder: 2, Salvation Army Archives; *Alternate Plan*, 11, 15, 24–30, 63–68.

39. "Moses Protests Cuts in U.S. Funds for Slum-Razing," *NYT*, 8 April 1957; Edwin L. Dale, Jr., "U.S. Hints at Halt in Slum Aid Here," *NYT*, 26 July 1957; "Wagner's Letter and Report by Moses," *NYT*, 3 May 1957; "City's Slum Unit Asks $10 Million," *NYT*, 27 August 1959; "Third Avenue Blossoms as El Disappears," *NYT*, 6 February 1956; Caro, *The Power Broker*, 984–1004; Moses to Waldo G. Bowman, 1 September 1959, Box 30,

Folder: 8, Commissioner Felt Subject Files, City Planning Commission Papers, New York City Municipal Archives; "Urban Renewal Stirs Up a Storm," *Engineering News-Record*, 9 July 1959, 21–23; "Scandal Charges Buffet Title I Projects in City," *NYT*, 1 July 1959; "Title I Slum Clearance Proves Spur to Cooperative Housing in City," *NYT*, 2 July 1959; "Oust-Moses Drive On," *NYT*, 17 October 1959; "Congress Urged to Study Moses' Housing Actions," *NYT*, 20 June 1959; "Mayor to Bolster Title I Committee," *NYT*, 8 July 1959; "Wagner Assails Shanahan Gloom on Title I Future," *NYT*, 9 July 1959; "Wagner Is Given Title I Findings on Housing Aide," *NYT*, 24 June 1959; "Ouster of Moses and Aide is Urged by Citizens Union," *NYT*, 10 July 1959; "Civic Unit Offers to Back Wagner if Moses Is Let Go," *NYT*, 11 July 1959; "Gerosa Advocates Open Title I Bidding," *NYT*, 29 June 1959; "House Unit Plans to Hold Hearings in City on Slums," *NYT*, 12 July 1959; "Wagner Pledges Inquiry in Slum Deals if Justified," *NYT*, 23 June 1959; "Moses Says Title I Is a 'Dead Duck,' Decries Charges," *NYT*, 4 July 1959.

40. Davies, *Neighborhood Groups*, 19; Panuch, *Building a Better New York*, 7; City Planning Commission, Designation Report, 1963, 12; see also Rexford Tugwell, "The Moses Effect," in *Urban Government: A Reader in Politics and Administration* , ed. Edward C C. Banfield (New York: Free Press, 1961), 462–72.

41. "1962–63 Urban Renewal Study Program," *Department of City Planning Newsletter*, May–June 1962, 1; Rehabilitation Report, The City of New York Department of City Planning—City Planning Commission, Community Renewal Program, 14 August 1963, 60, 29; "A Housing Program for the St. Mark's Area," Richard Pease, Chair of the St. Mark's Neighborhood Council, to Mayor Wagner, 17 June 1963, Ballard Subject Files, Box 3, Folder: 7, City Planning Commission Collection, New York City Municipal Archives; Thomas W. Ennis, "Cooper Square Plan Set for Decision," *NYT*, 31 August 1969; Iver Peterson, "Project in Bowery is Approved Following 10-Year Controversy," *NYT*, 14 February 1970. See Robert A. M. Stern, Thomas Mellins, and David Fishman, *New York 1960: Architecture and Urbanism Between the Second World War and the Bicentennial* (New York: Monacelli Press, 1995), 257.

42. "A State of Chassis: One Crisis After Another," Lovett Lecture by Robert Moses at Pierson College, Yale University, March 9, 1960, 14, Robert Moses Papers, Box 8, Bound Volume 1960, City Planning Commission Collection, New York City Municipal Archives.

43. Moses, "Remarks by Robert Moses at Seward Park," 11 October 1958, Box 7, Bound Volume 1958, City Planning Commission Collection, New York City Municipal Archives.

44. Jane Jacobs, *The Death and Life of Great American Cities* (1961; New York: Random House, 1989), 4, 15, 282; Herbert Gans, "The Failure of Urban Renewal: A Critique and Some Proposals," in *Urban Renewal: People, Politics, and Planning*, ed. Jewel Bellush and Murray Hausknecht (New York: Anchor Books, 1967), 465–79, orig. in *Commentary*, April 1965.

45. Jacobs, *Death and Life*, 92–100.

46. John F. Bauman, "The Eternal War on the Slums," 1–17, Robert B. Fairbanks,

"From Better Dwellings to Better Neighborhoods: The Rise and Fall of the First National Housing Movement," 21–42, and Alexander von Hoffman, "Why They Built Pruitt-Igoe," 180–205, all in *From Tenements to the Taylor Homes: In Search of an Urban Housing Policy in Twentieth-Century America*, ed. John F. Bauman, Roger Biles, and Kristin M. Szylvian (University Park: Pennsylvania State University Press, 2000); David R. Hill, "Jane Jacobs' Ideas on Big, Diverse Cities: A Review and Commentary," *Journal of the American Planning Association* 54, 3 (Summer 1988): 302–14.

47. Judge John M. Murtagh, "The Derelicts of Skid Row," *Atlantic Monthly* 209 (March 1962): 77–81, 80.

48. 36 U.S. (11 Pet.) 102, 142–43 (1837), quoted in William O. Douglas, "Vagrancy and Arrest on Suspicion," *Yale Law Journal* 70, 1 (November 1960): 1–14, 2; see Gary V. Dubin and Richard H. Robinson, "The Vagrancy Concept Reconsidered: Problems and Abuses of Status Criminality," *New York University Law Review* 37, 1 (1962): 102–36. In 1941, Miln had been reversed by the Court in *Edwards v. California*; 314 U.S. 160, 177 (1941); S. Rep. No. 821, 77th Cong., 1st sess. 2 (1941), quoted in Douglas, "Vagrancy and Arrest on Suspicion," 8; *Columbia v. Hunt*, 163 F.2d 833, 835 (D.C. Cir. 1947); Harry Simon, "Towns Without Pity: A Constitutional and Historical Analysis of Official Efforts to Drive Homeless Persons from American Cities," *Tulane Law Review* 66, 4 (March 1992): 632–76, 40; Jacqueline P. Wiseman, *Stations of the Lost: The Treatment of Skid Row Alcoholics* (Englewood Cliffs, N.J.: Prentice-Hall, 1970), 80.

49. Caleb Foote, "Vagrancy-Type Law and Its Administration," *University of Pennsylvania Law Review* 603 (1956): 104; Madeline R. Stoner, *The Civil Rights of Homeless People: Law, Social Policy, and Social Work Practice* (New York: Aldine, 1995), 23; Simon, "Towns Without Pity," 634, 642; *Fenster v. Leary*, 229 N.E. 2d 426, 430 (N.Y. 1967). The Supreme Court struck down vagrancy laws in *Papchristou v. City of Jacksonville* (405 U.S. 156 (1972)) and *Kolender v. Lawson* (461 U.S. 352 (1983)).

50. "Skid Row Cleanup: Some Big Cities Switch from Arresting Drunks to Try Rehabilitation," *Wall Street Journal*, 14 February 1967; *The Challenge of Crime in a Free Society: A Report By the President's Commission on Law Enforcement and the Administration of Justice* (Washington, D.C.: U.S. GPO, February 1967), 233–38.

51. *Easter v. District of Columbia*, 361 F.21 50 (D.C. Cir. 1966); *Driver v. Hinnant*, 356 F.2d 761 (4th Cir. 1966); *Robinson v. California*, 370 U.S. 660 (1962).

52. *Powell v. Texas*, 392 U.S. 514 (1968); Simon, "Towns Without Pity," 660–63; "Chronic Alcoholics' Jailing for Intoxication is Upheld," *NYT*, 18 June 1968; Gerald R. Garrett, "Alcohol Problems and Homelessness: History and Research," *Contemporary Drug Problems* (Fall 1989): 301–23.

53. Operation Bowery, *Third Report*, 1; Thomas A. Johnson, "Courts Praised on Vagrants Aid," *NYT*, 23 April 1966; "Police Here Halt Derelict Arrests," *NYT*, 29 July 1966.

54. Lucas A. Powe, Jr., "Policing the Police" and "Wealth and Poverty," in *The Warren Court and American Politics* (Cambridge, Mass.: Harvard University Press, 2000), 379–411, 445–62; Morton J. Horwitz, *The Warren Court and the Pursuit of Justice* (New York: Hill and Wang, 1998).

Chapter 5. Operation Bowery and Social Scientific Inquiry

1. Interview #006, conducted by R. Riday at the Uncle Sam on April 20, 1966, Folder: B1024 Interview Schedules, Source: 1–10 Bound Interview Schedules from the Bowery, Box 78, Bureau of Applied Social Research (BASR), Columbia University Archives.

2. Theodore Caplow, "The Sociologist and the Homeless Man," in *Disaffiliated Man: Essays and Bibliography on Skid Row, Vagrancy, and Outsiders*, ed. Howard M. Bahr (Toronto: University of Toronto Press, 1970), 6.

3. "Carmine De Sapio, Political Kingmaker and Last Tammany Boss, Dies at 95," *NYT*, 8 July 2004; Chris McNickle, "Wagner, Robert F.," in *The Encyclopedia of New York City*, ed. Kenneth T. Jackson (New Haven, Conn.: Yale University Press, 1995), 1231; "Group Protests Bums in Park," *New York World-Telegram and Sun*, 4 November 1961.

4. "Bowery Clean-Up Planned," *NYT*, 31 October 1961.

5. "Mayor Accused of Switch on Bowery Plan," *NYWTS*, 2 November 1961; "Lefkowitz Hails Series on Bums," *NYWTS*, 6 November 1961.

6. Thomas Furey, "New Wave of Derelicts Poses Menace in Parks and Streets," *NYWTS*, 1 November 1961.

7. "Grim Problems of the Bowery Complicate Clean-Up Drive," *NYT*, 20 November 1961.

8. Sara Harris, *Skid Row USA* (New York: Tower, 1961), 9.

9. Ibid., 12–30; 21, 15, 65–69, 31, 38; Samuel E. Wallace, *Skid Row as a Way of Life* (New York: Harper and Row, 1968), 125.

10. Harris, *Skid Row USA*, 57–58; Wallace, *Skid Row*, 203–4.

11. Harris, *Skid Row USA*, 58–81, 84.

12. *New Yorker*, 12 May 1962, 361; 3 November 1962, 111; 17 November 1962, 47; Bahr, *Skid Row*, 68, 79.

13. Edmund G. Love, *Subways Are for Sleeping* (New York: Signet, 1958); Dave Balch, "TA Nixes Merrick on Subway Sleeping," *NYWTS*, 2 November 1961; David Merrick, *Subways Are for Sleeping Soundtrack*, 1962 Stratford Music Corp., issued on CD by Fynsworth Alley, 2001.

14. Barnard L. Collier, "Down and Out on the Bowery: How it Feels," *New York*, 12 May 1969, 24–29.

15. Steve Lerner, "On the Bowery: Last Step Down or First Step Up?" *Village Voice*, 7 November 1968; Margaret Bourke-White, "At the Time of the Louisville Flood," 1937, George Eastman House Collection.

16. David McReynolds, "The Bowery: A Ghetto Without A Constituency," *Village Voice*, 5 December 1968, 25–26; see Maren Stange, *Symbols of Ideal Life: Social Documentary Photography in America, 1890–1950* (New York: Cambridge University Press, 1989).

17. Operation Bowery, *First Annual Report* (New York: New York City Department of Welfare, 1964), 3 September 1963–2 September 1964, 1; "Mayor Swears in James Dumpson as New Commissioner of Welfare," *Welfarer*, xi, 9 (September 1959): 1, Box

159, Folder: 1820, Mayor Wagner Papers, Department Files, New York City Municipal Archives; "Dumpson to Head Bowery Project," *NYT*, 11 May 1962 (Dumpson succeeded Henry L. McCarthy in August 1959); Operation Bowery, *First Annual Report*, 4.

18. Operation Bowery, *Third Annual Report*, 3 September 1965–2 September 1966, 6.

19. Howard Bahr and Theodore Caplow, *Old Men Drunk and Sober* (New York: New York University Press, 1973), 19; Operation Bowery, *Second Annual Report*, 3 September 1964–2 September 1965, 3–4.

20. Operation Bowery, *Second Annual Report*, *Third Annual Report*, 2.

21. Operation Bowery, *First Annual Report*, 3.

22. Theodore Caplow, "Columbia University—New York City Contract, October 29, 1963," Appendix I in *Summary Report of a Study Undertaken Under Contract Approved by the Board of Estimate, Calendar No. 14, 19 December 1963*, 1965, 38.

23. Donald Bogue, *Skid Row in American Cities* (Chicago: University of Chicago Press, 1963), 19–45, 17; Alice O'Connor, *Poverty Knowledge: Social Science, Social Policy, and the Poor in Twentieth-Century U.S. History* (Princeton, N.J.: Princeton University Press, 2001), 102–7.

24. Theodore Caplow, "Transiency as a Cultural Pattern," *American Sociological Review* 5, 5 (October 1940): 731–39; Wallace, *Skid Row*. Howard M. Bahr came on board at Columbia as project director in 1965. Howard M. Bahr, *Homelessness and Disaffiliation* (New York: Columbia University Press, 1968), 11; "Homelessness: Etiology, Patterns, and Consequences," was funded by the National Institute of Mental Health Grant MH_10861; *Summary Report*, 17.

25. Bahr, *Homelessness and Disaffiliation*, 24; Wallace, quoted in Bahr, *Skid Row*, 32–35; Howard M. Bahr and Gerald R. Garrett, *Women Alone: The Disaffiliation of Urban Females* (Lexington, Mass.: Lexington Books, 1976), 1.

26. The project's parameters were defined in two sources: Bahr and Caplow, *Old Men*, 3–4, and Bahr, *Homelessness and Disaffiliation*, 43–44, 294–95.

27. Bahr, *Skid Row*, 17. Quote from Theodore Caplow, Howard M. Bahr, and David Sternberg, "Homelessness," in *International Encyclopedia of the Social Sciences*, vol. 6, ed. David Sills (New York: Macmillan, 1968), 494–99. See also the synopsis of George Nash's "The Habitats of Homeless Men in Manhattan," 20 October 1964, in *Summary Report*; Bahr and Caplow, *Old Men*, 5.

28. Bahr, *Homelessness and Disaffiliation*, 67–69.

29. Interview #005, conducted by Myron Freier, 22 April 1966, at Andrews House, Box 78, Folder B1024, Bound Interview Schedules from the Bowery, 1, BASR Records, Columbia University Archive; Interview #009, conducted by M. Weiss, 19 April, at the Union Hotel; Interview #006, conducted by R. Riday, April 20; Howard M. Bahr and Kathleen C. Houts, "Can You Trust a Homeless Man? A Comparison of Official Records and Interview Responses by Bowery Men," *Public Opinion Quarterly* 35, 3 (Fall 1971): 374–82.

30. Caplow, "The Sociologist and the Homeless Man."

31. Kenneth L. Kusmer, *Down and Out, on the Road: The Homeless in American History* (New York: Oxford University Press, 2003), 73–97.

32. See Fred H. Matthews, *Quest for an American Sociology: Robert E. Park and the Chicago School* (Montreal: McGill-Queen's University Press, 1977); Robert Park, "Editor's Preface," in Nels Anderson, *The Hobo: The Sociology of the Homeless Man* (Chicago: University of Chicago Press, 1967; c. 1923), xxiii, 61–122; Bahr, *Skid Row*, 110;

33. Bogue, *Skid Row in American Cities*, 48; Kusmer, *Down and Out*, 230; Bahr, *Skid Row*, 113–17.

34. Bahr, *Homeless and Disaffiliation*, 11; Mathieu Defleur, "From Anomie to Anomia and Anomic Depression: A Sociological Critique on the Use of Anomie in Psychiatric Research," *Social Science & Medicine* 29, 5 (1989): 627–34; Robert Agnew and Nikos Passas, "Introduction," in *The Future of Anomie Theory*, ed. Passas and Agnew (Boston: Northeastern University Press, 1997), 3.

35. Merton's article appeared in *American Sociological Review* 3, 5 (Oct; 1938): 672–82 and, with substantial revisions, in "Continuities in the Theory and Social Structure and Anomie," in *Social Theory and Social Structure*, rev. enlarged ed. (Glencoe, Ill.: Free Press), 161–94; Elmer Bendiner, *The Bowery Man* (New York: Nelson, 1961), 217; Robert Agnew, "The Nature and Determinants of Strain: Another Look at Durkheim and Merton," in *The Future of Anomie Theory*, 27–51; 41.

36. Herbert McClosky and John H. Schaar, "Psychological Dimensions of Anomy," *American Sociological Review* 30, 1 (February 1965): 14–40, 19. On anomie, see Merton, "Continuities in the Theory and Social Structure and Anomie," 226–27. On anomia, see Leo Srole, "Social Integration and Certain Corollaries: An Exploratory Study," *American Sociological Review* 21, 6 (December 1956): 709–16; James T. Patterson, *America's Struggle Against Poverty, 1900–1985* (Cambridge, Mass.: Harvard University Press, 1981), 94; see Gunnar Myrdal, *An American Dilemma: The Negro Problem and Modern Democracy* (New York: Harper & Row, 1944).

37. Oscar Lewis, *Five Families: Mexican Case Studies in the Culture of Poverty* (New York: Basic Books, 1959); Lewis, *The Children of Sánchez: Autobiography of a Mexican Family* (New York: Random House, 1961); Susan M. Rigdon, *The Culture Façade: Art, Science, and Politics in the Work of Oscar Lewis* (Urbana: University of Illinois Press, 1988); Patterson, "A Culture of Poverty?" in *America's Struggle*, 115–25.

38. Rigdon, *The Culture Façade*, table, 114–15; Bahr, *Homelessness and Disaffiliation*, 290.

39. Rigdon, *The Culture Façade*, 80; Paul E. Peterson, "The Urban Underclass and the Poverty Paradox," in *The Urban Underclass*, ed. Christopher Jencks and Paul E. Peterson (Washington, D.C.: Brookings Institution, 1991), 3–27.

40. Bahr, *Skid Row*, 23–24.

41. James Rooney, "Group Processes Among Skid Row Winos," *Quarterly Journal of Studies on Alcohol* 22 (September 1961): 444–60; Charles Hoch and Robert A. Slayton, *New Homeless and Old: Community and the Skid Row Hotel* (Philadelphia: Temple University Press, 1989), 107–10; Jacqueline P. Wiseman, *Stations of the Lost: The Treatment of Skid Row Alcoholics* (Englewood Cliffs, N.J.: Prentice-Hall, 1970), 43–45; O'Connor, *Poverty Knowledge*, 4–22; Lewis, précis and response in "The Children of Sanchez, Pe-

dro Martinez, and La Vida," reviews by Nathan Ackerman, Mary Jean Aerni, K. Aoyagi, et al., *Current Anthropology* 8, 5, Part 1 (December 1967): 480–500.

42. Gerald R. Garrett, "Alcohol Problems and Homelessness: History and Research," *Contemporary Drug Problems* (Fall 1989): 301–23, 308.

43. See Rooney, "Group Processes Among Skid Row Winos."

44. Bahr, *Skid Row*, 154–65.

45. Gerald R. Garrett and Howard M. Bahr, "On Measuring Drinking Status: An Analysis of Self-Rating and Quantity-Frequency Classifications," paper presented at annual meeting of the Society for the Study of Social Problems, Montreal, 1974, 11–12, BASR Records, Box 76, Columbia University Archive.

46. Box 78, BASR, Folder B1024: Interview #004, conducted 21 April 1966 by Andrew Lewis, 25–26; Interview #006, by Myron Freier, 6 April 1966, 25–26; Interview #008, conducted by Andrew Lewis on 21 April 1966, 25–26; Interview #009, conducted by M. Weiss, 19 April 1966.

47. Howard M. Bahr, "Drinking, Interaction, and Identification: Notes on Socialization into Skid Row," *Journal of Health and Social Behavior* 8, 4 (December 1967): 272–85; Bahr, *Homeless and Disaffiliation*, 289.

48. Boris M. Levinson, "Some Aspects of the Personality of the Native-Born White Homeless Man as Revealed by the Rorschach," *Psychiatric Quarterly Supplement* 32, 2 (1958): 278–86.

49. "U.S. Remembers Forgotten Men," *NYT*, 12 May 1960; "Summary of Special Reports," Appendix III in *Summary Report*; "The Bowery in the Small Hours of the Morning," 43, 21, 26; Kusmer, Down and Out, 316, n. 26.

50. *Summary Report*, 29–31. Drawn from Nan Markel, "A Preliminary Study of New York City's Hospitals and their Contact with Homeless Men," submitted 30 November 1964, prepared for Department of Welfare, City of New York, 13.

51. *Summary Report*, 8. "Bowery Bars," in Appendix III, *Summary Report*, 42–47.

52. Bahr, *Homelessness and Disaffiliation*, 90–91.

53. Ibid., 258–62; Leonard Blumberg, Thomas E. Shipley, Jr., and Irving W. Shandler, *Skid Row and Its Alternatives: Research and Recommendations from Philadelphia* (Philadelphia: Temple University Press, 1973), 176, 179, 182–83; Theodore Caplow, Keith A. Lovald, and Samuel E. Wallace, *A General Report on the Problem of Relocating the Population of the Lower Loop Redevelopment Area* (Minneapolis: Minneapolis Housing and Redevelopment Authority, 1958), 112–14.

54. Bahr, *Homelessness and Disaffiliation*, 264–67; Interview #006, conducted by R. Riday, 20 April; Interview #004, Paul Bailey, conducted by Andrew Lewis, 21 April 1966, at Union House on Hester, Box 78, Folder B1024, BASR Records.

55. "1964 Voting Behavior in the Bowery," in Appendix III in *Summary Report*, 45; "Poll of Bowery Residents Shows 81% Expect Johnson Re-election," *NYT*, 1 February 1968; Robert F. Crawford, photos in Bahr and Caplow, *Old Men*.

56. Appendix III in *Summary Report*, 42; Rita Aronow, "Bowery Census, 1967," Box 79, BASR, Table 2, n.p.

57. Stanley K. Henshaw, *Camp LaGuardia: A Voluntary Total Institution for Homeless Men* (New York: Columbia University BASR, 1968), 2–9.

58. Ibid., 59–61.

59. Ibid., 67–69.

60. Ibid., 76–79.

61. Interviews #306, #302, conducted by Andrew Lewis, 25 May 1966, BASR Records, Box 78, Columbia Archive.

62. Henshaw, *Camp LaGuardia*, 91–102, 25, 22, 45, 94; Bahr, *Homelessness and Disaffiliation*, 33.

63. Henshaw, *Camp LaGuardia*, 102; Bendiner, *The Bowery Man*, 38, 90.

64. Henshaw, *Camp LaGuardia*, 27–28, 81–83.

65. Featherstone, Richard, and Mathieu Deflem; "Anomie and Strain: Context and Consequences of Merton's Two Theories," *Sociological Inquiry* 73, 4 (2003): 471–89.

66. Howard M. Bahr, *Skid Row: An Introduction to Disaffiliation* (New York: Oxford University Press, 1973); Blumberg et al., *Skid Row and Its Alternatives*. The Columbia University Bowery Project publications and unpublished reports addressed an array of subjects, including drinking and labor. On drinking, see Bahr and Stephen J. Langful, "Social Attachment and Drinking in Skid-Row Life Histories," *Social Problems* 14, 4 (Spring 1967); Bahr, "Drinking, Interaction, and Identification: Notes on Socialization into Skid Row," *Journal of Health and Social Behavior* 8, 4 (December 1967); Bahr, "Family Size and Stability as Antecedents of Homelessness and Excessive Drinking," *Journal of Marriage and the Family* 31, 3 (August 1969): 477–83; Bahr, "Lifetime Affiliation Patterns of Early- and Late-Onset Heavy Drinkers on Skid Row," *Quarterly Journal of Studies on Alcohol* 30, 3 (September 1969): 645–56; and Gerald R. Garrett and Bahr, "Comparison of Self-Rating and Quantity-Frequency Measures of Drinking," *Quarterly Journal of Studies on Alcohol* 35, 4 (December 1974): 1294–1306. On labor, see Bahr, "Worklife Mobility Among Bowery Men," *Southwestern Social Science Quarterly* (June 1968): 128–41; Bahr and Caplow, "Homelessness, Affiliation, and Occupational Mobility," *Social Forces* 47, 1 (September 1968): 28–33; George Nash and Patricia Nash, "The Non-Demanding Society: An Analysis of the Social Structure of a Skid Row," paper for Eastern Psychological Association, 14 April 1966, Box 79, BASR Records; Bahr, "A Funny Thing Happened on the Way to the Reservation," 20 July 1966, Box 79, BASR Records; Nan Markel Sigal, "The Unchanging Areas in Transition," *Land Economics* 43, 3 (August 1967): 284–93.

67. Kim Hopper, *Reckoning with Homelessness* (Ithaca, N.Y.: Cornell University Press, 2003), 45–46, 62–65; Bahr, *Homelessness and Disaffiliation*, 96–98, 396–98. See Bogue, *Skid Row in American Cities,* 109–10.

68. "Bowery Project Staff Meeting, 15 March 1965," n.p. (present: Dr. Caplow, Howard, Pat, George, Mark, Nan, Ann), Box 79, BASR Records; Bahr, *Homelessness and Disaffiliation*, 107, 117.

69. Blumberg et al., "Two Neglected Skid Row Populations: Blacks and Women," in Blumberg et al., *Skid Row and its Alternatives*; Kusmer, *Down and Out*, 232–33.

70. Bahr, *Homelessness and Disaffiliation*, 74, 72; Bahr, *Skid Row*, 105.

71. Bahr, *Skid Row*, 170.

72. Ibid., 123, 126.

73. Ibid., 129–32.

74. "Bowery Bars," in Appendix III, *Summary Report*, 42; also see George Nash, "Bowery Bars," September 1964, 37, Box 79, BASR Records; Bahr, *Homelessness and Disaffiliation*, 123–24, 54; Bahr, *Skid Row*, 168.

75. Henshaw, *Camp LaGuardia*, 37, 97, 33–34; "Welfare Aide Tied to Misuse of Funds," *NYT*, 1 May 1963.

76. Blumberg et al., chap. 6 in Blumberg et al., *Skid Row and Its Alternatives*, 92–107.

77. Interviews #306 and #308, Box 78, BASR Records.

78. Henshaw, *Camp LaGuardia*, 68–69; press release, 20 August 1963, Box 158, Folder, 1812, Wagner Papers, Department Files; Anne C. Rose, "Putting the South on the Psychological Map: The Impact of Region and Race on the Human Sciences During the 1930s," *Journal of Southern History* 71, 2 (May 2005): 321–56.

79. Nash, "Bowery Bars," September 1964, 29, 38, Box 78, BASR Records.

80. Bahr, *Skid Row*, 141–46; Wiseman, *Stations of the Lost*, 38; Bogue, *Skid Row in American Cities*, 64.

81. Harris, *Skid Row USA*, 15–20; Todd DePastino, *Citizen Hobo: How a Century of Homelessness Shaped America* (Chicago: University of Chicago Press, 2003), 85–91; Bendiner, *The Bowery Man*, 159.

82. Bahr, *Skid Row*, 168.

83. Regina G. Kunzel, "Situating Sex: Prison Sexual Culture in the Mid-Twentieth-Century United States," *GLQ: A Journal of Lesbian and Gay Studies* 8, 3 (2002): 253–70; Martin Hoffman, *The Gay World: Male Homosexuality and the Social Creation of Evil* (New York: Basic Books, 1968).

84. Subhead quoted from Bahr and Garrett, *Women Alone*, 94; Bahr, *Skid Row*, 176.

85. Bahr and Garrett, *Women Alone*, 85; Gerald R. Garrett, "Family Histories of Skid-Row Women and Men: Sex Differentials in Antecedents of Homelessness," Box 96, BASR Records.

86. Bahr and Garrett, *Women Alone*, 1–20.

87. Gerald R. Garrett and Dinah Hirschfeld Volk, "Homeless Women in New York City: Memorandum," 34, 64, Box 96, BASR Records; Bahr and Garrett, *Women Alone*, 15.

88. Morris Chase, "Historical Sketch of the Women's Emergency Shelter, 1970," Appendix C in Bahr and Garrett, *Women Alone*, 183–84; "Homeless Women-Emergency Assistance Unit," *Welfarer* xii, 5 (May 1960): 7–8, Wagner Papers, Department Files, Department of Welfare, Box 156, Folder 1788, January–July 1960.

89. Bahr, *Skid Row*, 203.

90. Bahr and Garrett, *Women Alone*, 116.

91. Garrett, *Family Histories of Skid-Row Women and Men: Sex Differentials in Antecedents of Homelessness*, 5, Box 96, BASR Records; Caplow, *Women Alone*, xvi;

92. Garrett, *Family Histories*, 5–6.

93. *Ibid.*, 7.

94. Bahr, *Skid Row*, 214–16.

95. Bahr and Garrett, *Women Alone*, 115–16.

96. Ibid., 57–61; Garrett and Volk, *Homeless Women in NYC: Memo*, 35–64.

97. Garrett and Volk, Case 333 in *Homeless Women in NYC: Memo*, 58–63.

98. Mary Lou Prentiss, in Ann Marie Rousseau, *Shopping Bag Ladies Homeless Women Speak About Their Lives* (New York: Pilgrim Press, 1981), 67.

99. Bahr and Garrett, *Women Alone*, 135, xvi-xvii.

100. Ibid., 89, 29, 31.

101. Harris, *Skid Row USA*, 9–11.

102. Gerald Markowitz and David Rosner, *Children, Race, and Power: Kenneth and Mamie Clark's Northside Center* (Charlottesville: University Press of Virginia, 1996).

103. Daniel Patrick Moynihan, "The Negro Family: The Case for National Action," Office of Policy Planning and Research, U.S. Department of Labor, March 1965, http:www.dol.gov/oasam/programs/history/webid-meynihan.htm.

104. Charles Murray, *Losing Ground: American Social Policy, 1950–1980* (New York: HarperCollins, 1986); Daryl Michael Scott, "The Politics of Pathology," *Journal of Policy History* 8, 1 (Winter 1996): 81–105; William Graebner, "The End of Liberalism: Narrating Welfare's Decline, from the Moynihan Report (1965) to the Personal Responsibility and Work Opportunity Act (1996)," *Journal of Policy History* 14, 2 (2002), 170–90.

105. "Police Here Halt Derelict Arrests," *NYT*, 29 July 1966; "Derelicts in City's Parks to Get a Boon of Sorts," *NYT*, 18 August 1966; "A Tour in Bowery Stirs Night Mayor," *NYT*, 6 October 1966.

106. Manhattan Bowery Project, *First Annual Report*, April 1969, 13, 16; George and Patricia Nash, "The Planning and Operation of the Experimental Detoxification Center, October 1966," 114, Box 79, BASR Records; Steven S. Manos, "The Manhattan Bowery Project," *Alcohol Health and Research World* (Winter 1975/76, experimental issue): 11–15.

107. MBP, *First Annual Report*, 25, 30–31, 56–57.

108. "City Helping Bowery Derelicts to Discover a New Way of Life," *NYT*, 22 June 1968; MBP, *First Annual Report*, 37, 40, 36, 26–27, 63–65; Manhattan Bowery Corporation, *Annual Report*, 1 July 1970–30 June 1971.

109. MBC, *Annual Report*, 1 July 1970–30 June 1971; Manos, "The Manhattan Bowery Project," 13–15.

110. Manos, "The Manhattan Bowery Project," 15.

111. Johnson cited in Patterson, *America's Struggle*, 147; Charles Brecher, Raymond D. Horton, with Raymond D. Horton, and Dean Michael Mead, *Power Failure: New York City Politics and Policy Since 1960* (New York: Oxford University Press, 1993), 83–84; Vincent J. Cannato, *The Ungovernable City: John Lindsay and His Struggle to Save New York* (New York: Basic Books, 2001), 539, 542.

112. Lewis, précis in "The Children of Sanchez," 486, 497, 499.

113. Wiseman, *Stations of the Lost*, 10–14.

Chapter 6. The End of the Skid-Row Era

1. Lee Stringer, *Grand Central Winter: Stories from the Street* (New York: Washington Square Press, 1998), 57.

2. Randy Young, "The Homeless: The Shame of the City," *New York*, 21 December 1981, 26–32; Iver Peterson, "New Hard Times Fill Soup Kitchens," *NYT*, 3 January 1982.

3. Jonathan Soffer, *Ed Koch and the Rebuilding of New York City* (New York: Columbia University Press, 2010).

4. Lawrence K. Altman, "Release of Mentally Ill Spurring Doubts," *NYT*, 20 November 1979.

5. Christopher Jencks, *The Homeless* (Cambridge, Mass.: Harvard University Press, 1994); Brendan O'Flaherty, "An Economic Theory of Homelessness and Housing," *Journal of Housing Economics* 4, 1 (1995): 13–49. See John M. Quigley, "The Homeless," *Journal of Economic Literature* 34 (December 1996): 1935–41; Sarah Connell, Director, NYC Regional Office, State Office of Mental Health, "Albany's Concern for the Mentally Disabled and Homeless," Letter to the Editor, *NYT*, 27 October 1982; "The Danger of Dumping the Mentally Ill," *NYT*, 26 December 1979.

6. Mrs. Naomi Young to Mayor Wagner, 20 August 1962, Box 157, Folder 1800, Wagner Papers, Department Files.

7. Deirdre Carmody, "The City Sees No Solutions for Homeless," *NYT*, 10 October 1984; Steven Vanderstaay, *Street Lives: An Oral History of Homeless Americans* (Philadelphia: New Society, 1992), 117–36.

8. Lawrence D. Maloney, "Take Mental Patients Off Streets, Back to Hospitals?" *U.S. News & World Report*, 1 July 1985, 55.

9. Max H. Seigel, "Relief Cuts Evict Old and Disabled," *NYT*, 30 September 1974.

10. "For S.R.O. Hotel Roomers, It's a Precarious Life," *NYT*, 27 June 1973; "Illegal Evictions Charged at Welfare Hotels," *NYT*, 11 November 1980; "Influx of Former Mental Patients Burdening City, Albany Is Told," *NYT*, 23 November 1980.

11. "S.R.O. Hotel: Rare Species," *NYT*, 20 November 1981; "50 S.R.O. Tenants Charge Harassment," *NYT*, 28 December 1979; "Bills for Revision of J–51 Program Pass in Council," *NYT*, 28 April 1981; "Koch Wants S.R.O. Hotels Barred from J–51 Program," *NYT*, 22 July 1982; "Koch Is Seeking Retroactivity on Ending S.R.O. Tax Breaks," *NYT*, 13 August 1982.

12. "Carey Says City Worsens Plight of the Homeless," *NYT*, 29 December 1980; "Aide Denies Carey Assailed City Policy," *NYT*, 31 December 1980.

13. Glenda Riley, *Divorce: An American Tradition* (New York: Oxford University Press, 1992), 156–82.

14. Rayne Landry, quoted in Ann Marie Rousseau, *Shopping Bag Ladies* (New York: Pilgrim Press, 1981), 41.

15. Ellie Fredricks, quoted in Rousseau, 106.

16. Rayne Landry, in Rousseau, 43.

17. "Bag Ladies," *NYT*, 29 September 1981; "Alone and Homeless, 'Shutouts' of Society Sleep in Doorways," *NYT*, 26 October 1971.

18. Young, "The Homeless: The Shame of the City," 28.

19. "Facilities for 'Shopping-Bag Ladies' and Battered Women Are Planned," *NYT*, 26 May 1979; Ellen Baxter, Kim Hopper, and Institute for Social Welfare Research, *Private Lives/Public Spaces: Homeless Adults on the Streets of New York City* (New York: Community Service Society, Institute for Social Welfare Research, 1981), 63, 65.

20. Baxter and Hopper, *Private Lives*, 46; Young, "The Homeless: The Shame of the City," 26–32, 29.

21. Kenneth L. Kusmer, *Down and Out, On the Road: The Homeless in American History* (New York: Oxford University Press, 2002), 243; Kim Hopper, *Reckoning with Homelessness* (Ithaca, N.Y.: Cornell University Press), 169–71.

22. James T. Patterson, *America's Struggle Against Poverty, 1900–1985* (Cambridge, Mass.: Harvard University Press, 1981), 210–23.

23. William Julius Wilson, "The Truly Disadvantaged," in *Color, Class, Identity: The New Politics of Race*, ed. John Arthur and Amy Shapiro (Boulder, Colo.: Westview Press, 1996), 109–22, 110–11.

24. "Vagrants and Panhandlers Appearing in New Haunts," *NYT*, 6 August 1976; John R. Coleman, "Diary of a Homeless Man," *New York* 16, 8, 21 February 1983, 26–35.

25. "Maze of Tunnels Remains Refuge of the Homeless," *NYT*, 17 March 1980; "Hobo Colony Lives Mole-Like in an Inferno of Pipes under Park Avenue," *NYT*, 29 November 1977; Baxter and Hopper, *Private Lives*, 75–77; Hopper, *Reckoning*, 52, n. 57; "Some of City's Homeless Gather in Convention's Shadow," *NYT*, 14 August 1980.

26. Jonathan Alter, "Homeless in America," *Newsweek*, 2 January 1984, 20–23, 25–29; 25; Martin Kasindorf, "A New Breed of Hobos," *Newsweek*, 16 August 1982, 30; William L. Chaze, "Behind Swelling Ranks of America's Street People," *U.S. News & World Report*, 30 January 1984, 57; "Surge of Homeless People in Nation Tests Cities' Will and Ability to Cope," *NYT*, 3 May 1982.

27. Jonathan Alter, "Fighting Back," *Newsweek*, 2 January 1984, 26.

28. Edward M. Gramlich, "The New York City Fiscal Crisis: What Happened and What is to be Done?" *American Economic Review* 66, 2 (May 1976): 415–29; Andrew Glassberg, "The Urban Fiscal Crisis Becomes Routine," *Public Administration Review* 41 (January 1981): 165–72.

29. Demetrios Caraley, "Washington Abandons the Cities," *Political Science Quarterly* (Spring 1992): 1–30; 9; Tom Morganthau, "Down and Out in America," *Newsweek*, 15 March 1982, 28; see Joseph Dillon Davey, "The New Homelessness: The Reagan Legacy," in *The New Social Contract: America's Journey from Welfare State to Police State* (Westport, Conn.: Praeger, 1995): 39–54; Alter, "Homeless in America," 21.

30. Baxter and Hopper, *Private Lives*.

31. Kim Hopper, Ellen Baxter, and Institute for Social Welfare Research, *One Year Later: The Homeless Poor in New York City, 1982* (NY: Community Service Society, 1982); "A Journey into the City's Netherworld," *NYT*, 11 March 1981; "Two Homeless Persons Adrift in Grand Central," *NYT*, 20 March 1981.

32. Baxter and Hopper, *Private Lives*, 8–10; "City to Make a Count of Homeless

People," *NYT*, 30 December 1981; "Mayor Defends City's Handling of Its Homeless," *NYT*, 20 November 1981.

33. Baxter and Hopper, *Private Lives*, 10, 52–53.

34. Ibid., 69–70, 19–20.

35. "Wanderers Find Shelter and a New Life," *NYT*, 21 April 1981; Baxter and Hopper, *Private Lives*, 110–16, 7, 73.

36. Thomas J. Main, "The Homeless of New York," *Public Interest* 72 (Summer 1983): 3–28, 5.

37. Patricia Siebert, "Homeless People: Establishing Rights to Shelter," *Law and Inequality* 4 (1986): 393–407; Christine Robitscher Ladd, "A Right to Shelter for the Homeless in New York State," *NYU Law Review* 61, 272–99.

38. Charles Kaiser, "A State Justice Orders Creation of 750 Beds for Bowery Homeless," *NYT*, 9 December 1979; *Callahan v. Carey*, N.Y. County Supreme Court, Index #42582/79; *Eldredge v. Koch*, 469 N.Y.S.2d 744 (A.D. 1 Dept. 1983). The Eldredge case extended the consent decree to homeless women. In 1986, *McCain v. Koch* expanded the right to shelter to homeless families, *McCain v. Koch*, 523 N.Y.S.2d 112 (A.D. 1 Dept. 1988); "Koch Pays Visit to New Shelter on Wards Island," *NYT*, 4 January 1980; "New York City Psychiatric Wards Overflow as Albany Changes Its Mental Health Role," *NYT*, 8 December 1980; "Year's Extension for 3 City Taxes Is Voted by Council Finance Panel," *NYT*, 21 July 1981.

39. "New York City Resists State on Shelters for Homeless in Residential Areas," *NYT*, 30 December 1980; "City's Homeless Rejecting Shelter in the Catskills," *NYT*, 9 September 1981; "In Armory, Tenants and Homeless, Too, Find Shelter," *NYT*, 9 January 1981; "Nightly Dramas Unravel at City's Shelters in Cold," *NYT*, 15 January 1981.

40. "Pact Requires City to Shelter Homeless Men," *NYT*, 27 August 1981.

41. Robert C. Coates, "Legal Rights of Homeless Americans," *University of San Francisco Law Review* 24 (1989–90): 297–362; Gary Blasi, "Rights on the Homeless: Litigation Concerning Homeless People," *Public Law Forum* (1985): 433–43; David W. Crosland, "Can Lawyers Really Help the Homeless?" *Human Rights* 14 (1987): 16–19; Geoffrey Mort, "Establishing a Right to Shelter for the Homeless," *Brooklyn Law Review* 50: 939–94; Inez Smith Reid, "Law, Politics and the Homeless," *West Virginia Law Review* 89 (1986–87): 115–47; Lillian Gelberg, "Federal Aid to the Homeless," *National Black Law Journal* 12 (1990–93): 163–75; James K. Langdon II and Mark A. Kass, "Homelessness in America: Looking for the Right to Shelter," *Columbia Journal of Law and Social Problems* 19 (1985): 305–92.

42. "Providing Shelter for New York City's Homeless," *NYT*, 18 September 1981; "Proposed Referral Center for Homeless Disturbs West Side Neighborhood," *NYT*, 25 May 1981; "Center to Help Vagrants wins West Side Vote," *NYT*, 4 June 1981; "Koch Hears Complaints on Midtown," *NYT*, 10 June 1981; "Church's Program for Homeless Upsets Its Neighbors," *NYT*, 14 June 1981; "New York is Facing 'Crisis' on Vagrants," *NYT*, 28 June 1981; "Residents Assail City Proposal to House Derelicts in Gateway Park," *NYT*, 14 August 1981.

43. "Residents Balk at City Shelter on Harlem Site," *NYT*, 20 November 1982; "Lawyer Says City Fails to Comply with Pact on Sheltering Homeless," *NYT*, 8 December 1981.

44. "Who Will Take New York's 36,000 Outcasts," *NYT*, 22 August 1981.

45. "House Homeless in Armory, Judge Orders City and State," *NYT*, 21 October 1981; "Shelter for Men Opened by City at Brooklyn Site," *NYT*, 22 October 1981; "Problems Grow in Sheltering Homeless in City," *NYT*, 18 November 1981; "City Plans to Expand Use of Armories to House Homeless Men," *NYT*, 1 December 1981.

46. "Religious Groups Lukewarm to City Homeless Plan," *NYT*, 11 December 1981; "Some Churches Answer Koch's Bid on Homeless," *NYT*, 28 December 1981; "Koch, Reagan, and The Poor," *NYT*, 31 January 1982; "New York Clergy Fault Government for Failures in Housing Homeless," *NYT*, 25 December 1982.

47. "City Picks 10 Private Agencies to Assist Homeless," *NYT*, 2 December 1982; "Havens for the Homeless," *NYT*, 16 February 1984.

48. "Hidden Resource for the Homeless," *NYT*, 22 December 1981.

49. Christopher Mele, *Selling the Lower East Side: Culture, Real Estate, and Resistance in New York City* (Minneapolis: University of Minnesota Press, 2000), 180–254.

50. "Self-Help Is the Goal of a Skid-Row Project," *NYT*, 10 July 1973; "City Subsidizes 6 Hotels on the Bowery," *NYT*, 30 March 1976.

51. Stephen Petrus, "From Gritty to Chic: The Transformation of New York City's SoHo, 1962–1976," *New York History* (Winter 2003): 50–87; "Downtown Scene: Art in the Bowery," *NYT*, 5 December 1970; "Brightening Up the Bowery," *NYT*, 23 July 1972.

52. See Mele, *Selling the Lower East Side*, 217–19; "A New Life for the Bowery," *NYT*, 15 April 1977.

53. Hilly Kristal, *CBGB's: Thirty Years from the Home of Underground Rock* (New York: Harry Abrams, 2005), not paginated; Tommy Ramone quoted in Monte A. Melnick and Frank Meyer, "It's Alive: CBGB, the Look, the Sound," in *On the Road with the Ramones* (London: Sanctuary Publishing, 2003), 48–63.

54. David Byrne, "The Creative Algorithm," afterword in Kristal, *CBGB's*.

55. "The Bowery Would Be Chic, They Said—Ha!" *NYT*, 29 May 1977; "Decline in Derelicts Hurting Bowery Flophouses," *NYT*, 27 March 1978.

56. "Problems Grow in Sheltering Homeless in City," *NYT*, 18 November 1981; "NoHo Residents' Opposition Kills Plan for Homeless Shelter," *NYT*, 26 December 1982.

57. Byrne, "The Creative Algorithm."

58. "Koch Revises Plan on Aiding Homeless," "Scoring the Mayor," *NYT*, 28 March 1981.

59. William Chaze, "Street People: Adrift and Alone in America," *U.S. News & World Report*, 8 March 1982, 60; "Woman Refuses Aid, Dies in Carton Street," *NYT*, 27 January 1982; "One of City's Homeless Goes Home—in Death," *NYT*, 31 January 1982; "City Steps Up Court Action To Aid Homeless and Others," *NYT*, 12 February 1982; "Charities and Citizens Lend a Hand to City's Homeless," *NYT*, 16 February 1982.

60. "Suit on Homeless Mental Patients Asks New York State for Housing," *NYT*, 21

May 1982; "Lawyer Terms Shelters for Women Inadequate," *NYT*, 8 January 1982; Herman, "Suit Seeking to Upgrade City Shelters for Women," *NYT*, 25 February 1982.

61. John D. Skrentny, "Introduction: How War and the Black Civil Rights Movement Changed America," *The Minority Rights Revolution* (Cambridge, Mass.: Harvard University Press, 2002), 1–20; Hugh Davis Graham, "Conclusion," *The Civil Rights Era: Origins and Development of National Policy, 1960–1972* (New York: Oxford University Press, 1990), 450–76.

62. "The Main Civil Liberty: A Right Not to Starve," *NYT*, 18 July 1984; Main, "The Homeless of New York," 5, 27.

63. J. Phillip Thompson, "The Failure of Liberal Homeless Policy in the Koch and Dinkins Administration," *Political Science Quarterly* 111, 4 (Winter 1996–97), 659.

64. Wolf von Eckardt, "The Greening of Skid Row," *Time*, 19 July 1982.

65. "Report Says City Homeless May Double in Two Years," *NYT*, 24 December 1983; "Fairness of Reagan's Cutoffs Of Disability Aid Questioned," *NYT*, 9 May 1982; "Study on Hunger Stirs Skepticism," *NYT*, 4 August 1983.

66. "U.S. Seen Curbing Help for Homeless," *NYT*, 12 June 1983.

67. Patterson, *America's Struggle Against Poverty*, 210–14.

68. "Reagan's Homeless," *NYT*, 4 February 1984; "Reagan's Homeless (Cont'd)," *NYT*, 3 April 1984.

69. "Youth Shelter Wins Praises from Reagan," *NYT*, 26 January 1984.

70. "'Reaganville' Camp Erected to Protest Plight of the Poor," *NYT*, 27 November 1981; "National Group Formed to Help the Homeless," *NYT*, 9 May 1982.

71. "Mondale Accuses Reagan of Lacking Compassion," *NYT*, 3 February 1984; "Tents Set Up in Capital in Protest on Homeless," *NYT*, 16 August 1984; see Leonard C. Feldman, *Citizens Without Shelter: Homelessness, Democracy, and Political Exclusion* (Ithaca, N.Y.: Cornell University Press, 2004), 138–48; "Fasting Wins Concessions on Shelter for Homeless," *NYT*, 5 November 1984.

72. "Homeless in U.S. Put at 250,000, Far Less Than Previous Estimates," *NYT*, 2 May 1984; "The Depression Army," *NYT*, 15 February 1983.

73. Stringer, *Grand Central Winter*, 220.

74. Donna Wilson Kirchheimer, "Sheltering the Homeless in New York City: Expansion in an Era of Government Contraction," *Political Science Quarterly* 104, 4 (Winter, 1989–90): 607–23; 608; "Providing Shelter for New York City's Homeless," *NYT*, 18 September 1981.

75. "Community Care for Mentally Ill Termed a Failure," *NYT*, 13 September 1984.

76. Mary Ellen Holmes, "Federal Policy for the Homeless," *Stanford Law and Policy Review* (Fall 1989): 57–68; see also Christina Victoria Tusan, "Homeless Families from 1980–1996: Casualties of Declining Support for the War on Poverty," *Southern California Law Review* 70 (1996–97): 1141–237. For comparative information on the policies adopted during this era in Great Britain, see Amy B. Corday, "Great Britain's Answer to Homelessness: The Housing (Homeless Persons) Act of 1977," *Washington University Journal of Urban and Contemporary Law* 31 (1987): 201–23.

77. William Chaze, "Street People: Adrift and Alone in America," *U.S. News & World Report*, 8 March 1982, 60; Margot Hornblower, Andrea Sachs, and James Will Werth, "Ethics: Not in My Backyard You Don't," *Time*, June 27, 1988.

Conclusion: Whither the Homeless

1. "Murtagh Depicts Revived Bowery," *NYT*, 30 March 1956; "Mrs. Simon Scores City on Alcoholics," *NYT*, 24 October 1957; "Alcoholism Aid Urged," *NYT*, 23 January 1957; "Penitentiary Ban on Addicts Eased," *NYT*, 3 July 1958.

2. "Forcibly Hospitalized Woman Identified," *NYT*, 5 November 1987.

3. "In Hospital Courtroom, Plea for Freedom," *NYT*, 6 November 1987.

4. Richard Campbell and Jimmie L. Reeves, "Covering the Homeless: The Joyce Brown Story," *Critical Studies in Mass Communication* 6, 1 (1989): 21–42; "Four Women Reach Out to Their Homeless Sister," *NYT*, 7 November 1987; "Though Homeless, She Copes, She Is Fit, She Survives," *NYT*, 13 November 1987.

5. "Homeless Woman Sent to Hospital Under Koch Plan Is Ordered Freed," *NYT*, 13 November 1987; "Court Bars the Release of Woman," *NYT*, 14 November 1987; "The Poor a Major Concern of Judge in Homeless Case," *NYT*, 14 November 1987; "Fate of Homeless Woman Is Debated in Court," *NYT*, 28 November 1987; "Court Backs Treatment of Woman Held Under Koch Homeless Plan," *NYT*, 19 December 1987; "Homeless Woman to Be Released After Being Forcibly Hospitalized," *NYT*, 19 January 1988.

6. "TV Anchorman Gets Suspension for Harsh Report," *NYT*, 21 January 1988; "Can't We Aid New York's Homeless Without Locking Them Up?" *NYT*, 26 November 1987; "Thousands March Against Homelessness," *NYT*, 21 December 1987.

7. "Koch, in Washington, Criticizes Civil Libertarians over Homeless," *NYT*, 7 January 1988.

8. "Razing of Shanties Starts Confrontation in Tompkins Square," *NYT*, 6 July 1989.

9. "City Moves to Clean Up Tompkins Sq. After Raid," *NYT*, 7 July 1989; "Worlds Collide in Tompkins Sq. Park," *NYT*, 31 July 1989; "Tent Cities Becoming the Front Lines," *NYT*, 11 September 1989; "36 Arrested During Protest over Squatters," *NYT*, 27 October 1989.

10. "Removal of Tompkins Sq. Homeless is Set," *NYT*, 16 November 1989; "Neighbors' Attitudes Shift as Park Declines," *NYT*, 7 December 1989; "Tent City in Tompkins Square is Dismantled by Police," *NYT*, 15 December 1989; "New York Closes Park to Homeless," *NYT*, 4 June 1991; "Tompkins Square, (Almost) United," *NYT*, 6 August 1993; Don Mitchell, *The Right to the City: Social Justice and the Fight for Public Space* (New York: Guilford, 2003), 161–94; 189.

11. "For Homeless, A Last Haven Is Demolished," *NYT*, 18 August 1993; "New York City Bulldozes Squatters' Shantytowns," *NYT*, 16 October 1991; "Tougher Campaign Is Vowed Against Homeless in Subway," *NYT*, 19 October 1991.

12. "Evicting the Homeless," *NYT*, 22 June 1991; "Ray of Hope for Homeless Penetrates Meager Walls of Miami Shantytown," *NYT*, 6 July 1991; "2 Views of the Home-

less, One Aggressive, One Gentle," *NYT*, 2 October 1991; "City Ousts Homeless From Encampment," *NYT*, 28 August 1992.

13. Leonard C. Feldman, *Citizens Without Shelter: Homelessness, Democracy, and Political Exclusion* (Ithaca, N.Y.: Cornell University Press, 2004), 27–56; James Q. Wilson and George L. Kelling, "Broken Windows: The Police and Neighborhood Safety," *Atlantic Monthly*, March 1982, 29–36; Mitchell, *The Right to the City*, 195–226.

14. "Citywide Sweep Leads to 23 Arrests of the Homeless," *NYT*, 22 November 1999; Andrew Kirtzman, *Rudy Giuliani: Emperor of the City* (New York: HarperCollins, 2000), 39–40, 84–90; "The Homeless Huddle at City's Margins," *NYT*, 12 November 1995; "Police Remove Encampment of Homeless," *NYT*, 28 February 1997; "Still Homeless, Just Harder to See," *NYT*, 30 March 1997. On the broader trend of corporations controlling and regulating "public" spaces, see Lizabeth Cohen, *A Consumers' Republic: The Politics of Mass Consumption in Postwar America* (New York: Vintage Books, 2004); Timothy A. Gibson, *Securing the Spectacular City: The Politics of Revitalization and Homelessness in Downtown Seattle* (Lanham, Md..: Lexington Books, 2004); Leonard Feldman, *Citizens Without Shelter: Homelessness, Democracy, and Political Exclusion* (Ithaca, N.Y.: Cornell University Press, 2004).

15. "Giuliani Offers Strategy to Help City's Homeless," *NYT*, 10 October 1989; "Giuliani to Call for Curtailing Services." "New York Rivals Differ Strikingly on Dealing with City's Poorest," *NYT*, 2 October 1993; "Homeless Plan Would Require that Families Accept Services," *NYT*, 7 May 1994; "Burden of Proof Is Shifted to Applicants for Shelter," *NYT*, 4 January 1995; "Mayor Tightens Screening of People Seeking Shelter," *NYT*, 27 August 1996.

16. "Homeless Parents in New York Face a Work Mandate," *NYT*, 17 August 1996; "New York City Plans to Extend Workfare to Homeless Shelters," *NYT*, 20 February 1999; "Work-for-Shelter Requirement Is Delayed by New York Judges," *NYT*, 9 December 1999; "Shelters Vow to Defy Mayor on Work Rule," *NYT*, 18 December 1999; "City's Rules for Shelters Held Illegal," *NYT*, 23 February 2000; "Bullying the Homeless," *NYT*, 29 November 1999; Richard Goldstein, "Sanctioned Sadism: Why the Right Needs the Homeless," *Village Voice*, December 1999, 8–14.

17. Michael Winerip, "Bedlam on the Streets," *New York Times Magazine*, 23 May 1999; "History of Mental Illness Detailed for Man held in Subway Attack," *NYT*, 30 April 1999.

18. "A Young Life Ripped Apart, Just as It Was Coming Together," *NYT*, 18 November 1999; "Citywide Sweep Leads to 23 Arrests of the Homeless," *NYT*, 22 November 1999; "In Wake of Attack, Giuliani Cracks Down on Homeless," *NYT*, 20 November 1999; "Police Scour Shelters for Man Who Hit Woman with Brick," *NYT*, 18 November 1999; "Sharpton Assails Crackdown on Homeless," *NYT*, 28 November 1999; "Mayor Rebuts Policy Attack on Homeless by First Lady," *NYT*, 2 December 1999.

19. "Labeling the Homeless, in Compassion and Contempt," *NYT*, 5 December 1999; "Panhandler Is Arrested in Brick Attack," *NYT*, 1 December 1999.

20. Ralph Nunez, "Family Homelessness in New York City: A Case Study," *Political Science Quarterly* 116, 3 (2001): 367–79; "Judge Cites New York City on Homeless," *NYT*,

28 September 1994; "A Judge Cites New York City for Contempt," *NYT*, 15 May 1996; "Judge Orders City to Stop Housing Homeless in Office," *NYT*, 14 January 1999.

21. Darlene, quoted in Steven Vanderstaay, *Street Lives: An Oral History of Homeless Americans* (Philadelphia: New Society, 1992), 30.

22. "New Mayor, New Focus," *NYT*, 17 January 2002; "Bloomberg Plans More Housing Aid for the Homeless," *NYT*, 18 June 2002; "Quiet Move to Settle Giuliani Era Cases over City's Policies," *NYT*, 19 April 2002; "Bloomberg to Fight Ban on Shelter Evictions," *NYT*, 19 June 2002.

23. "A Victory over 'Homeless' Hooey," *New York Post*, 2 October 2003; Joel Schwartz, *Fighting Poverty with Virtue: Moral Reform and America's Urban Poor, 1825–2000* (Bloomington: Indiana University Press, 2000).

24. "With Skid Row Fading, Change Sweeps the Bowery," *NYT*, 29 July 1986.

25. Guy Lawson, "Down and Out at the Hotel Providence: Scenes from a Bowery Flophouse," *Harper's*, December 1999, 66–82; Darren Reidy, "The Last of the Mohicans," *Village Voice*, 1 March 2005.

26. National Coalition for the Homeless and the National Law Center on Homelessness & Poverty, *A Dream Denied: The Criminalization of Homelessness in U.S. Cities*, January 2006, 9.

27. U.S. Interagency Council on Homelessness, Opening Doors: Federal Strategic Plan to End Homelessness, 2010, 10–24, http://www.usich.gov.

28. National Coalition for the Homeless, Summary of 2010 Public Policy Recommendations; Hopper, *Reckoning with Homelessness*, 181–82.

INDEX

ACKNOWLEDGMENTS

I am indebted to many sources of financial, intellectual, and personal support that enabled me to write this book. A Larry J. Hackman Research Residency Award facilitated a trip to the New York State Archives. The History Department, the Dean's Office of the College of Liberal Arts, and the Faculty Research Grant Program of Armstrong Atlantic State University in Savannah, Georgia, have contributed travel funding, course reductions, and a summer stipend.

I am grateful to many historians for their suggestions and criticisms. Bruce Schulman generously offered wisdom, encouragement, and humor at all the right times. The insightful comments of Julian Zelizer, Marilyn Halter, Brooke Blower, and Thomas Whalen were most useful. As I began this project, Mike Wallace and Joshua Freeman welcomed me into the City University of New York Graduate Center Gotham Institute Postwar New York City History Symposium, where I learned more than I thought possible from all participants, but especially Samuel Zipp, Joshua Guild, and Eric Schneider. Kenneth Kusmer, Elaine Abelson, Alan Bloom, Nicolas Bloom, and Brad Hunt posed useful questions at an Organization of American Historians session and a meeting of the Urban History Association, as did everyone involved with the Cityscapes in History conference sponsored by the Center of Advanced Studies at Ludwig Maximilian University, Munich, Germany. More recently, I benefited from the comments offered by Kim Sichel and Claire Dempsey at the Boston University American Conversations series House and Home in American Culture. I am grateful to Michael Price for his close reading and helpful comments on this manuscript. Readers and editors for this press have also offered extremely useful suggestions, as have Jonathan Bell, Tim Stanley, Katrina Gulliver and Helena Toth.

Many librarians and archivists provided valuable assistance, including Susan Mitchem and Scott Bedio of the Salvation Army National Archives and Research Center in Alexandria, Virginia, Kenneth Cobb of the New York City Municipal Archive, and Ann Fuller, Caroline Hopkinson, and all the members of the reference and interlibrary loan teams of Lane Library at Armstrong.

My partner, Susan Hacker, spun microfilm wheels, braved the New York Public Library photocopy pen, formatted footnotes, and listened to painfully early drafts. She did not resent the space this work occupied in our lives, and has embraced our move to Savannah with good cheer. I am forever in her debt. Family and friends were also patient with me, especially James Howard, Tanya Koukeyan, Samantha Khosla, Jason Tatlock, and Chris Hendricks. My parents, Lynn and Lola Howard, did not see this project begun, but I hope that traces of their compassionate worldview emerge in its pages.